Studies in Philosophy
and the
History of Philosophy

Founded in 1960 by John K. Ryan

Volume 4

STUDIES IN PHILOSOPHY
AND THE
HISTORY OF PHILOSOPHY

Edited by

JOHN K. RYAN

THE CATHOLIC UNIVERSITY OF AMERICA PRESS
Washington, D. C. 20017

Paperback Edition Copyright © 2018
The Catholic University of America Press
All rights reserved

The paper used in this publication meets the minimum requirements of the
American National Standards for Information Science – Permanence of paper for
Printed Library Materials, ANSI Z39.48-1984.
∞

Cataloging-in-Publication Data available from the Library of Congress

ISBN 978-0-8132-3106-8 (pbk)

TABLE OF CONTENTS

                                                                         page

1. Prayer for Plato and Plutarch...................... 1
   Ioannes Mauropous. Translated by John K. Ryan

2. The Philosopher-Monk According to the
   Pseudo-Areopagite 3
   Caroline Canfield Putnam, R.S.C.J.

3. The Logic of Confucian Dialogues 18
   A. S. Cua

4. Lessons from the History of Science and Technology... 34
   Jude P. Dougherty

5. Does Acquired Moral Virtue Entail Facility?.......... 51
   Gilbert B. Arbuckle

6. Ancients and Moderns: Notes on Interpreting Hume... 69
   Thomas Prufer

7. The Concept of Time in St. Augustine.............. 75
   John M. Quinn, O.S.A.

8. Duns Scotus and St. Anselm's Ontological Argument.. 128
   Bernardino M. Bonansea, O.F.M.

9. The Anachronism of Certain Neothomistic Physical
   Doctrines 142
   Marius G. Schneider, O.F.M.

10. Thomas Aquinas and the Problem of Universals:
    A Re-examination 174
    B. Ryosuke Inagaki

11. Radical Reality According to José Ortega y Gasset..... 191
    Felix Alluntis, O.F.M.

12. Scholasticism, Nominalism and Martin Luther........ 207
    Richard P. Desharnais, C.S.C.

NOTES ON CONTRIBUTORS 229

INDEX 231

1

A PRAYER FOR PLATO AND PLUTARCH

by

IOANNES MAUROPOUS

Lord Jesus Christ, if Thou wouldst deign
    to release any pagans from Thy just judgment,
  then at this prayer of mine
    Plato release, and Plutarch!

In what they taught and what they did
    each one was near Thy Law,
  and if they were unable to see that
    Thou art God and Lord of all,
  there is need but for Thy gift of grace,
    wherein doth lie Thy will
        to save all humankind.

        Translated by John K. Ryan

The Greek text of this prayer by Ioannes Mauropous, an 11th-century Metropolitan of Euchaeta, is given in the Migne edition of his works, *Patrologia graeca*, CXX, 1156-57, as follows:

    Εἴπερ τινὰς βούλοιο τῶν ἀλλοτρίων
    τῆς σῆς ἀπειλῆς ἐξελέσθαι, Χριστέ μου,
    Πλάτωνα καὶ Πλούταρχον ἐξέλοιό μοι.

    ἄμφω γάρ εἰσι καὶ λόγον καὶ τὸν τρόπον
    τοῖς σοῖς νόμοις ἔγγιστα προσπεφυκότες.

    εἰ δ'ἠγνόησδ'ν ὡς θεὸς σὺ τῶν ὅλων
    ἐνταῦθα τῆς σῆς χρηστότητος δεῖ μόνον
    δι' ἣν ἅπαντας δωρεὰν σῴζειν θέλεις.

Migne also gives a Latin translation of the prayer:

Si quosdam alienos e tuis minis excipere velles, Christe mi, Platonem et Plutarchum excipe, quaeso. Ambo enim more ac sermone tuis legibus maxime paruerunt. Si vero te Deum universorum esse non cognoverunt, hic tua benignitate sola qua cunctos vis salvare gratis, opus est.

The prayer has been put into English in rhymed couplets by John Oakesmith in his *The Religion of Plutarch as Expounded in His Ethics* (London: Sheppard and St. John, 1901), p. 203. His translation is reprinted in the Loeb Classical Library edition of Plutarch's *Moralia,* Vol. I, p. xvii.

2

THE PHILOSOPHER-MONK ACCORDING TO DENIS THE PSEUDO-AREOPAGITE

by

CAROLINE CANFIELD PUTNAM, R.S.C.J.

In considering the problems raised by the writings of Denis the Pseudo-Areopagite, it is tempting to look on the persons and events he mentions as disguises rather than as clues. However, since Vanneste has pointed out the obvious link between the Areopagus speech of Acts 17 and the dionysian teaching about the "unknown God,"[1] it may be helpful to follow up other hints which Denis has given us.

I.

The Areopagus speech in its entirety is one of these. Viewed as a whole, it furnishes a more complete outline for *The Divine Names* than any of the other sources from which its author may have borrowed.[2] Aside from the concept of μετάνοια,[3] which he neglects altogether, the topics of the exhortation not only appear in *The Divine Names*, but are also enlarged upon: ἀγνωσία as a condition of human perfection and a quality of man's awareness of God, transcendent causality, the nature of limit and duration, the function of justice, and the oneness of mankind.

Denis also takes over the methods of the discourse. He begins as a philosopher talking to philosophers, laying down fundamental

---

[1] J. Vanneste, *Le Mystère de Dieu: Essai sur la structure rationnelle de la doctrine mystique du Pseudo-Denys l'Aréopagite* (Brussels: Desclée De Brouwer, 1959), p. 14.

[2] C. Pera, in *S. Thomae Aquinatis in librum beati Dionysii De divinis nominibus expositio* (Turin: Marietti, 1950), pp. 156-226, gives full notes on the relationship of *D.N.* IV to *De malorum subsistentia* of Proclus. E. von Ivanka in "Der Aufbau der Schrift 'De divinis nominibus' des Ps.-Dionysios," *Scholastik*, XXV (1940), pp. 389-99, shows the dependence of *D.N.* IX on the *Parmenides*.

[3] See Pera, *op. cit.*, p. 225, n. 3. He refers to *E.H.*, 561D.

points of natural theology and avoiding Jewish doctrine. He never refers to the Messiah or to the crucifixion; Christ is not named but is spoken of as the man who saves by the power of his resurrection.[4] We are left with the question clearly asked by Vanneste: Is Denis a Christian convert trying to present to fellow Christians a neoplatonic system compatible with faith, or is he an apologist attempting to show neoplatonists how their doctrines fit into the Christian creed?[5]

The authorship of the Areopagus speech itself is also open to question. In the pattern of New Testament historical narrative, such discourses serve literary ends and evade definite attribution. This is especially true of the greeting to the people of Lystra[6] and the sermon on the Aeropagus,[7] both of which are ascribed in the text to Paul.[8] At Lystra, the speaker points to the living God whose vitality is shown in his production of the universe and whose providence is shown in his care for it. At Athens, with the Stoics and Epicureans in mind, he makes a more prolonged effort to treat divine matters philosophically. His brilliant appeal to the Greeks "intent on their philosophy"[9] is met with irony at the outset and with mockery at the finish. Athenian dilettantes, perhaps a small group to begin with (if the Areopagus seats were to hold them), wished to hear something new, but of course could not stomach the notions of judgment, repentance, and resurrection.

If the text of the speech is followed verse by verse, its general relationship to the *Areopagitica* will stand out along with some of the particular interpretations.

v. 23. The speaker alludes to the dedication of an altar "to the unknown God (ἀγνώστῳ θεῷ)" who is worshipped by the Greeks "unknowingly (ἀγνοῦντες)."

---

[4] There are, of course, references to Christ in the *Areopagitica,* but they are minimal in a system which purports to be Christian.

[5] Vanneste, *op. cit.*, p. 180.

[6] Acts 14, 14-17.

[7] Acts 17, 22-31.

[8] Those who favor Pauline authorship include Curtius, Schmid, Prat, and Cerfaux; those who reject it are represented by Schweitzer, Pohlenz, and Dibelius. See J. Dupont, *Les problèmes du Livre des Actes d'après les travaux récents* (Louvain: 1950), pp. 88-91, and W. D. Davies, *Paul and Rabbinic Judaism* (London: S.P.C.K., 1962), pp. 187-88. Denis never alludes directly to the Areopagus speech. He does, however, cite the following epistles: I Cor. (13 times), II Cor. (twice), Rom. (6 times), I Tim. (3 times), II Tim. (twice), Gal. and Col. (once each).

[9] I Cor., 1, 22.

Denis turns this literal ignorance into a required frame of mind according to which the man who considers God is to view him. Through the "power of the Spirit" he shall be joined "ineffably and unknowingly" to the "ineffable and unknown (τοῖς ἀφθέγκτοις καὶ ἀγνώστοις ἀφθέγκτως καὶ ἀγνώστως)."[10] This "unknowing" is beyond reason (ὑπὲρ λόγον), intellect (νοῦς), and essence (οὐσία) and of course beyond sense (αἰσθητός). Repeatedly the terms "hidden (κρύφιος)," "invisible (ἀόρατος)," "incomprehensible (ἄληπτος)," and "uncontemplatable (ἀθεώρητος)" crop up as the only valid words to describe the God who is the object of this negative knowledge. This is the burden of Ch. I, the introduction to *The Divine Names* and also of the section in Ch. VII in which he deals with wisdom as a name of God.[11] He speaks of it as a light which is ineffable (ἄρρητον) and unnamable (ἀνώνυμον), which cannot be investigated (ἀνεξιχνίαστον), to which man must turn.

v. 24. God is maker of the world and lord of heaven and earth.

In the presentation of creation which Denis gives, God is the creative cause (ποιητικὸν αἴτιον).[12] He fashions all things,[13] through his goodness,[14] through his beauty,[15] through his life,[16] and through exemplars.[17] There is no reciprocity between the transcendent cause and its effects.[18] As "Lord of lords,"[19] he orders the universe perfectly and provides for it.[20]

v. 25. God does not dwell in temples as an idol would; he is transcendent. He has no need of men, yet he gives life to all. (This is opposed to both the Stoic and the Epicurean view of the world. For both, the material world is the real one, and reality is somewhat divine.)

Denis repeatedly emphasizes the superlative status of the divinity. God is beyond all that is and in full and entire possession of all the qualities of the beautiful-and-good. This typically Greek way of presenting ideal reality is put forth in Ch. IV in which the disposi-

---

10 *D.N.*, 585A-588B.
11 *D.N.*, 865BC.
12 *D.N.*, 704A, 705D.
13 *D.N.*, 872B.
14 *D.N.*, 717C.
15 *D.N.*, 704A.
16 *D.N.*, 856B.
17 *D.N.*, 824C.
18 *D.N.*, 916C. See also 893A and the generative stillness (γόνιμον στάσις) 916D.
19 Ps. 135, 3; Apoc. 19, 16.
20 *D.N.*, 969AB, and 816BC.

tion of all things, efficient, formal, final, and exemplary, falls to the beautiful-and-good.[21] Both Ch. V and Ch. VI treat of the being which produces all being and the life which gives all life.[22] All things exist or pre-exist in God and he alone is the principle of existence.[23] However, in the dionysian scheme, being parallels knowledge; the former is a positive reality, while the latter is chiefly a negative experience.[24]

v. 26. Men are brought to unity by God, and their times and limits are ordered by him.

Unification and oneness through consistency in being, through conformity to the analogy fixed on for each creature, and through an ordered arrangement in the hierarchy of being are primary tendencies for Denis. Not only is there an ontic urge in every being which impels it toward oneness, there is at the same time an equally fundamental intellectual urge toward union by knowledge.[25] God is also the lord of times and seasons,[26] while the circumvolutions of fire, earth, air and water, the original elements of the early cosmogonies, receive their impetus from God as their beginning and their end.[27] Although the notion of hierarchic order and pre-defined limits for both spiritual and material beings belongs more particularly to *The Celestial Hierarchy* and *The Ecclesiastical Hierarchy*, the assigning of limits and definitions are here considered as the function of the transcendent cause. Good order ($εὐταξία$) and harmony are measured out by divine justice,[28] while divine wisdom, the active, shaping word, reaches to the limits of all that is.[29]

v. 27. Men seek to find God. He is near to every one of them.

The neoplatonic law of loving desire and of return to the One, which Denis adopts, finds expression in Ch. IV, in the discussion of the power of the beautiful-and-good to call beings into existence and then attract them to itself.[30] It is the goal of all, their love, and

---

[21] *D.N.*, 704A-705D. See also 969B.
[22] *D.N.*, 816BC and 856A-857B.
[23] *D.N.*, 817C, 820CD.
[24] Vanneste, *op. cit.*, p. 131, provides a helpful diagram of the relationship between causality and transcendence.
[25] *D.N.*, 588B; 980B-981A.
[26] *D.N.*, 821B.
[27] *D.N.*, 821B-824A; 892D.
[28] *D.N.*, 893D.
[29] Sap., 18, 15; cited in *D.N.*, 872C.
[30] *D.N.*, 704B. In the Areopagus speech, a positive wish on the part of God is implied.

their final cause. Love and then ecstasy lead men to a realization of their potential union.³¹ This is the mode by which the lower is drawn to the higher. The final return will be to a perfect and immortal life.³²

v. 28-29. In God we "live and move and are."³³ "For, we are also his offspring."³⁴

The notion of "all things in God" is a recurrent theme for Denis. Speaking, in Ch. IV, of the divine causality, of the cohesion and communion of the various beings which exist, he supports neoplatonic expressions with words from Scriptures: "Of him and through him and to him are all things."³⁵ This theogony combines a divine unity with an equally divine fecundity.³⁶ Man moves in a triple motion of knowledge which reaches its climax in the endless circle of divine movement.³⁷

v. 30-31. The speaker comes to the abrupt conclusion that faith and repentance must be practiced to prepare for the judgment and resurrection in Christ. (This is quite different from the fortuitousness of Stoic doctrine.)

The resurrection and its foreshadowing in the transfiguration are important mysteries for Denis; the latter event, probably because of its connection with light, illumination, and divine knowledge.³⁸ We are "sons of the resurrection."³⁹ The giving of life after death, along with life here and now, is the work of the Trinity.⁴⁰ The action and the nature of Christ stem from the divine-informing ($\theta\epsilon o\pi\lambda\alpha\sigma\tau\iota\alpha$) which he assumed out of love.⁴¹

God is not only our efficient cause and final cause, he is our exemplar. We are made in his image and will be most perfectly like him when we exercise the spiritual powers of intellection which raise us higher than we are.⁴² Justice is an aspect of salvation

---

31 *D.N.*, 708A-712B.
32 *D.N.*, 856CD.
33 This phrase seems to be inspired by Epimenides of Cnossos.
34 This half-line is from the *Phenomena* of Aratus the Stoic poet. Cleanthes writes similarly in his *Hymn to Zeus*. The former stresses the transcendence of God, while the latter deals with man's creaturehood.
35 Rom. 11, 36.
36 *D.N.*, 981A. $\dot{\epsilon}\nu\dot{o}\tau\eta s\ \ddot{\eta}\ \gamma o\nu\iota\mu\dot{o}\tau\eta s$.
37 *D.N.*, 705AB. See also: 712D, 817C, 820CD, 857B, 980BC.
38 *D.N.*, 592A-C.
39 Luke 20, 36; *D.N.*, 592C.
40 John 5, 21; *D.N.*, 637AB.
41 *D.N.*, 640C-648A.
42 *D.N.*, 704.

which somehow redeems and orders all reality, not merely the ranks of men; Denis connects this with the release of liberation which purified and perfected creatures will enjoy.[43]

II.

In drawing on themes from the Areopagus speech, Denis has shown himself a philosopher rather than a theologian. His statements are descriptive rather than polemical, dispassionate rather than personal; they seem to epitomize the intellectual attitude which he expects of certain members of the ecclesiastical hierarchy. These are the monks who form the highest rank among the initiated and whose position enables them to carry on the life of the spirit which Denis admires. In order to verify this proposal, we must consider his description of the role of the monk in *The Ecclesiastical Hierarchy* and then look at the letters he has addressed to individual monks.

He treats of the consecration of monks and of the significance of their life in Ch. VI of *The Ecclesiastical Hierarchy*. There, the monk is depicted as the servant (θεραπευτής) of God.[44] That is, he attends on God, he serves him, he worships him. As servant, he is not involved in the active ministry but in the task of contemplation. He is one of the illumined and is thereby admitted to intellectual contemplation (νοερᾶθεωρία).[45] His service, one might say, is detachment. Yet Denis does not mean by this the sort of separation which a hermit has. In fact, he prefers to derive the term "monk," not from μοναχός (an isolated person), but from μόνος (one).[46] Thus, the monk becomes a force for unity, a small monad who exemplifies the transcendent unity of the One. It is his chief duty to remain united with the One, renouncing all division and communing in a manner different from that of the other initiates.[47]

Philosophy is the means to this union; so the monk must live by philosophy. Denis reveals what he understands by this in Letter VII to the bishop Polycarp.

---

[43] *D.N.*, 896A-897B.
[44] *E.H.*, 533C.
[45] *E.H.*, 532D.
[46] Denys Rutledge, *Cosmic Theology* (Staten Island: Alba House, 1965), presents a translation of *The Ecclesiastical Hierarchy* with an introduction and commentary. He singles out this etymology, p. 172. R. Roques, *L'Univers dionysien* (Paris: Aubier, 1954), p. 187, notes the equivalence of certain concepts in the monk's life: purification, light, interior unity, conformity to God.
[47] *E.H.*, 533D-536C.

This kind of knowledge of things (τῶν ὄντων γνῶσις), which the sophist Apollophanes well names 'love of wisdom' (φιλοσιφία) and which Paul calls 'the wisdom of God'[48] (σοφία Θεοῦ) should raise the true philosophers to the cause of beings (αἴτιον τῶν ὄντων) and of knowledge (τῆς γνώσεως).[49]

At the conclusion of the letter, Denis proposes the fitting attitude of mind for such a person. He should learn "humbly and meekly" the "more-than-wisdom of our religion (τὴν ὑπέρσοφον τῆς θρησκείας)."[50] Human dialectic is therefore not to be considered for its own sake; instead, revelation and the knowledge of God are the components of philosophy.[51] In *The Ecclesiastical Hierarchy*, this outlook takes on a moral dimension. Denis speaks of the "powerful and unshakable philosophy (ἀκατάσειστον ἐν καρτερίᾳ φιλοσοφίαν)" which enabled men to put up with many vicissitudes.[52]

Of the five letters addressed to monks, Letter VIII, to the monk Demophilus,[53] stands apart for its practical and human qualities. Its theme is gentleness and charity and the need to recognize one's status in the hierarchy. No man should arrogate to himself the duties of those above him or set himself up as the judge of others. To do so would reverse the right order of things and run counter to the specific calling of a monk: that of establishing a perfect inner unity and a spirit of love toward God and man.

The four letters (I-IV) written to Caius, on the other hand, have none of the moral tone or the personal savor which make the letter to Demophilus so lively. Instead, we find a compact little group of essays which sum up the main teachings of *The Divine Names* and *The Mystical Theology*. Letter I parallels the opening chapters of *The Divine Names* and provides a summary of *The Mystical Theology*. Letter II returns to the all-pervading theme of the transcendence of the One; a theme which appears in Chapters II, XI, and XIII of *The Divine Names*. The letter also takes up the concept of participation treated in Chapters II and V and the status of intermediary principles described in Ch. V. Letter III brings out

---

[48] Paul's "wisdom of God" is the person of Christ, I Cor. 1, 24. It is interesting to see in *D.N.*, 868A the Pauline attribution of wisdom to Christ (Colos. 2, 3) applied more generally to the divine wisdom which is the cause of all wisdom.
[49] 1080B.
[50] 1081C.
[51] *D.N.*, 640A.
[52] *E.H.*, 429C. See Roques, *op. cit.*, p. 188, nn.
[53] 1084B-1100D.

the mystery of the incarnation and stresses Christ's overriding love for men as the basis for his action, and thus finds echoes in *The Mystical Theology* and in Ch. II of *The Divine Names*.[53a] Finally, Letter IV, the so-called Christological letter, should be read in conjunction with the similar passage in Ch. I of *The Divine Names*.[54] The language of both passages does not permit us to decide whether Denis is tainted with monophysite doctrine or not.[55] As Vanneste suggests, this is beside the point. Denis has no concern with polemics. The letter is much more profitable as a demonstration of the method of mystical knowledge, where negation is as much true as affirmation.[56] Thus, the final sentence of the letter, once treasured by medieval theologians for its precise doctrine about the theandric action of Christ, is in fact based on the process of *The Mystical Theology* where one negates in order not to know and in order ultimately to transcend.[57]

Looking back on the matter covered, it is easy to discover a certain consistency in the selection of topics and in their presentation. From the Scriptures, the author of the *Areopagitica* seems to have chosen a passage which is in harmony with his own neoplatonic cast of mind, and to have associated his major philosophic work with it; from the types of human activity, he has singled out the function of the philosopher, in his case, a philosopher-about-God, and provided a special place in his hierarchic order for this activity. Not only that; he has emphasized the rank of monk by addressing to the unknown Caius four letters which form a compendium of his favorite doctrines. One can conjecture further: if Denis were not such a monk, he would certainly like to be, so that what has all along been theory might then become a true and personal experience.

III.

The following translation of the first four letters is meant to allow the reader to judge for himself.[58]

[53a] *D.N.*, 640-648.
[54] 592.
[55] Neither Roques (*op. cit.*, pp. 303-339; esp. 313-15), nor Vanneste (*op. cit.*, p. 121), nor M. Schiavone, *Neoplatonismo e cristianesimo nello Pseudo Dionigi* (Milan: Marzorati, 1963), p. 167, seems to favor a monophysite interpretation.
[56] *Op cit.*, pp. 122-23.
[57] Vanneste, *op. cit.*, p. 128. See also his more recent article, "Is the Mysticism of Pseudo-Dionysius Genuine?" *International Philosophical Quarterly*, III (1963), pp. 286-306.
[58] Letters I and II have been translated by A. B. Sharpe, *Mysticism: Its True*

LETTER I, TO THE MONK CAIUS

Darkness vanishes[59] before light,
   and the more so the greater the light;
Unknowing[60] is dispelled by knowledge,
   and the more so by much knowledge.

You must understand this not as a privation
   but as something transcendent
   and affirm above all truth
     that the unknowing which concerns God
     is hidden from those who have the light of being[61]
     and the knowledge of beings;
     and that his transcendent darkness remains veiled from all light
     and concealed from all knowledge.

If someone, seeing God, has grasped what he has seen,
   he has not seen God himself
   but one of his works which exist and can be known;
for he remains above every mind and every essence;
he is neither known nor exists,
   save as being beyond all essence and all thought.

And this complete unknowing, in a higher sense,
   is the knowledge of him who is beyond all that is known.

Nature and Value (London: Sands and Company, 1910), pp. 224-227. The present translation is new.

[59] De Gandillac prefers a more literal, and at the same time bolder, translation: "Darkness is invisible to light." *Oeuvres Complètes du Pseudo-Denys l'Aréopagite* (Paris: Aubier, 1943), p. 327. "Les mots *aphanès* et *aphanizein* signifient à la fois la non-vision et l'invisibilité. Nous adoptons une interprétation devant laquelle la plupart des traducteurs ont hésité . . . mais qui correspond exactement au paradoxe de la *Théologie mystique* (supériorité de l'apophase intégrale)." *Ibid.*, n. 2.

[60] $\dot{\alpha}\gamma\nu\omega\sigma\iota\alpha$ or ignorance. "Unknowing," the term used by the English writer of *The Cloud of Unknowing*, pertains exclusively to the type of experience described here and does not carry the privative or derogatory connotations which "ignorance" conveys.

[61] This expression may indicate the notion of created light or, as Vanneste translates it, "light (at the core) of being." J. Vanneste, *Le Mystère de Dieu: Essai sur la structure rationnelle de la doctrine mystique du Pseudo-Denys l'Aréopagite* (Brussels: Desclée De Brouwer, 1959), p. 243.

ΕΠΙΣΤΟΛΗ Α΄ ΓΑΙΩ ΘΕΡΑΠΕΥΤΗ

Τὸ σκότος ἀφανὲς γίνεται τῷ φωτὶ
καὶ μᾶλλον τῷ πολλῷ φωτί.
τὴν ἀγνωσίαν ἀφανίξουσιν αἱ γνώσεις
καὶ μᾶλλον αἱ πολλαὶ γνώσεις.

Ταῦτα ὑπεροχικῶς
ἀλλὰ μὴ κατὰ στέρησιν ἐκλαβών,
ἀπόφησον ὑπεραληθῶς
ὅτι λανθάνει τοὺς ἔχοντας ὂν φῶς
καὶ ὄντων γνῶσιν
ἡ κατὰ Θεὸν ἀγνωσία.
καὶ [ὅτι] τὸ ὑπερκείμενον αὐτοῦ σκότος
καὶ καλύπτεται παντὶ φωτὶ
καὶ ἀποκρύπτεται πᾶσαν γνῶσιν.

Καὶ εἴ τις, ἰδὼν, θεόν, συνῆκεν ὃ εἶδεν,
οὐκ αὐτὸν ἑώρακεν
ἀλλά τι τῶν αὐτοῦ τῶν ὄντων
καὶ γιγνωσκομένων.
αὐτὸς δὲ ὑπὲρ νοῦν καὶ ὑπὲρ οὐσίαν ὑπεριδρυμένος,
αὐτῷ τῷ καθόλου μὴ γινώσκεσθαι, μηδὲ εἶναι,
καὶ ἔστιν ὑπουσίως καί ὑπὲρ νοῦν γινώσκεται.

Καὶ ἡ κατὰ τὸ κρεῖττον παντελὴς ἀγνωσία
γνῶσίς ἐστι τοῦ ὑπὲρ πάντα τὰ γινωσκόμενα.

LETTER II, TO THE MONK CAIUS

How can he who surpasses everything
  be also beyond the principle of divinity
    and the principle of the good?

Only if we understand by deity and goodness
  the very largesse of a gift
    which produces the good and the divine;
  and if we think of the inimitable imitation[62]
    of him who is more than god and more than good.

---

[62] τὸ ἀμίμητον μίμημα one of the many plays on words by which Denis brings out the paradox of the situation he describes. In the same context, he juxtaposes ἄσχετος free, unconditioned with σχέσις condition, share.

And if such becomes, in fact,
   the source of the divinizing and of the rendering-good
     of what is divine and good,
   then he who is beyond all principles and the principle of all
     transcends deity and goodness thus understood,
   insofar as he is the transcending principle
     of divinity and goodness.

And insofar as he is inimitable and unpossessable,
   he exceeds all imitation and possession
   as well as those who imitate and those who share.

ΕΠΙΣΤΟΛΗ Β΄ ΤΩ ΑΥΤΩΓΑΙΩ ΘΕΡΑΠΕΥΤΗ

Πῶς ὁ πάντων ἐπέκεινα
   καὶ ὑπὲρ θεαρχίαν ἐστὶ
   καὶ ὑπὲρ ἀγαθαρχίαν;

Εἰ θεότητα καὶ ἀγαθότητα νοήσαις
   αὐτὸ τὸ χρῆμα
     τοῦ ἀγαθοποιοῦ καὶ θεοποιοῦ δώρου.
   καὶ τὸ ἀμίμητον μίμημα
     τοῦ ὑπερθέου καὶ ὑπεραγάθου
     καθ᾽ ὃ θεούμεθα καὶ ἀγαθυνόμεθα.

Καὶ γὰρ εἰ τοῦτο ἀρχὴ γίνεται
   τοῦ θεοῦσθαι καὶ ἀγαθύνεσθαι
     τοὺς θεουμένους καὶ ἀγαθυνομένους,
   ὁ πάσης ἀρχῆς ὑπερύρχιος,
     καὶ τῆς οὕτω λεγομένης θεότητος καὶ ἀγαθότητος,
   ὡς θεαρχίας καὶ ἀγαθαρχίας ἐστὶν ἐπέκεινα.

καθ ὅσον ἀμίμητος καὶ ἄσχετος,
   ὑπερέχει τῶν μιμήσεαν καὶ σχέσεων,
   καὶ τῶν μιμουμένων καὶ τῶν μετεχόντων.

LETTER III, TO THE MONK CAIUS

The *sudden*[62a] is that which was once hidden
   and which is now brought to light
      in a way beyond all expectation.

In applying this to the love of Christ for men,
   I think the Scriptures[63] give us to understand
   that he, who exceeds all essence,[64]
      came forth from his hiddenness and showed himself to us
      by assuming a human essence.

And he remains hidden even after this revelation,
   or (to use more divine words) within this revelation.

Indeed, the mystery of Jesus remains concealed:
   no word or thought can attain him as he is;
although we speak of him, he remains inexpressible;
although we think of him, he remains unknown.

ΕΠΙΣΤΟΛΗ Γ ΤΩ ΑΥΤΩ ΓΙΑΩ

Ἐξαίφνης ἐστὶ τὸ παρ ἐλπίζα,
καί ἐκ τοῦ τέως αφανοῦς
εἰς τὸ ἐ'μφανὲς ἐξαγόμενον.

Ἐπὶ δὲ τῆς κατὰ Χριστὸν φιλανθρωπίας,
καὶ τοῦτο οἶμαι τὴν θεολογίαν αἰνίττεσθαι,
τὸ ἐκ τοῦ κρυφίου τὸν ὑπερούσιον
εἰς τὴν καθ' ἡμᾶς ἐμφάνειαν ἀνθρωπικῶς
οὐσιωθέντα προεληλυθέναι.

Κρύφιος δέ ἐστι καὶ μετὰ τὴν ἔκφανσιν,
ἤ, ἵνα τὸ θειότερον εἴπω, καὶ ἐν τῇ ἐκφάνσει.

[62a] ἐξαίφνης. See Plato's *Symposium*, 210 E. On several occasions, Denis is occupied with the meaning of words, giving to them a particular significance which they had not hitherto received. See, for instance, the etymology of the term κάλλος, which he derives from Plato's *Cratylus*, 416 C (*D.N.*, 701 C) and his bold use of the term ἔρως, *D.N.*, 709 BC.

[63] *Mal.*, 3, 1. "Suddenly the Lord whom you seek will enter his temple."

[64] οὐσία. Cordier and the medieval translators usually render this as *substantia*; however, "essence" is closer to the original meaning.

καὶ τοῦτο γὰρ Ἰησοῦ κέκρυπται,
καὶ οὐδενὶ λόγῳ οὔτε νῷ τὸ κατ᾽ αὐτὸν ἐξῆκται μυστήριον,
ἀλλὰ καὶ λεγόμενον ἄρρητον μένει,
καὶ νοούμενον ἄγνωστον.

LETTER IV, TO THE MONK CAIUS

You ask how Jesus, who is beyond all that is,
   should align himself by his essence with men.

He is not called a man because he is the maker of men,
   but as being, wholly and in essence, truly man.
We do not limit Jesus by a human description,
   for he is not merely a man
     (he would not be beyond all essence if he were a mere man):
   but, out of his surpassing love for men, truly man.
Yet, being truly man,
   he who is more-than-man and, at the same time, really man,
     out of his exceeding love for men,
     while transcending all essence, took on a human essence.
Nor is he any the less abounding in his transcendent essence,
   he who is forever the transcendent and superabundant.

In assuming an essence in a superessential fashion,
   he accomplishes human actions in a more-than-human way.
This is shown by his marvellous birth of a virgin
   and by the fact that unsteady water,
     remaining firm and compact by a power beyond its nature
     instead of yielding,
     could bear the weight of his material and earthbound feet.[65]

Who can recount his numerous other marvels?
In considering them from a divine point of view,
   we shall know beyond all intelligence
that what is affirmed positively about the love of Jesus for men
   has the value of a transcendent negation.

To sum up, we should say
   that he was in fact neither a mere man
     nor not a man;

---

[65] Matt., 14, 25. See *D.N.*, 648 A, for a listing of the same miracles.

for he was born of man, yet greater than man;
and, in a manner greater than man, he became man.

For the rest, he did not carry out divine actions as God
and human actions as man;
but rather, as God-made-man,
he lived among[66] us in an unheard of way of acting,
at once human and divine.[67]

ΕΠΙΣΤΟΛΗ Δ' ΤΩ ΑΥΤΩ ΓΑΙΩ ΘΕΡΑΠΕΥΤΗ

Πῶς, φῇς, Ἰησυῦς ὁ πάντων ἐπέκεινα,
πᾶσίν ἐστιν ἀνθρώποις οὐσιωδῶς συντεταγμένος;

Οὐ γὰρ ὡς αἴτιος ἀνθρώτων ἐνθάδελέγεται ἄνθρωπος,
ἀλλ' ὡς αὐτὸς κατ' οὐσίαν ὅλην ἀληθῶς ἄνθρωπος ὤν.

Ἡμεῖς δὲ τὸν Ἰησοῦν οὐκ ἀνθρωπικῶς ἀφορίζομεν.
οὐδὲ γὰρ ἂν θρωπος μόνον
(οὐδὲ ὑπερούσιος, ἢ ἄνθρωπος μόνον),
ἀλλ' ἄνθρωπος ἀληθῶς ὁ διαφερόντως φιλάνθρωπος ὑπεράνθρώπους
καὶ καιὰ ἀνθρώπους
ἐκ τῆς τῶν ανθρώπων ουσίας
ὁ ὑπερούσιος οὐσωμενος.

Ἔστι δὲ οὐδὲυ ἧττον ὑπερουσιότητος ὑπερπλήρης
ὁ ἀεὶ ὑπερούσιος, ἀμέλει τῇ ταύτης περιουσίᾳ.
Καὶ εἰς οὐσίαν ἀληθῶς ἐλθὼν, ὑπὲρ οὐσίαν οὐσιώθη,
καὶ ὑπὲρ ἄγθρωπον ἐνήργει τὰ ἀνθρώπου.
Καὶ δηλοῖ παρθένος ὑπερφυῶς κύουσα,
καὶ ὕδωρ ἄστατον,
ὑλικῶν καὶ γεηρῶν ποδῶν ἀνέχον βάρος,
καὶ μὴ ὑπεῖκον.
ἀδδ' ὑπερφυεῖ δυνάμει πρὸς τὸ ἀδιάχυτον συνιστάμενον.
Τί ἄν. τις τὰ λοιπὰ, πάμπολλα ὄντα, διέλθοι;
δι' ὧν ὁ θείως ὁρῶν,

---

[66] Schiavone notes that the use of the term πολιτεύω is significant. It "recalls the concept of the right of citizenship. It is evident that the Pseudo-Dionysius alludes to the redemptive rapprochement beween God and man brought about by the Incarnation and Redemption of Christ." *Op. cit.*, p. 167, n. 2. Denis uses this expression only one other time to describe the initiation of baptism. *E.H.*, 396A.

[67] θεανδρικός. This term is not repeated in the *Areopagitica*.

ὑπὲρ νοῦν γνώσεται,
καὶ τὰ ἐπὶ τῇ φιλανθρωπίᾳ τοῦ Ἰησοῦ καταφασκόμενα,
δύναμιν ὑπεροχικῆς ἀποφάσεως ἔχοντα.

Καὶ γὰρ, ἵνα συνελόντες εἴπωμεν,
οὐδὲ ἄνθρωπος ἦν,
οὐχ ὡς μὴ ἄνθρωπος,
ἀλλ' ὡς ἐξ ἀνθρώπων, ἀνθρώπων ἐπέκεινα,
καὶ ὑπὲρ ἄνθρωπον ἀληθῶς ἄνθρωπος γεγονώς.

Καὶ τὸ λοιπὸν, οὐ κατὰ Θεὸν τὰ θεῖα δράσας,
οὐ τὰ ἀνθρώπεια κατὰ ἄνθρωπον,
ἀλλ' ἀνδρωθέντος Θεοῦ,
καινήν τινα τὴν θεανδρικὴν ἐνέργειαν
ἡμῖν πεπολιτευμένος.

3

THE LOGIC OF CONFUCIAN DIALOGUES

by

A. S. Cua

I. *Introduction*

It is a noteworthy characteristic of Chinese philosophical thought that its theses are rarely stated and expounded in the form of systematic discourse. In many classical Chinese philosophical writings, one may observe the absence of orderly and connected reasoning that obeys the strict canons of either inductive or deductive logic. Fung Yu-lan succinctly explains that, "Chinese philosophers were accustomed to expressing themselves in the form of aphorisms, apothegms, or allusions and illustrations." He adds that the insufficiency of linguistic articulateness is "compensated for, however, by their suggestiveness."[1] This way of thinking and expression appears to be more congenial to a poetic rather than a logical and analytical mind. This feature is particularly striking in the Confucian *Lun Yü* or the *Analects* and *Lao-tzu* or *Tao Teh Ching*. In the case of the *Analects*, it is primarily a record of dialogues between Confucius and his disciples and other purportedly historical persons. Hajime Nakamura remarks that, "in the *Analects* of Confucius there are many separate examples of moral conduct from which certain lessons are inductively drawn. There are many aphorisms, but there is no dialectic such as one finds in Plato."[2] As aphorisms, the remarks of Confucius are thereby interpreted as short sayings embodying universal truths. The remarks are thus amenable to orderly exposition in terms of certain explicit sayings that seem to form the underlying theme of the *Analects*. The interesting question is whether or not the *Analects* possess a logical

---

[1] Fung Yu-Lan, *A Short History of Chinese Philosophy* (New York, 1950), p. 12.
[2] Hajime Nakamura, *Ways of Thinking of Eastern Peoples: India, China, Tibet, and Japan* (Honolulu, 1964), p. 188.

structure or method that has philosophical significance. The affirmative answer to this question would be important from the point of view of philosophical exposition and evaluation of a work of non-logical form.

In a recent essay, Donald Holzman convincingly argued that the *Analects* in fact portray a philosophical method distinct from that depicted in the Socratic dialogues of Plato. Holzman writes that, "the *Conversations* (or *Analects* as they are commonly, but improperly, called after Legge's translation) of Confucius are the source of the tradition and one of its most perfect examples."[3] As exhibiting a philosophic method of conversation, the *Analects* contain two essential features: (1) with the exception of Book X, there are "a record of spoken words, whether in conversations or not, and certain peculiarities of style prove clearly that the object of the recorder or recorders of the words has been to preserve as much as the recalcitrant Chinese character was willing to preserve of the colloquial flavor of the original speech," and (2) "they are usually very short" and present "an attempt to capture the living speech of Confucius, the implication being that it was there that lay the real meaning of his philosophy and not in any perhaps clearer and more systematic exposition of his thought."[4] In this essay, I would like to discuss certain characteristics of the *Analects* in the use of general remarks with a view of developing a conceptual map that will hopefully provide an explanation, and perhaps also a justification for the Confucian use of dialogues as a philosophical method. A dialogue, being a conversation between two or more persons, is here conceived in terms of the logic of questions and answers. Dialogue is thus a *genus* that embraces the Confucian and Socratic uses as *differentiae*.

II. *Some Characteristics of Confucian Dialogues*[5]

Before proceeding to set forth a conceptual map for the Confucian use of dialogues, it is important and illuminating to examine cer-

---

[3] Donald Holzman, "The Conversational Tradition in Chinese Philosophy," *Philosophy East and West* (Vol. VI, No. 3, 1956), p. 224.
[4] *Ibid.*, p. 225.
[5] For the purpose of this paper, I shall use the term "Confucian dialogues" to refer to the conversations in the *Analects*. Unless otherwise indicated, all translations from the *Analects* are taken from *A Source Book in Chinese Philosophy*, translated and compiled by Professor Wing-tsit Chan (Princeton, 1963).

tain characteristics of the use of general remarks in the *Analects* that constitute, as it were, some of the principal features of Confucian logic or methodology. These features are ultimately related to a pragmatic and humanistic intention. In the last analysis, Confucian logic and ethics are merged in a way of thinking in which truth and goodness are seen as aspects of the same concern. The prime exemplar is Wang Yang-ming's doctrine of the unity of knowledge and action.

A closer study of the use of certain general remarks in the Confucian dialogues discloses at least the following formal but related characteristics: (1) the use of general remarks for making fundamental ethical declarations, (2) the frequent occurrence of contrasting pair of concepts for elucidation, and (3) the explanation of concepts by particular rules. I hope to show that these three characteristics represent the varying degrees of specification of meanings of concepts. I shall gather certain dialogues as illustrating these characteristics without claiming to give an adequate and connected exposition of Confucian ethics.

1. In a work that contains largely logically independent dialogues with neither an explicit nor seemingly implicit control of a subject matter, the acute problem relates to that of coherence or unity of discourse. This should at once despair of any attempt to regard the work as exhibiting an orderly system of thinking. The *Analects,* being a record of dialogues, appear to be tied to the particular contexts or situations in which the utterances were made. As utterances, the remarks of Confucius were speech-acts in the Austinian sense in that they were temporal occurrences viewed as significant in terms of their capacity to inform the hearers of their relevance to concrete situations, or as in the case of dialogue, to concrete questions.[6] Concrete questions are, ultimately, tied up with the situations in which the questions arise. In the Confucian dialogues, certain utterances of Confucius have been generally accepted as fundamental ethical declarations. The following dialogues may be presented as support for this interpretation of the *Analects:*

[6] I do not mean to suggest here that Austin's theory of speech-acts in *How To Do Things With Words* (Cambridge, 1963) is applicable *in toto* to Confucian dialogues. However, certain Austinian insights are relevant here, for example, the appropriateness of linguistic utterances and performances as governed by rules. In Confucian *Analects,* the rules, as we shall later see, are ethico-semantic rules. This interpretation owes much to the incisive work of Hu Shih in *The Development of the Logical Method in Ancient China* (Shanghai, 1922, Paragon Reprint Corp., 1963).

a. Confucius said, "T'san, there is one thread that runs through my doctrines." Tseng Tzu said, "Yes." After Confucius had left, the disciples asked him, "What did he mean?" Tseng Tzu replied, *"The way of our Master is none other than conscientiousness (Chung) and altruism (Shu)"* (4:15).

b. Tzu-Kung said, "If a ruler extensively confers benefit on the people and can bring salvation to all, what do you think of him? Would you call him a man of humanity?" Confucius said, "Why only a man of humanity? He is without doubt a sage. Even (sage-emperors) Yao and Shun fell short of it. *A man of humanity, wishing to establish his own character, also establishes the character of others, and wishing to be prominent himself, also helps others to be prominent. To be able to judge others by what is near to ourselves may be called the method of realizing humanity"* (6:28).

c. Tzu-Kung asked, "Is there one word which can serve as the guiding principle for conduct throughout life?" Confucius said, "It is the word altruism *(Shu). Do not do to others what you do not want them to do to you"* (15:23).

d. Tzu-chang asked Confucius about humanity. Confucius said, *"One who can practice five things wherever he may be is a man of humanity."* Tzu-chang asked what the five are. Confucius said, *"Earnestness, liberality, truthfulness, diligence,* and *generosity.* If one is earnest, one will not be treated with disrespect. If one is liberal, one will win the hearts of all. If one is truthful, one will be trusted. If one is diligent, one will be successful. And if one is generous, one will be able to enjoy the service of others" (17:6).

The italicized expressions in the above dialogues may be construed as a series of general remarks that explicates the concept of *jen* or humanity or human-heartedness.[7] It must be observed that all the general remarks are embedded in particular contexts of dialogue. None amounts to an analytic definition that purports to establish a semantic equivalence between the definiens and the definiendum. As general remarks, they require further explication since the purported explanation of *jen* contains general concepts as in passages a and d. The remark in c appears to be a statement of a moral rule—the Golden Rule that has been equated

[7] For an interpretation and development of this concept in the history of Chinese philosophy, see Wing-tsit Chan, "The Evolution of the Confucian Concept *Jen,*" *Philosophy East and West* (Vol. IV, No. 4, 1955).

with b.[8] The relation between a, b, and c is quite clear to students of the *Analects*. One may state that Confucius' basic ethical doctrine is based on the concept of *jen* which may be explicated in terms of conscientiousness and altruism. Altruism is essentially the Golden Rule: "Do not do to others what you do not want them to do to you." Passage b may be regarded not so much as another expression of a, but a method of moral achievement which is essentially that of self-cultivation—a prominent concept in Confucian philosophy. Moreover, all the general remarks do not function in abstract discourse, they are an ingredient in the Confucian dialogues that occur in living, concrete, and particular contexts. In the words of Holzman, "he [Confucius] never quite gives a definition or an abstraction of goodness [*jen*]; all his replies concern different concrete facets, immanent in specific vital contexts, of this supreme virtue."[9] These general remarks may be viewed as normative insights into the human reality. Their ultimate significance lies in their relevance to the problematic texture of our moral life.

One problem relates to passage d. In this passage the concept of humanity is explained in terms of the practice of "earnestness, liberality, truthfulness, diligence, and generosity."[10] These "five things" appear to be desirable qualities required of a man of humanity. The desirability of these qualities is appealed to what the characters of the dialogue approved of and implies that all men would approve of the same qualities. These moral qualities, if my interpretation of the passage is correct, constitute the criteria of personal merit. These criteria are related to the Golden Rule in that the rightness of an act is to be judged not merely in conformity with the propriety of the act but also the qualities of the moral agent. In this sense, Confucius is more concerned with the

---

[8] Chan, *A Source Book in Chinese Philosophy*, p. 27.

[9] Holzman, p. 226.

[10] I have here omitted a key passage on *jen:* "to love all men" (*Analects*, 12:22). Professor Chan points out that the concept *jen* is subject to both a general and particular interpretation. As a general virtue, *jen* means humanity, as a particular virtue it means love. (Wing-tsit Chan, "The Evolution of the Confucian Concept *Jen*," pp. 299-300; and *Source Book on Chinese Philosophy*, p. 40.) If love is interpreted as a quality of behavior, which is ultimately a quality of moral character, it seems to have the same status as those in passage d, i.e., earnestness, liberality, truthfulness, diligence, and generosity. It may well be true that Confucius has a scheme for grading these qualities in the order of merit. However, the Confucian dialogues do not appear to indicate such a grading scheme, since they are responses to particular questions in particular situations.

character of moral agents as it is displayed in rule-governed behavior rather than human actions independent of the motives of the actors.

If the above comments on the passages are not far from the mark, what appear as general remarks in some Confucian dialogues function as fundamental ethical declarations aiming at an exposition of a moral ideal of humanity or human-heartedness. The ideal is to be understood in terms of moral rules and criteria. The former as guiding maxims of conduct and the latter as standards for evaluating the merit of the moral agent. These rules and criteria, as we shall later see, are to be comprehended by reference to the particular contexts of questions and answers. It is unfortunate that the living and vital contexts of the Confucian dialogues were not recorded for our scrutiny. This absence of living and vital contexts sets a task for an hypothetical construction of actual contexts—a task that lies beyond the scope of this essay. There is no question of verification or retrodiction here, but a question of the plausibility of constructed contexts as relevant to our actual situations. The normative insights of Confucius, if any, owe to their relevance to concrete contexts, not to any claim to a privileged apprehension of universal and abstract principles. This may account for the enthusiasm of a recent translator, who states that:

> Confucius speaks to all men as man to man.... Confucius has much to say to us today. Through him we could, if we so willed, achieve a more valid synthesis of the facts available to our generation—they are far more vast than ever before—and thus formulate for ourselves a better Truth.[11]

2. Another feature of the Confucian dialogues is the frequent occurrence of contrasting pair of concepts. This is particularly evident in the elucidation of the notion of the superior man *(Chün-tzu)*. We may note the following explanatory passages:

a. Confucius said, "The superior man is broadminded but not partisan; the inferior man is partisan but not broadminded" (2:14).

b. Confucius said, "The superior man thinks of virtue; the inferior man thinks of possessions. The superior man thinks of sanctions; the inferior man thinks of personal favors" (4:11).

c. Confucius said, "The superior man understands righteousness (*i*); the inferior man understands profit" (4:16).

---
[11] James R. Ware (tr.), *The Sayings of Confucius* (Mentor Books, 1955), p. 7.

d. Confucius said, "The superior man brings the good things of others to completion and does not bring the bad things of others to completion. The inferior man does just the opposite" (12:16).

These passages show a method of explanation by the use of contrasting concepts. The concept of the superior man—the moral ideal of Confucius—is elucidated by way of contrast with the concept of the inferior man in terms of a man's moral qualities. These qualities are dispositions or characteristic tendencies toward actions in the living problematic contexts that call for moral behavior. The remarks of Confucius here, like those in section 1, are again general remarks as answers to questions asked by his disciples. But these remarks appear to be less general in that they appear to set a limitation or division of concepts, explaining one by indicating that the extension of one term differs from that of the other. The method here resembles the method of explanation by exclusion rather than by positive explication. Again, the general remarks must be viewed as answers to concrete questions presumably varying from one occasion to another. Thus there is here no "essential definition" of the "superior man." The understanding of this concept may be contrasted with that of an "inferior man." But these contrasts are embedded in the living contexts of questions in concrete situations.

3. A very significant feature of the Confucian dialogues is the explanation of concepts by the use of particular rules. This is particularly instructive in the following passages concerning filial piety *(Hsiao)*:[12]

a. Confucius said, "When a man's father is alive, look at the bent of his will. When his father is dead, look at his conduct. If for three years [of mourning] he does not change from the way of his father, he may be called filial" (1:11).

b. Meng I Tzu asked about filial piety. Confucius said: "Never disobey." [Later] when Fan Ch'ih was driving him, Confucius told him, "Meng-sun asked me about filial piety, and I answered him, 'Never disobey'." Fan Chi'ih said, "What does that mean?"

[12] To Confucius, filial piety is ultimately related to *jen* as in his remark that, "filial piety and brotherly respect are the root of humanity *(jen)*" (1:2). For the exposition of this Confucian concept see Hsieh Yu-Wei, "Filial Piety and Chinese Society," in *Philosophy and Culture: East and West*, ed. C. A. Moore (Honolulu, 1962).

Confucius said, "When parents are alive, serve them according to the rules of propriety. When they die, bury them according to the rules of propriety and sacrifice to them according to the rules of propriety" (2:5).

c. Meng Wu-po asked about filial piety. Confucius said, "Especially be anxious lest parents should be sick" (2:6).

d. Tzu-yu asked about filial piety. Confucius said, "Filial piety nowadays means to be able to support one's parents. But we support even dogs and horses. If there is no feeling of reverence, wherein lies the difference?" (2:7).

Unlike the Confucian dialogues in sections 1 and 2, the above passages are more specific in that they draw attention to special rules (*li* or rules of propriety) as in a and b, and the required attitude in c and d in the application of these rules in actual conduct. Here the ethics of Confucius as an ethics of human character emerges in a clear outline. Being a filial son implies the attitude of reverence in the performance of actions conforming to rules of propriety which are accepted and recognized in one's moral tradition.

It is interesting to note here that the special rules or rules of propriety constitute an explanation of the conduct of filial piety, because these rules are assumed to be directly regulative of the actions called "filial." A complete description of filial actions would thus include an account of such actions in terms of the normative context of rules as relevant to certain types of situation. Although the above dialogues are more specific and definite than those in sections 1 and 2, they still require further specification for assuring their concrete relevance to the characters and participants in the *Analects*, since the utterances were intended as answers to questions of vital concern. Owing to the fact that most of the questions asked concerned conduct, the answers to these questions must finally be elucidated in terms of particular examples that can serve as guides to conduct.

The *Analects* to some scholars do in fact portray a mental attitude that emphasizes the particular and the concrete as a way of explaining concepts.[13] This is quite evident in the frequent occur-

---

[13] "The way of thinking in which the Chinese prefer particular, concrete, and intuitive explanations may be seen in their way of explaining ideas and teaching people by the use of particular examples. To most Chinese, therefore, ethics

rence of proper names intended as exemplars of the Confucian ideal. Yao and Shun, regarded by Confucius as sage-emperors, were frequently commended as models of virtue.[14] Other purportedly historical personages were also cited as particular exemplars of conduct as in the following dialogue:

> Tzu-lu asked what was meant by, "the perfect man." The master said, If anyone had the wisdom of Tsang Wu Chung, the uncovetousness of Meng Kung Ch'o, the valour of Chuang Tzu of P'ien and the dexterity of Jan Ch'iu, and had graced these virtues by the cultivation of ritual and music, then indeed I think we might call him "a perfect man" (14:13).[15]

This dialogue is interesting in that it explains the notion of a perfect man by way of the persons that were judged to have concretely embodied the ideal qualities. These persons, if we take them seriously, appear to be the paradigms that individuals should aspire, although none of them seems to be a complete and sufficient embodiment of perfection. On the whole, Yao and Shun were more heartily taken as paragons of virtue rather than the persons mentioned in the dialogue.

In this part of the essay I hope I have adequately illustrated three characteristic uses of general remarks in the Confucian dialogues. These uses may be viewed in terms of a method of explanation of concepts commencing with an apparently universal statement and then specifying the meaning of the concepts by the method of exclusion. The final determination of the meaning of concepts rests on their specific relevance to concrete situations and persons. Being dialogues, the *Analects* contain a great many questions and answers. Since a dialogue is a living discourse, the apparently general questions must be answered in terms of particulars. In a different context, Collingwood incisively points out that questions and answers must be conceived as strictly correlative. "A proposition was not an answer, or at any rate could not be the right answer, to any question which might have been answered otherwise. A highly detailed and particularized proposition must be the answer, not to a vague and generalized question, but to a question as detailed and particularized as itself."[16] This apt state-

---

is not understood or taught as part of a universal law, but is grasped on the basis of particular experiences, and is then utilized to realize human truth" (Nakamura, p. 198).

[14] See *Analects*, 6:28, 14:45, 20:1.
[15] Arthur Waley's translation, *The Analects of Confucius* (London, 1938).
[16] R. G. Collingwood, *An Autobiography* (Oxford, 1939), pp. 31-2.

ment perhaps lies at the heart of the highly practical character of Chinese philosophy, which, as Professor Chan has recently shown, is related to the Chinese concept of truth. In the Chinese way of thinking, "truth is not understood as something revealed from above or as an abstract principle, however logically consistent, but as a discoverable and demonstrable principle in human affairs. In other words, the real test of truth is in human history."[17] Confucius' appeal to Yao and Shun and his general respect for antiquity exemplify this concept of truth. This is not offered as a justification but only as an explanation for the varying and sometimes highly detailed and particularized answers to apparently general questions in the Confucian dialogues. Moreover, the various features of the dialogues discussed may be used as a way of presenting a logical map for an adequate understanding of the Confucian dialogues, and perhaps also used as a means for giving an orderly exposition of the *Analects* in terms of a structure of a way of thinking rather than a substantive ethics.

As an example, one may attempt a coherent exposition of the *Analects* by utilizing the three formal features as stages in the explanation of the general concepts used in the fundamental ethical declarations in the Confucian dialogues. If one takes the moral concept *jen* or humanity as the most general Confucian concept by virtue of its frequent occurrence, the concept requires explanation in terms of moral rules and criteria. To explain these, one is required to set a limit to the domain of application of the concept by the method of exclusion. The delimitation of the domain has value in vital contexts only if the concept can be explained in terms of recognized and accepted rules. This would account for Confucius' emphasis on *li* or rules of propriety. Ultimately, however, these rules of propriety must be shown to have concrete relevance to situations involving moral agents. Some moral agents do embody the concept of *jen*. These agents are then to be regarded as paradigms comparable to *li* or rules of propriety. The structure of Confucian ethics is in this way amenable to an orderly treatment. I do not claim here that this is the only possible method of exposition, but as a plausible method that attempts to do justice to the various features of Confucian dialogues. In the next part of the essay, I shall attempt to sketch a conceptual map

---

[17] Chan, "Chinese Theory and Practice," in Moore's *Philosophy and Culture: East and West*, pp. 81-2.

for the Confucian use of dialogues, briefly termed the Confucian logic.

III. *The Confucian Logic: The Rectification of Names (Cheng Ming)*

Hu Shih has forcefully argued that the locus of Confucian logic lies in the doctrine of rectification of names. The doctrine arises because Confucius conceived of "the problem of philosophy as essentially one of intellectual reorganization."[18] In the *Analects,* the most extensive dialogue on the rectification of names is the following:[19]

> Tzu-lu said, "The ruler of Wei is waiting for you to serve in his administration. What will be your first measure?" Confucius said, "It will certainly concern the rectification of names. . . . If names are not rectified, then language will not be in accord with truth. If language is not in accord with truth, then things cannot be accomplished. If things cannot be accomplished, then ceremony and music will not flourish. If ceremonies and music do not flourish, then punishment will not be just. If punishments are not just, then the people will not know how to move hand or foot. Therefore the superior man will give only names that can be described in speech and say only what can be carried out in practice. With regard to his speech, the superior man does not take it lightly, that is all" (13:3).

This is the paradigm source of the well-known doctrine of rectification of names. From the recent point of view of logic of ethics or ethical methodology, we may restate this doctrine as follows: Ethical concepts are governed by moral rules which define offices and functions. The names of these offices and functions pragmatically imply corresponding duties and obligations. Failure to "live up to" the names is a moral failure that requires rectification. To rectify a name is to make "the real relationships and duties and institutions conform as far as possible to their *ideal* meanings."[20] The moral rules thus function as ethico-semantic rules that determine the contents of these ideal meanings. The task of Confucian logic is to make certain that actual conduct does not deviate from

---
[18] Hu Shih, p. 24.
[19] "To govern is to rectify" *(Analects,* 12:17). Dialogues relevant to rectification of names are found in *Analects,* 6:23, 12:11, 13:6, 2:13, 4:5, 5:9.
[20] Hu Shih, p. 26.

the ethico-semantic rules. The success of this task would depend on our ability to discover these ideal meanings. This is the underlying motive, perhaps, in the disturbing use of argument from history in Chinese philosophy. This historicism as a form of argument is justly regarded as suspect, but it plays an important role in the conceptual map that I shall sketch in accordance with the distinctive features of the Confucian dialogues that we have discussed. The elements in this conceptual landscape are elucidated by contrast with those in the Socratic use of dialogues. What I have to offer may in effect provide a conceptual base for the doctrine of the rectification of names.

1. The priority of problematic context over general principles.

The Confucian use of dialogues presupposes a living and vital context in which problems and questions arise. Unlike the Socratic dialogues of Plato, they are not utilized for the dialectical purpose of arriving at universal and essential definitions which are logically independent of spatial and temporal conditions. We may formulate this basic conceptual element in the Confucian methodology as *the actual priority existence over essence*. Because of its pragmatic and humanistic intention, existence is viewed as human existence or any existence that is endowed with a normative status. Every existence is an actual existence, since normative endowment is possible only with respect to actual living entities. Existence in this sense has a spatio-temporal dimension. However the Confucian concepts of *space* and *time* are primarily cultural. Cognitive understanding of any principle is thus a species of cultural and historical understanding rather than an intuitive apprehension of non-spatial and non-temporal essences. This draws our attention to the second element of the Confucian logic.

2. General principles as constituted by functioning rules.

In the Socratic dialogues, concepts are determined not by particular examples of their uses or denotation. It is the concept that must ultimately determine the significance and classification of examples. In principle the range of variables is specified by the concepts or general principles governing the uses of concepts. In this methodology, the examples of the use of concepts are extraneous to their content or principles. The Confucian methodology, on the other hand, regards the examples as inherent in the use or understanding of concepts. The concepts of *jen* or humanity and *hsiao* or filial piety, as we have seen, are understood and explained by way of the ethico-semantic rules or the rules of propriety. The absence of essential definitions shows that concepts or general principles are incompletely specified by examples. Inherent in this conceptual scheme is the allowability of the range of variables to take care of present and future contingencies. Although examples in terms of rules and personalities are constitutive of the content of principles, they do not exhaustively determine the range of application. Another way of expressing this is that the so-called examples are not really exemplifications of concepts or general principles but are *exemplars*. The exemplars may either take the form of ethico-semantic rules *(li)* or historical personages. Unlike the Socratic essentialist, the Confucian regards form and content as united in the living problematic situation. Principles are thereby understood with reference to rules and rules with reference to concrete situations. One cannot adequately understand principles and rules apart from these concrete situations.

3. General principles as open-textured.

In Socratic essentialism, the sort of content is thus deduced from the cognitive definitions of concepts. In the Confucian use of dialogue, on the other hand, the content is tied up with the form of concepts and principles—it is altogether contingent upon the situations and the persons involved. In spite of the constant use of appeal to history, the Confucian principles were not meant as absolute determinants of every concrete and problematic situation. In the *Analects,* we may note the varying emphasis on flexibility. As H. E. Creel has shown, Confucius' "thinking was characterized by an absence of dogma, a clear realization of the necessity of suspended judgment, and an espousal of intellectual democracy that, in its forthright acceptance of the minimal philosophic conditions of scientific thinking, is altogether remarkable."[21] Or in the words of a recent historian of Confucian philosophy:

> Confucianism excels in its adaptability to varying circumstances and its magnetism, which attracts whatever is good and useful. . . . Hence the chief strength of Confucianism is its flexibility, a remarkable quality that enables it to resist all

[21] H. G. Creel, *Confucius and the Chinese Way* (New York and Evanston, 1960), p. 137.

pressures and to face all adversities. For this reason, though suffering eclipse from time to time, it has always emerged with renewed brilliance.[22]

The element of flexibility lies ultimately in the open-textured principles. The rules which constitute their content are not free from exceptions and qualifications. Thus it is said in *Chung Yung* that "the moral man conforms himself to his life circumstances; he does not desire anything outside of his position. . . . In one word, the moral man can find himself in no situation in life in which he is not master of himself."[23] To assure the nonarbitrariness in the exercise of flexibility with respect to principles and rules, the Confucian methodology requires the use and appeal to history. For good or for ill, the burden of individual decision is placed on the context of a historic tradition. In this way the use of historic personages as exemplars of moral ideals provides the orbit upon which individual choices are to be made. Principles and rules are thus ultimately interpreted and understood in the light of the historic exemplars. Consequently, the dimensions of moral choice are clothed in a historical and cultural milieu. Every departure from this moral tradition would be justified only by an appeal to the particular living problematic context. Every action or decision, if it is to be justified at all, must contain an historical reference. The principles, being open-textured, need to be particularized by the exercise of *good sense* or sense of reasonableness or appropriateness. The approach radically differs from the Socratic burden of self-knowledge which is viewed as logically independent of tradition. The Confucian burden of individuality is thus an existential and cultural burden, whereas the Socratic burden implies primarily the use of cognitive or intellectual capacities.

4. Philosophy as rectification of names.

In the light of the above elements of the conceptual map, the Confucian concept of philosophy is reconstructive or rectificatory of names. It is primarily a progressive process of enrichment of the content of principles by individual decisions in harmony with history. In principle every name or concept implies a norm that purports to regulate actions in living contexts. Rectification thus

---

[22] Liu Wu-chi, *A Short History of Confucian Philosophy* (New York, 1964), p. 11.
[23] Lin Yutang (ed. and tr.), *The Wisdom of Confucius* (New York, 1938), p. 111.

consists in the specification of the ideal norms by way of action. The Socratic conception, on the contrary, regards philosophy as constructive criticism and a means to self-knowledge. Knowledge in unison with actions is a progressive realization of the self. Norms are in this sense self-imposed in the light of the progressive search for adequate definitions. In the Confucian sense, the philosophic use of reason is reasonableness rather than abstract rationality. It is a sense of appropriateness of the relevance of philosophical theses to the human condition. The philosophical theses are finally to be appraised in the light of human nature. Since philosophy is primarily ethics, the moral principles enunciated by philosophers must in the last analysis be vindicated by their plausible relevance to the human problems and the capacity of the moral agents to fulfill them in concrete situations. Lin Yutang recently expresses thus: "While reason [as rationality] is always abstract, analytical, idealistic, and inclined toward logical extremes, the spirit of reasonableness is always realistic, in closer touch with reality, more truly understanding and appreciative of the true situation."[24] The use of reasonableness is thus a dynamic use, not an exercise in deduction or induction. Unlike the Socratic concepts which are statically universal, the Confucian concepts tend to be universalizable. But every universalization is tied to a cultural and historic environment. Meanings of concepts are not definitions but contextual fields. Philosophy, in the Confucian sense, may thus be described as the search for particulars that hopefully will serve as paradigms for individual decision in the light of history.

IV. *Conclusion*

I have begun this essay by noting and illustrating certain characteristic uses of Confucian dialogues. These uses amount to a method of ethico-semantic rules. This method can now be more clearly seen in the conceptual map. Concepts and general principles are explained by way of examples and rules, for the latter are constitutive of the content of the former. The Confucian use of dialogues is primarily *ethical;* the sort of ethical theory that emerges would be one that is essentially evolutionary, since morality is bound to cultural history. The task for ethics is the search for paradigmatic rules or models. Since moral theory is to be ultimately

---

[24] Lin Yutang, *The Pleasures of a Nonconformist* (London, 1962), p. 109.

vindicated in practice, moral knowledge is ultimately moral achievement. The Confucian use of dialogues is a device to preserve the sense of the concrete—a testimony to the inherently dynamic spirit of Chinese Philosophy.[25]

State University of New York
College at Oswego

[25] This paper was presented before a symposium on "The Spirit of Chinese Philosophy" sponsored by the School of Philosophy, The Catholic University of America, Washington, D.C., May 5-6, 1967. The writer is indebted to the Research Foundation of the State University of New York for a Summer Faculty Research Fellowship to work on a project to which this essay is a partial report.

4

LESSONS FROM THE HISTORY OF SCIENCE AND TECHNOLOGY

by

JUDE P. DOUGHERTY

Introduction

Ideas rejected at the professional level have a tendency to linger beyond their time in the popular mind. One such idea is the view that nothing of intellectual moment occurred between the collapse of Greek culture and the rise of modern science in the sixteenth century. Frequently this view of history is used to support the positivistic thesis that the experimental method, ideally practiced by the modern mathematical physicist, is the only reliable method of obtaining genuine knowledge. It is often flatly asserted that when philosophy reigned supreme, as in the Middle Ages, it was to the detriment of science. Thinking in the Middle Ages, the argument goes, was so confined within theological and metaphysical fences that science which demands a spirit of free inquiry and direct observation was all but extinguished. The Middle Ages consequently was a period of obscurantism, dominated by an other worldly spirit and a blind faith in authority, which prevented men from exercising their reason about natural things. The positivist will argue that the success of his own view in vanquishing the ecclesiastically oriented philosophy of the Middle Ages was responsible for the birth of modern science.

Examples of this view are numerous and not without reason[1] It was until lately the prevalent one in histories of science and tech-

[1] To offer one example which must be regarded as notorious, because its author, a highly respected physicist, could be expected to know better. George Gamow, writing as late as 1961 in *Biography of Physics* (New York: Harper and Brothers), characterizes medieval learning by the following: "'Scientific' discussions were mostly limited to such problems as to how many angels can dance on the end of a needle and whether Almighty God could make a stone which is so heavy that He cannot lift it Himself," p. 25.

nology. As recently as 1934, the London University historian of science A. Wolf has written in his work on science and technology in the sixteenth and seventeenth centuries:

> The chief obstacle in the path of science during the Middle Ages was the Christian Church. Concerned mainly with the lowly, disdainful of the world and flesh, and believing itself in proud possession of divinely revealed truth concerning all that mattered, the church was at first contemptuous and then hostile towards all those who sought knowledge of nature by the independent light of reason.[2]

According to Wolf's interpretation, modern science emerged rapidly out of the Renaissance because it revived certain classical modes of thought opposed to the medieval outlook. Medieval thinkers followed one set of Greek ideas, whereas the pioneers of modern science embraced another set of Greek views. Scholasticism had set up Aristotle as its authority on matters which did not involve religious dogmas, whereas the founders of modern science were thoroughly imbued with the Pythagorean spirit.

Wolf informs us that:

> The tendency of medieval Christianity was toward a self-repression and other worldliness. The ideal Christian, conforming to the vows of the religious life, had his thoughts fixed on Heaven. Nature and natural phenomena had no intrinsic interest for him. Natural desires had to be transmuted into mystical ecstasy; spontaneous personal thought had to be subordinated to authority.[3]

> (The scholastics) . . . were always kept within the bounds of premises based on authority; they never attempted to exercise, or permitted others to exercise, that wider rationality which seeks to embrace the whole of human experience without such arbitrary boundaries as dogmas prescribed by authority.[4]

> The (Renaissance) stress laid on experience and more particularly on experiment was largely prompted by the spirit of naturalism exemplified and encouraged by the recovered literature of pagan antiquity, as contrasted with the spirit of supernaturalism which pervaded the intellectual atmosphere of the Middle Ages.[5]

---

[2] *A History of Science, Technology and Philosophy in the Sixteenth and Seventeenth Centuries* (New York: Harper Torchbooks, 1959), 2 vols., I, p. 8.
[3] *Ibid.*, pp. 1-2.
[4] *Ibid.*, p. 2.
[5] *Ibid.*, p. 3.

> The naturalist outlook may be regarded as essentially secular and matter of fact; the supernaturalist outlook is apt to be rather mysterious. The former view expects regularity in nature, the latter is prepared to find miracle and magic in natural phenomena.[6]

To anyone acquainted with the history of medieval thought these statements are obviously unfounded. Yet this view is still the popular one of the Middle Ages and of the medieval Church's relation to science. No doubt this view has been abandoned by the genuinely informed, but it has in the past been repeated so often and on so many platforms that it still lingers in many academic halls as well as in the popular press.

Historical research in the last forty years, particularly the pioneering work of Pierre Duhem, as continued by his disciples, Lynn Thorndike, Anneliese Maier and Alistair Crombie, and others such as Marshall Clagett, E. J. Dijksterhuis, A. Koyré, Lynn Whyte, and W. C. Bark, has shown the factual errors embodied in the attitude exemplified by Wolf.[7] To review briefly some of their investigations is the purpose of this paper. That research firmly establishes the historical continuity of scientific thought and attests to the contribution which Christian theology and philosophy made by their teachings to the advancement of science and technology. Recent scholarship has also shown that the decline of scholasticism was not a *condito sine qua non* for the birth of natural science, but rather that through its discussion of the nature of scientific methodology the much despised scholasticism actually did much to prepare the way for modern science. This same scholarship suggests that seventeenth century science can best be regarded as the second phase of an intellectual movement begun in the thirteenth century; that medieval technological accomplishments actually amounted to a revolution; and that the orthodox theologian did much to make modern science possible by challenging the exaggerated authority

---

[6] *Ibid.*

[7] Pierre Duhem, *Le Système du monde. Histoire des doctrines cosmologiques de Platon à Copernic* (Paris, 1913-17), 5 vols.; vols. 6-10 (Paris, 1954-59); Anneliese Maier, *Studien zur Naturphilosophie der Spätscholastik* (Rome, 1949-1958), 5 vols.; Lynn Thorndike, *A History of Magic and Experimental Sciences* (New York: Columbia University Press, 1923-58), 8 vols.; Alistair Crombie, *Medieval and Early Modern Science* (New York: Doubleday Anchor, 1959), 2 vols.; Crombie, *Robert Grosseteste and the Origins of Experimental Science* (Oxford, Clarendon, 1953); W. C. Bark, *Origins of the Medieval World* (New York: Doubleday Anchor, 1960); E. J. Dijksterhuis, *The Mechanization of the World Picture* (Oxford, Clarendon, 1961).

of Aristotle, thus asserting that other points and other approaches to natural phenomena were possible.

After reviewing this research it is clear that empiricism jumped on a bandwagon that it did not invent and that it tends to take credit for accomplishments that it did not make possible but perhaps would have prevented if it had been dominant. It should be evident that as a knowledge of medieval science and technology becomes more widespread, empiricism's claim that it liberated the human mind from an assertedly Christian hostility to physical science becomes more untenable. Research of the last forty years has shown that modern science has deep roots which are largely Christian.

Medieval Contributions to Technology

Though history records no gap in the development of either science or technology, the continuity of technology is more evident than that of science. It will therefore be well to review medieval technological achievement before we turn our attention to the science of the period.

The medieval contribution to technology has been recognized since the researches of Commandant Lefebvre des Noëttes, a onetime cavalry officer who upon retirement from military life turned his professional training to account by making a historical study of animal power.[8] This work, published in the early 1930's eventually led him to accumulate an impressive body of evidence on medieval technical developments and their social consequences. The result of his work, which has been praised as one of the capital historical discoveries of recent decades, was of general interest for the history of medieval technology. Today most historians look upon the early Middle Ages as a period of impressive technical achievement.

Lynn Whyte in an article entitled "Dynamo and Virgin Reconsidered" calls attention to the significant role that the Benedictines played in the history of Western technology, saying of St. Benedict that he was probably the pivotal figure in the history of labor.[9] Whyte compares the status of labor in ancient Greece with its status in the later Middle Ages. He finds that in the classical tradition

[8] *L'Attelage et le cheval de selle à travers les âges* (Paris, 1931); *De la marine antique à la marine moderne* (Paris, 1935).
[9] "Dynamo and Virgin Reconsidered," *American Scholar*, Vol. 27 (1958), p. 187.

there is scarcely a hint of the dignity of labor. The civilization of ancient Greece and Rome had rested on the backs of slaves. Work was the lot of the slave and any free man who dirtied his hands with it, even in the most casual way, demeaned himself. Even Plato once rebuked two friends who had constructed an apparatus to help themselves solve a geometrical problem. Plutarch states that Archimedes was ashamed of the machines he had built.

Reversing this Greek attitude toward labor was St. Benedict. By making labor a part of the corporate life of his monastery, by adopting it, not merely as a regrettable necessity, but rather as an integral and spiritually valuable part of monastic discipline, Benedict did much to increase the prestige of labor and the self-respect of the laborer. Whyte suggests that the Benedictine regard for the dignity of labor "marks a revolutionary reversal of the traditional attitude toward labor; it is the high peak along the watershed separating the modern from the ancient world."[10] An interesting passage reads:

> Moreover, although St. Benedict had not intended that his monks should be scholars, a great tradition of learning developed in the abbeys following his *Rule*: for the first time the practical and the theoretical were involved in the same individuals. The monk was the first intellectual to get dirt under his fingernails. He did not immediately launch into scientific investigation, but in his very person he destroyed the old artificial barrier between the empirical and the speculative, the manual and the liberal arts, and thus helped to create a social atmosphere, favorable to scientific and technological development.[11]

The significance of this Benedictine contribution is recognized by no less a figure than Alfred N. Whitehead in his *Science and the Modern World:* "The alliance of science with technology, by which learning is kept in contact with irreducible and stubborn facts owes much to the practical bent of the early Benedictines."[12] This practical bent of the Benedictines is witnessed in their interest in medicine, concern for the improvement of farm instruments, harnessing natural power, and promotion of the crafts. For instance, some abbeys had as many as four or five water wheels, each powering a different shop.

No doubt medieval technological achievement was slow, but a

---

[10] *Ibid.*, p. 188.
[11] *Ibid.*, pp. 188-189.
[12] *Science in the Modern World* (New York: Macmillan, 1951), p. 22.

steady progress can be detected from the sixth to the twelfth century. This progress is evidenced primarily in the increased utilization of the elemental forces of water and wind. Commenting upon this period Frederick Klemm observes: "The medieval changeover to the application of natural sources of power betokened technical progress which had important results, comparable in modern times only to those following the introduction of the steam engine in the eighteenth century and the utilization of atomic energy in our day."[13]

Achievement was not limited to agricultural needs. Medicine was studied in the earliest Benedictine monasteries and initiated a long series of works which continued without a break until the sixteenth century. Beginning with Bede in the seventh century a series of treatises was written on astronomy by scholars for purely practical purposes, such as determining the date of Easter, fixing latitude and showing how to determine true north, and tell time with an astrolabe. Another series of practical treatises is that dealing with the preparation of pigments and other chemical substances. Technical treatises were among the first to be translated out of the Arabic and Greek into Latin. In the thirteenth century the encyclopedias of Alexander Neckham, Albertus Magnus and Roger Bacon contain a great deal of accurate information about the compass, the calendar, chemistry, and agriculture and reflect a long tradition of learning. Mention should also be made of the development of mines, saltworks, foundries and glassworks, in Bohemia, Germany, and Hungary.[14]

Reviewing the total achievement of medieval technology, Crombie writes:

> In the field of technology, the Middle Ages saw the most rapid progress since prehistoric times. Beginning with the new methods of exploiting animal-, water-, and wind-power, new machines were developed for a variety of purposes, often requiring considerable precision. Some technical inventions, for instance, the mechanical clocks and magnifying lenses, were to be used as scientific instruments. Measuring instruments such as the astrolabe and quadrant were greatly improved as a result of the demand for accurate measurement. In chemistry, the balance came into general use. Empirical advances were made

---

[13] *A History of Western Technology* (New York: Scribners, 1959), p. 80.
[14] Crombie, *Augustine to Galileo*, pp. 143 ff.

and the experimental habit led to the development of special apparatus.[15]

We can see that Wolf's description of the other-worldly characteristic of the medieval mind is wholly without foundation. As Bark points out, "If the decline of the classical interest in science had been due to a systematic obscurantism on the part of the church, we could confidently expect to find science snuffed out altogether."[16] The evidence shows that Western science did not die, although it developed slowly by modern standards. Bark suggests that it developed to meet the needs of an impoverished agrarian society. Hence he can write: "The early medieval way of tackling science, that is, by first getting down to earth and working out practical devices, and only then turning to theory turned out to be vastly superior to the too speculative Greek approach, by air, which never got around to coping with crude necessities."[17]

Benjamin Farrington attributes the success of Renaissance science to the technological revolution of the Middle Ages. According to Farrington, when the classic Greek works arrived in the West, the West was prepared. Medieval man had learned the use of natural resources and upon this had built a society in which humans were free from a large part of their former drudgery. Technical advance had led to social change. The slave had been replaced by the serf and the craftsman.[18]

Concerning this relation of the new technology to slavery there are a number of theses. Lynn Whyte has been especially concerned with this subject and suggests that the development of medieval technology owes its impetus to the Christian teaching of the infinite worth of the individual and the Church's opposition to slavery.

In the article cited above, Whyte notes that if Henry Adams can symbolize an age by the concept of "dynamo," the early Middle Ages can be characterized by the devotion shown to Our Lady. "St. Bernard's Cistercian monks were so devoted to the Virgin that every one of their hundreds of monasteries was dedicated to her; yet these White Benedictines seem often to have led the way in the

---

[15] "From Rationalism to Experimentalism," *Roots of Scientific Thought*, ed. by P. Wiener and A. Noland (New York: Basic Books, 1957), p. 133.
[16] *Origins of the Medieval World*, p. 115.
[17] *Ibid.*, p. 148.
[18] *Greek Science* (London: Penguin, 1953), pp. 307 ff.

use of power."[19] Whyte uses the concept "Virgin" to symbolize the theology which, by its opposition to slavery, contributed to the development of medieval technology. In another article he observes:

> The chief glory of the later Middle Ages was not its cathedrals or its epics or its scholasticism: it was the building for the first time in history a complex civilization whch rested not on the backs of sweating slaves or coolies but primarily on non-human power ...
>
> The labor saving power machines of the later Middle Ages were produced by the implicit theological assumption of the infinite worth of even the most degraded personality, by the intrinsic repugnance towards the subjecting of any man to monotonous drudgery which seems less human in that it requires the exercise neither of intelligence nor choice. It has often been remarked that the Latin Middle Ages first discovered the dignity and spiritual value of labor—that to labor is to pray. But the Middle Ages went further: they gradually and very slowly began to explore the practical implications of an essentially Christian paradox: that just as the heavenly Jerusalem contains no temple, so the goal of labor is to end labor.[20]

In defining this thesis, Whyte is developing Lefebvre des Noëttes argument that the new inventions destroyed slavery by making it unnecessary and undesirable. On the other hand, Marc Bloch has argued that the end of slavery came first and created a necessity to which such devices as the new harness and the water mill were the response. Both Crombie and Bark defend a middle point of view, suggesting that the Church, although it never succeeded in completely stamping out slavery, was greatly aided in its opposition to slavery by the new labor-saving devices.

Medieval Contribution to the Philosophy of Science

If the history of Western technology displays no gaps, neither does the history of science. This does not mean that there was a uniformity in progress at every stage of the medieval period. The later Middle Ages which witnessed the rise of the universities and the merging of Greek and Christian thought experienced a period of intellectual accomplishment previously unknown. Of particular

[19] "Dynamo and Virgin Reconsidered," *American Scholar*, Vol. 27 (1958), p. 190.
[20] "Technology and Invention in the Middle Ages," *Speculum*, Vol. 15 (1940). p. 156.

significance for the history of science are the thirteenth- and fourteenth-century discussions of science and scientific method. This is not to neglect the concrete advances made in the special sciences during this period. It is fruitful to consider both the theoretical and concrete developments of this period.

Crombie's wide study has convinced him that the most significant changes in the history of science are nearly always brought about by new conceptions of scientific procedure. This he holds is especially true of medieval discussions of science and what flowed from them. In telling the story of science from Augustine to Galileo, from its decay after the collapse of the Roman Empire in the West to its full flowering in the seventeenth century, he has emphasized what he believes are the two most significant results of recent scholarship: the essential continuity of Western scientific traditions from Greek times to our own, and the significance of the medieval discussions of scientific methodology. What Whitehead dimly saw, Crombie has made explicit in his well-documented *Medieval and Early Modern Science*.

It is Crombie's thesis that the natural philosophers of the thirteenth and fourteenth centuries created the experimental science characteristic of modern times. He argues that if modern science owes most of its success to the use of inductive and experimental procedure, then it owes a great deal to the medieval philosopher who first produced an understanding of that experimental procedure. According to Crombie, it was thirteenth-century philosophers who transformed the Greek geometrical method into the experimental science of the modern era. Although the conception of scientific explanation accepted by Galileo, Harvey, and Newton is a theory of formal proof developed by the Greek geometers and logicians, the distinctive feature of the seventeenth century, Crombie writes, is non-Greek in origin. It is a scientific method based on "a conception of how to relate a theory to the observed facts it explained, the set of logical procedures . . . for constructing theories and for submitting them to experimental tests."[21]

The outstanding scientific event of the twelfth and early thirteenth centuries, Crombie suggests, was the confrontation of the empiricism of the West in the practical arts with the conception of rational explanation continued in scientific texts recently translated from Greek and Arabic. Whereas Aristotle distinguished

[21] *Robert Grosseteste and the Origins of Experimental Science*, p. 1.

natural science on the basis of subject matter, deriving three orders of science—physics, mathematics, and metaphysics—the medieval mind tended to look upon his distinction as one not of subject matter but of method of inquiry. The philosophers of the thirteenth century distinguished clearly between the kinds of questions to be asked under each heading. Crombie likens this to the role of linguistic analysis in our own time. The object of the experimental method worked out during this period was to discover and define the conditions necessary and sufficient to produce the experimental facts. It was recognized that a theory defining those conditions could never be certain; it was sufficient to "save the appearance" but it was not "necessarily true" in the sense of being a necessary conclusion from the analysis of experimental fact and therefore final.

The effect of this tendency to regard mathematics as a method rather than a domain or province of study was to change the kind of question asked. Interest gradually shifted from the physical or metaphysical to the kind of question that could be answered by a mathematical theory within the reach of experimental verification. The rest of the history of medieval science consists of the working out of the consequences of this new approach to nature. Examples of this shift in emphasis are seen in the sciences of statics, optics, and astronomy.[22]

Crombie is not alone in his view. Whitehead implies as much when he writes: "The Middle Ages formed one long training of the intellect of Europe in the sense of order."[23] Lynn Thorndike and Bark take similar views.[24] Dawson makes much the same point when he compares the utilitarian view of science propounded by Roger Bacon in the fourteenth century with the speculative view of science entertained by the Greek mind. Bacon is obviously close to the modern mind when he makes science an instrument of world conquest and exploitation. Dawson suggests that both the utilitarian and the Greek view of science contributed to the formation of the European scientific tradition: "The pragmatic experimentation of the Baconian ideal could have borne no fruit apart from the intellectual training and discipline which were provided by Aristotelian scholasticism."[25]

[22] *Ibid.*, pp. 2-3.
[23] *Science and the Modern World*, p. 12.
[24] See especially Bark, *op. cit.*, pp. 115 f.
[25] "Origins of European Scientific Tradition," *The Clergy Review*, Vol. 2 (1931), p. 203.

Recent scholarship has discovered that it is from Grosseteste that Bacon derives his distinctive philosophical and scientific views. Both Dawson and Crombie accord Grosseteste a major role in the history of scientific theory. Grosseteste is a symbol of the fusion of two traditions. Crombie writes:

> From the almost pure empiricism of such practical sciences of the twelfth century as practical mathematics, astronomy, and medicine, and the almost pure rationalism of theoretical speculation in contemporary philosophy on scientific method, he produced a science in which he tried to show the principles according to which the world of experience could be experimentally investigated and rationally explained.[26]

Other important elements of Grosseteste's thought are his conceptions of physical nature in which the essence of "form" itself is mathematically determined and his conception of the immediate objective of inquiry as mathematical and predictive laws instead of the Aristotelian essential definition.

These concepts were not without their effect. In the fourteenth century we find the development of mathematical techniques designed to take advantage of the new methodology and conception of explanation. At the same time, extension of the use of experiment and mathematics led to an increase in positive knowledge. By the beginning of the seventeenth century the speculative use of the new methods of experiment and mathematical abstraction had produced results so striking that this movement has been given the name scientific revolution. These new methods, initially expounded in the thirteenth century, were first used with completeness and maturity and effectiveness by Galileo.

Wolf's thesis that the new science grew out of a Pythagorean, or Platonic, rather than an Aristotelian conception of science is only partly true. Science viewed as essentially mathematical explanation is no doubt Pythagorean. Owing to the influence of Grosseteste, such a spirit was strong at Oxford in the first half of the fourteenth century. Yet the distinctive feature of modern science, according to most historians, is the practical use of mathematics to understand nature.

The greatest medieval contribution to modern science is no doubt in the realm of theory, yet there are many concrete contributions made in the fields of mathematics, mechanics, dynamics, and

---

[26] *Robert Grosseteste*, p. 43.

biology which attest to the continuity of scientific enterprise. We will attempt to list only a few of the accomplishments in each of these fields.

Western mathematics developed with Leonard of Pisa, John Nemorarius, and Robert Grosseteste. According to Dirk J. Struid, scholastic speculations regarding the continuum, the possibility of an infinite series, and the nature of minima "had their influence on the inventors of the infinitesimal calculus in the seventeenth century and on the philosophers of the transfinite in the nineteenth: Cavalieri, Tacquet, Bolzano, and Cantor knew the scholastic authors and pondered over the meaning of their ideas."[27] He continues:

> These churchmen occasionally reached results of more immediate mathematical interest. Thomas Bradwardine, who became Archbishop of Canterbury, investigated star polygons after studying Boetius. The most important of these medieval clerical mathematicians was Nicholas Oresme, Bishop of Lisieux in Normandy, who played with fractional powers .... He also wrote a tract called "De Latitudinibus formarum" (c. 1360) in which he graphs a dependent variable (latitudo) against an independent one (longitude), which is subject to variation. It shows a kind of vague transition from coordinates on the terrestrial or celestial sphere, known to the ancients, to the modern coordinate geometry. This tract was printed several times between 1482 and 1515 and may have influenced Renaissance mathematics including Descartes.[28]

Summarizing the medieval contribution to mathematics, Carl Boyer writes:

> If we regard the broadest aspects of mathematics, the speculations and investigations which lead up to the propositions which are in the end deductively demonstrated, it will appear that this so-called barren period furnished points of view of significance in the development of the calculus. In this respect, as in others, there was perhaps as much originality in medieval times as there is now.[29]

In the biological sciences, various considerable technical advances were made. Important works were written on medicine, surgery, and the symptoms of diseases, and descriptions of the flora and fauna of different regions were given. A beginning of classification was

---

[27] *A Concise History of Mathematics* (New York: Dover, 1948), p. 107.
[28] *Ibid.*
[29] *The History of the Calculus* (New York: Dover, 1959), p. 65.

made and the possibility of accurate illustrations was introduced by naturalistic art. Perhaps the most important medieval contribution to theoretical biology was the elaboration of the idea of a scale of animate nature.[30]

In the realm of physics many topics were discussed. In the sciences of meteorology and optics, we can mention the work of William Merlie, Robert Grosseteste, Roger Bacon, Witelo, John Pecham, and Theodoric of Freiburg; in mechanics and magnetism, Jordanus Nemorarius, Petrus Peregrinus, and John of St. Armand; in dynamics and kinematics, Gerard of Brussels, Thomas Bradwardine, William Ockham, John Buridan, Albert of Saxony, Nicholas Oresme, and Nicholas of Cusa. In dynamics, some of the topics discussed were projectile motion and trajectory, free fall, impressed power, and the motion of the earth. Crombie spends the greater part of two volumes reviewing these medieval discussions, so it is neither possible nor necessary to consider them here in detail. Suffice it to say that they are ample evidence of a continuity of scientific thought.[31] Crombie's emphasis on continuity is also supported by A. Maier and M. Clagett.

These and many other studies show that if the Middle Ages were dominated by an "other-worldly" spirit, it did not preclude a mathematical inquiry into the laws of nature or a machine technology. The other-worldly spirit of Christendom, though motivated by the promise of a heavenly Jerusalem, did what it could do to alleviate the temporal lot of man. If this was to be accomplished by the harnessing of nature, then the harnessing of nature was to be encouraged. Furthermore, encouragement of rational inquiry into the nature of things was implicit in St. Augustine's rational theology, which had long predisposed Western Christendom to value the natural world as sacramental and symbolic of spiritual truths. The same attitude is found even more forcefully expressed in the writings of Albert, Aquinas, and Scotus.

Some writers accuse the Church of exalting Aristotle to the point where no other authority on nature was admitted and of preferring the opinion of Aristotle even to direct experience. The truth is that the extreme regard for Aristotle had nothing to do with religion. This exaggerated appreciation was far more characteristic of the Aristotelian rationalism of the Averroists than of the Chris-

[30] Crombie, *Roots of Scientific Thought*, p. 134.
[31] *Medieval and Early Modern Science*, cf. especially I, ch. 3 & 4; II, ch. 1.

tian Aristotelians. Dawson maintains that the Aristotelianism of the Averroists proved a greater obstacle to science than the obscurantism of certain conservative theologians. Elaborating on this point, he writes:

> If the new scientific and philosophical culture of the West had been purely Aristotelian it would probably have been no less sterile than the scientific culture of Islam in the later Middle Ages. But medieval Aristotelianism never possessed a monopoly in Western thought. It was counterbalanced by another intellectual tradition—that of Christian Platonism—which contributed no less to the new scientific development, and which is equally characteristic of medieval culture.[32]

In schoolmen of the fourteenth century, i.e., William of Ockham, John Buridan, Albert of Saxony and Nicholas Oresme, we find not only a critical reaction against the authority of Aristotle and Arabic tradition, but also an original movement of scientific research which prepares the way for the coming of Leonardo da Vinci and Copernicus and the whole science of the Renaissance.[33]

No doubt the condemnations, particularly the condemnation of 1277, had much to do with the lessening of the prestige of Aristotle. If Aristotle could be wrong on some things, he could be wrong on others. Duhem attaches such importance to the condemnation of 1277, that he goes so far as to mark the beginning of modern science with its date. Crombie, commenting on Duhem, observes:

> With the condemnation of the Averroist view that Aristotle had said the last word on metaphysics and natural science, the bishops in 1277 left the way open for criticism which would, in turn, undermine his system. Not only had natural philosophers now through Aristotle a rational philosophy of nature, but because of the attitude of Christian theologians they were made to form hypotheses regardless of Aristotle's authority, to develop the empirical habit of mind working within a rational framework.[34]

The condemnations are evidence of conflicting schools of thought in the Middle Ages and of different attitudes taken toward the work of Aristotle. To describe the medieval mind as monolithic, as Wolf does, is to be guilty of gross oversimplification.

---
[32] *Medieval Essays*, p. 153.
[33] George Sarton, *A Guide to the History of Science*, p. 35.
[34] *Medieval and Early Modern Science*, p. 35.

Humanism and Science

Many scholars now agree that fifteenth-century humanism, which arose in Italy and spread northwards, was an interruption of the development of science. The so-called revival of letters deflected interest from content to literary style, and in turning back to classical antiquity, many humanists affected to ignore the progress of the previous three centuries. Unaware of how much they owed to their immediate predecessors, these humanists, by their contempt for scholasticism, did much to initiate the Dark Age myth. Crombie suggests that:

> The same absurd conceit that led the humanists to abuse and misrepresent their immediate predecessors for using Latin constructions unknown to Cicero and to put out the propaganda, which in varying degrees has captivated historical opinion until quite recently, also allowed them to borrow from scholasticism without acknowledgment. The habit affected almost all the great scientists of the sixteenth and seventeenth centuries, whether Protestant or Catholic, and it has required the labors of a Duhem or a Maier to show that their statements on matters of history cannot be accepted at their face value.[35]

Whitehead has written that the natural scientists of the sixteenth and seventeenth centuries were anti-intellectualistic in the same way that the religious reformers of the period were anti-intellectualistic. Whitehead has gone so far as to describe modern science as "a recoil from the inflexible rationality of medieval thought."[36] Herbert Butterfield recalls how the humanists of the Renaissance, Erasmus included, were accustomed to complaining of the boredom of scholastic lectures and suggests that this was due to the ignorance of the humanists more than anything else.[37] The humanists derided their scholastic teachers, but these despised scholastic disciplines now hold a remarkable key position in the story of the evolution of the modern mind. Butterfield writes, "Perhaps the lack of mathematics, or the failure to think of mathematical ways of formulating things, was partly responsible for what appeared to be verbal subtleties and an excessive straining of language in these men who were almost yearning to find the key to the modern science of mechanics."[38]

[35] *Augustine to Galileo*, pp. 268-269.
[36] *Science in the Modern World*, p. 12.
[37] *Origins of Modern Science* (New York: Macmillan, 1957), p. 2.
[38] *Ibid.*

This Renaissance attitude toward scholasticism took hold and has held sway ever since. Largely because of it the philosophical and theological roots of modern science are unknown to the contemporary mind. For complex reasons positivism has come to be associated with modern science. The theology and philosophy which in effect provided the rationale of modern science have been dismissed as "anti-empirical superstition and obscurantism." Yet the positivism which has been so long associated with science is beginning to show a decline. The tendency to restrict knowledge to that attained by physico-mathematical methods or to reduce science to description has begun to wane. Many are now coming to regard it as anti-intellectualistic. With remarkable insight, Christopher Dawson writes: "The disease of modern civilization lies neither in science nor in machinery, but in the false philosophy with which they have been associated .... Though these ideas accompanied the rise of the machine order, they are in reality profoundly inconsistent with that order and with scientific genius."[39] Elsewhere he remarks that "we cannot be sure that the world which science has made will be as favorable to the production of scientific genius as the world that made science."[40]

Karl Popper likewise indicts the positivistic attitude toward science in which the emphasis is placed on description and practical results:

> Instrumentalism is unable to account for the importance to pure science of severely testing even the most remote implications of its theories, since it is unable to account for the pure scientist's interest in truth and falsity. In contrast to the highly critical attitude requisite in the pure scientist, the attitude of instrumentalism (like that of applied science) is one of complacency at the success of application. Thus it may well be responsible for recent stagnation in theoretical physics.[41]

It is to be observed that the more versed in history a philosopher is, the less he tends toward an outright positivistic interpretation of knowledge. To paraphrase a remark of Newman, to be steeped in history is to cease to be a positivist. The historical defense of positivism simply does not bear scrutiny. If it is true that medieval discussion of science and scientific method actually laid the foundation

---

[39] *Christianity and the New Age* (London: Sheed and Ward, 1931), p. 102.
[40] *The Modern Dilemma* (London: Sheed and Ward, 1933), p. 49.
[41] "Three Views Concerning Human Knowledge," *Contemporary British Philosophy* (New York: Macmillan, 1960), p. 381.

for modern experimental science and provided a defense of it, then the positivist loses face on at least two accounts. He cannot take credit for something which he did not produce, and he is haunted by the suspicion that the philosophical climate which paved the way for modern science may be its proper rationale even today.

Furthermore, if historical research discloses that medieval theology and philosophy were far from preventing modern science and actually contributed to its development, then it is evident that experimental knowledge cannot be identified with all reliable knowledge. Other modes of inquiry and other types of procedure will have to be accorded their proper place.

5

DOES ACQUIRED MORAL VIRTUE ENTAIL FACILITY?

by

GILBERT B. ARBUCKLE

The definition of virtue as a good operative habit has stood as the basis of discussion of virtue and the moral life since the Middle Ages. Virtue is commonly described as the habit of performing a morally good action, just as vice is the habit of performing a morally evil action. Since it is a habit, virtue is not acquired by performing the appropriate good act once or even a few times and it cannot be obtained by any effort of resolution. Only the performance of many good acts can bring about the habit and facility in the act that is characteristic of virtue.

Thus the man of virtue is commonly represented as one who by the performance of many good acts has acquired habit and facility in them. He is distinguished from the vicious man, and also from the neophyte on the road to moral perfection, by the fact that he no longer has to contend as they do with tendencies and impulses to the contrary evil acts. To the beginner the performance of good acts is more painful and difficult and requires greater effort "because he is still in the state of imperfect virtue; were his state of virtue perfect he would experience pleasure, not pain, in practicing the virtue."[1] The virtuous man, on the other hand, finds good acts pleasurable and, as it were, second nature. The development of a state in which such salutary tendencies to good actions predominate is thus a part of his success in the pursuit of moral perfection.

I submit that in this notion of virtue and the virtuous man there is a radical error. It joins in the concept of virtue elements that are incoherent and it collides with the findings of studies in the psychology of habit and depth psychology.

---

[1] George P. Klubertanz, *Habits and Virtues* (New York: Appleton-Century-Crofts, 1965), p. 168.

It is commonly acknowledged by exponents of the traditional view that since acquired moral virtue is a habit it is subject to the same psychological laws that govern the formation of all habit.[2] Indeed, a great part of the traditional doctrine of virtue has been constructed on the basis of its generic character as habit. However, the mechanics of the process by which habits are formed and deteriorate have in recent years been the subject of considerable scientific investigation and illumination, and the results compel a reexamination of the traditional doctrine of virtue.

At this point we may remove some confusion surrounding the concept of facility itself. Facility is generally understood by authors on the subject as "nothing more than a readiness or promptitude of action, a tendency to repeat the same action constantly, easily, and almost unconsciously."[3] Typical examples cited are the trained athlete and skilled musician who through much practice have acquired facility in the performance of difficult tasks. These are offered as cases illustrative of the facility that is developed in the performance of a virtuous act.

In this notion of facility there is great imprecision. First of all, the concept of facility must be separated from that of readiness or promptitude. A man may experience inertia and even aversion to the performance of an act and yet be capable of performing it with great facility. An accomplished musician whose tastes have changed may be loathe to perform a piece in which he once acquired, and still retains, great facility. Secondly, facility cannot be said to imply a tendency to repeat an act constantly. A man may be very inconstant in the performance of an act which, when he does perform it, he performs with ease. These distinctions apply as well to the field of moral action which the examples are intended to illustrate.

In assessing the true character of the relation between virtue and facility it will be necessary to appreciate fully the material character of the process of habit formation. It is easy to fail in this because the relevant difference between a man before and after he has acquired a habit is so far from visible. This difference consists for the most part in the neural and other subtle and vastly complex changes of the brain and nervous system that are brought

---

[2] Robert F. Coerver, *The Quality of Facility in the Moral Virtues* (Washington: The Catholic University of America Press, 1946), p. 20. ". . . the acquired virtues are habits in the strict sense, and as such they are governed by the psychological rules of habit."

[3] *Ibid.*, p. 19.

about chiefly by the many performances of the act. The extreme delicacy of these changes, reaching as they do to the very atoms of the brain, must not obscure from us the fact that they are material phenomena.

The psychological process of habit formation which these changes constitute acquires a special significance because of its bearing on moral behavior, but in itself it is as indifferent to morality as the vegetative activities of a man. This aspect of habit is forcefully brought out by William James in a passage touching on the familiar error of the man who is resolved to break a bad habit but allows himself an exception with the mental note that "this time he will not count it."

> ... he may not count it, and a kind Heaven may not count it; but it is being counted none the less. Down among his nerve-cells and fibres the molecules are counting it, registering and storing it up to be used against him when the next temptation comes. Nothing we ever do is in strict scientific literalness, wiped out.[4]

The brain path theory of habit formation that James held is now discredited and we shall see later that tendencies to virtuous and vicious actions may be determined by events quite unrelated to the performance of good and bad actions. Nevertheless, the above passage remains a valid expression of the inexorability and the material character of the forces at work in the development of virtues and vices.

It may be urged that the acquisition of virtue involves more than a change in the material side of man. It includes a development of will and hence certain immaterial changes as well. However, this offers no stumbling block to our approach, for whatever virtue may imply in the spiritual side of man, facility in the virtuous act demands a certain congruent state of his material side. A good act will be performed with facility only where there is freedom from conflict in the forces bearing directly on it.

In this connection we may consider the thesis recently argued with some independence of thought by Servais Pinckaers that virtue is not a habit at all in the psychological sense. According to Pinckaers, confusion on this point has been engendered by the fact that the definition of virtue as a good operative habit is a mis-

---

[4] William James, *The Principles of Psychology*, 3 vols. (London: Macmillan & Co., 1891), Vol. I, p. 127.

leading translation of the Latin *habitus boni operativus* from which it derived much of its authority.[5] The Latin *habitus* is a much broader term than the vernacular *habit* and comprehends not only material qualities and conditions like psychological habit but immaterial qualities of the soul and its faculties as well.[6]

Pinckaers argues that psychological habit implies "a state of mental indifference, and even the gradual substitution of a progressive automatism for consciousness."[7] This automatism "deprives an action of precisely the thing that gives it its moral dimension" and hence is a source of amorality.[8] To the degree that an action proceeds from habit it does not "entail that attentive presence of reason and that personal engagement of free will which give our actions their whole worth and their entire human value."[9] Consequently, virtue cannot be described as a habit if we wish to hold at the same time that it adds to the moral character of an act.

Yet Pinckaers does not question either the assumption that virtue entails facility or the thesis that facility involves the material side of man. Facility, he writes, is "the result of the perfect ordination and unification of the interior principles of man's action," a state in which the sense appetite not only obeys reason and will but makes its own appropriate contribution to the act they command. "For the action to be performed with ease, it is essential that all interior conflict be resolved and that the whole human organism act in a harmonious way."[10] According to Pinckaers, this harmony is always attainable, being the result of many actions

---

[5] Servais Pinckaers, "Virtue is not a Habit," *Cross Currents*, Vol. 12 (1962), p. 68. This is a translation of an article originally published in *Nouvelle Revue Théologique*, Vol. 82 (1960). Probably the most influential definition of virtue has been that of St. Thomas Aquinas: "*Unde virtus humana, quae est habitus operativus, est bonus habitus et boni operativus.*" *Summa theologiae*, ed. P. Caramello (Romae: Marietti, 1952), I-II, q. 55, art. 3, c.

[6] Pinckaers is speaking, of course, of the difference between the meaning of the Latin *habitus* and the French *habitude*. The same difference exists between *habitus* and the English *habit* which, in the field of scientific psychology, is a very exact translation of the French *habitude*. Pieper notes that the German language has no word accurately expressing the meaning of the Latin *habitus*. "*Das Wort* habitus *lässt sich kaum völlig genau ins Deutsche übertragen. Fertigkeit, Gewohnheit, Gehaben, 'Verhabung'—des alles sind wenig glückliche übersetzungen.*" J. Pieper, "Tugend," *Handbuch Theologischer Grundbegriffe*, 2Bde., (Kösel-Verlag: München, 1963) Bd. 2, p. 716.

[7] Servais Pinckaers, *op. cit.*, p. 67.

[8] *Ibid.*, p. 68.

[9] *Ibid.*, p. 67.

[10] *Ibid.*, p. 75.

in which the will triumphs over the tendencies of matter in performing the good act.

This harmony is indeed essential to facility, but I propose to show that both it and the facility consequent on it are very far from being always possible of attainment. Moreover, even where they do exist they are accidental to the moral character of the virtuous act. To make them a part of virtue is to tie virtue to the domain of the material in such a way as to make it impossible to retain many of the most fundamental principles respecting the freedom and merit of virtuous action.

It is too evident to require discussion that in countless cases the performance of a good act many times has led to habit and facility in it. However, it is also a fact that the exercise of a long standing virtue may on occasion become markedly more difficult than before. The difficulty may arise without any waning of moral convictions and without any antecedent negligence in the performance of the good act. It may arise suddenly, as difficulty with the virtue of patience during the first stages of radiation poisoning, or it may develop gradually, as the difficulty with the virtues of obedience and docility that comes with old age or the gaining of experience.

Moreover, the state in which the virtue is practiced with difficulty is not necessarily more transient or unstable than the state in which it is practiced with facility. The loss of facility may be due to changes as irreversible and as permanent as those which, in the beginning, accounted for the development of facility. Indeed, it is possible, as in the case of zeal, for fervor and ease to characterize a relatively short period during the life of the virtue, and this during the earlier stages of its existence.

Exponents of the traditional doctrine of virtue as facility in the performance of a good action have been conspicuously remiss in recognizing such cases and in facing the question they suggest. How can virtue include, or even entail, facility in the performance of a good action when this facility can fluctuate as unpredictably as the state of a man's fortunes? Virtue has been presented throughout the ages as a good accessible to every man and dependent solely upon the will of the one who would acquire it. It is supposed to be distinguished from the lesser goods of this world by the assurance a man has that nothing can take it away from him as long as he maintains only the will to keep it. If attaining and preserving virtue thus rest entirely with the individual, how can it be identified with or linked to a facility which may turn out to be as transient as any of the other uncertain possessions of this life?

It may be answered that the apparent difficulty in the practice of a long standing virtue and the sudden need for heroic effort do not mean that the virtue or facility has diminished. It means simply that the virtue is put to a greater test by the special circumstances accounting for the difficulty. If the virtue and facility were not as great as ever, the virtuous act would have even less likelihood of being performed under the new and more trying conditions. As with Milo and the calf, the strength and facility with which a man does something may steadily increase even though the resistance an object gives him also increases.

Such a resolution of the problem is untenable. It bases itself upon a distinction between the external and internal forces bearing upon the performance of an action. Facility is kept an essential part of virtue by referring both to an inner domain not subject to the vicissitudes of the external material world. In this inner realm the will presumably enjoys absolute dominion and can attain to virtue in whatever degree it chooses.

This explanation collides with the fact that the circumstances accounting for the increased difficulty in performing the virtuous act may be as internal by any definition of the term as those that once made the act easy. It was a material change, we must remember, that made possible the acquisition of facility in the first place. The virtuous man was not able in the beginning to acquire facility by any act of will alone. He could only elicit many good actions and await the neural and other material changes that later allowed him to perform the act with facility. As long as facility is dependent upon a certain harmony between the spiritual and the material, it cannot be referred to any realm that is immune to the vicissitudes of the material world. When the existence of a state or property S depends upon a relation between two terms, then anything that can affect this relation by affecting one of the terms can also affect the existence of S. We must remember, moreover, that it makes no essential difference to the material character of a change, whether that change consists in more or less outward alterations of environment or whether it consists in the enormously complex and delicate neural changes produced by a given set of experiences.

Some light may be shed on the true character of the relation between virtue and facility if we consider how these two concepts came to be fused in the first place.

First of all, I suggest that there has been a confused identification of the class of men who perform a certain good act with great constancy and the class of men who have developed facility in the performance of that act. There is no doubt a high degree of positive correlation between the two classes. The virtuous act is the reasonable act and most men do what it is rational to do when there is no disinclination arising from the material side of their nature. However, there are instances of men who are constant in a good act though it continues to be very difficult. There are also some who are very inconstant in an act which, if they chose to do so, they could perform without difficulty. These cases which fall in one class but not the other would by themselves compel us to separate as incommensurate the elements of constancy and facility.

Secondly, beyond the mistaken association of constancy and facility, there has been a further assumption that when a man becomes very constant in the performance of a good act it is because frequent practice has given him facility in it. In most cases this may be the chief reason, or even the only reason, but there are also cases in which it plays no role whatever. It is possible for a man to become more constant in an act even as it becomes more difficult. Facility is due more to the absence of conflict in the forces bearing upon an act than to the strength of forces that favor it. Constancy, on the other hand, can be due to the strength or decisive character of forces favoring the act, and these may co-exist with others that make the act painful and difficult. Indeed, the forces responsible for constancy and those responsible for pain and difficulty in the performance of an act may increase at the same time. Thus, assuming that constancy in performing a virtuous act is necessarily linked to facility in that act is very much like assuming that the more consistently a man wins election at the polls, the easier it must be becoming for him to do so.

It should also be noted that there may be no opposition even between the forces tending to constancy and those responsible for difficulty in the performance of an act. It is entirely possible for the painful or difficult aspect of an act to combine with other conditions in such a way as to favor performance of the act. This will often be the case where masochistic tendencies influence the agent on the unconscious level and it may sometimes be the case even where we are dealing solely with conscious motivations. Thus Cellini writes: "It had always been my ambition to do those things which offer the greatest difficulties to men. . . ."[11]

We may notice here another reason for the assumption that virtue brings facility in the performance of a good act. Performing an act of virtue, it is commonly taught, is a pleasurable operation. It "produces the deepest, the most complete and the truest sort of human joy . . . a triumphant kind of joy, resulting from the creation of a personal achievement."[12] This joy is sometimes declared to be an essential component of virtue. "This also is an essential element of the concept of virtue," writes Pieper, "that it allows the good to be done *with joy.*"[13] This position naturally encourages the view that virtuous acts are always performed with facility.

However, I submit that virtue is very far from assuring its possessor a joy which makes the virtuous act easy to perform. A man may perform an act of the greatest virtue with no more joy than that which Abraham experienced as he went about preparations to kill his son. The only joy absolutely assured a man in the exercise of acquired moral virtue is, at most, that which derives from the purely rational knowledge that he is doing a good thing. However exalted it may be in some respects, such joy is extremely tenuous in others, and it is quite compatible with great mental distress and anguish. It is far from sufficient to guarantee facility in the performance of the virtuous act.

Closely connected with the concept of moral virtue as facility is the traditional teaching that acquired moral virtue is developed by the repetition of the appropriate good act. The usual doctrine on this point is found in Coerver:

[11] Benvenuto Cellini, *Vita*, trans. John A. Symonds (New York: Washington Square Press, 1963), Book I, Ch. 107, p. 210.

[12] Servais Pinckaers, *op. cit.*, p. 76.

[13] J. Pieper, *op. cit.*, p. 718. "*Auch dies gehört als wesentlichen Element zum Begriff der Tugend: das sie das Gute* mit Freuden *tun lasse.*" St. Thomas Aquinas appears to hold the same view, since he teaches that virtue is a habit and that actions performed from habit are pleasurable. "*Operationes ex habitu procedentes delectabiles sunt, et in promptu habentur, et faciliter exercentur, quia sunt quasi connaturales effectae.*" *Quaestiones Disputatae, De Veritate* (Romae: Marietti, 1953), q. 20, art. 2, p. 365. It is certainly not the case that operations proceeding from habit are always pleasurable. Workers on mass assembly lines perform actions from habit to a degree seldom equalled by others, yet many such workers find this activity extremely distasteful. Actions proceeding from morally evil habits, or vices, are also not necessarily pleasurable.

> ... the practice of the acquired virtues will follow the principles of natural habits, and the more frequently and the more perfectly their acts are exercised, the easier they become, until finally, the subject is disposed toward a constant manner of action and exercises acts of the acquired virtues easily and readily.[14]

If acquired moral virtue follows the principles of natural habits, this is rather a reason why it cannot be described simply as resulting from repetition. There are many cases in which the difficulty experienced in performing a good action is not diminished in the slightest by the repeated performance of that action. Indeed, it is possible for the performance of a good act to increase rather than decrease the difficulty with which it is performed the next time. A soldier who must cross enemy mine fields many times in a day may find each successive exercise of this virtue of courage more, not less, difficult than before. After years of peaceful life he may find the prospect of renewing such experiences still more painful than the original ones.

Further, clinical studies have shown that in some instances a habit may be most effectually developed by performing the act directly opposed to it. Habits of stuttering and stammering, for example, have sometimes been eradicated or diminished, and the contrary habit of speech developed, by therapeutic techniques that include deliberate acts of stuttering or stammering. Similarly, certain kinds of typing errors are most responsive to corrective drills that involve the deliberate typing of the erroneous combination of letters.[15] The psychological principles involved here will obviously not be suspended where the action in question has a dimension of moral good or evil to it.

Above all it should be pointed out that the natural inclination to perform a certain good action is not determined merely by the principles of natural habits. Depth psychology has revealed a vast world of forces that operate in determining the inclinations and aversions men have to different actions. These forces are often far more significant than those that tend to arise out of habit formation and sometimes so strong as to eclipse them entirely. When, because of the peculiar traumatic experiences of childhood and the dynamisms of the unconscious, feelings of intense hostility and aggressiveness predominate in a man, meekness and patience will

---
[14] Robert F. Coerver, *op. cit.*, pp. 20, 21.
[15] Knight Dunlap, *Habits* (New York: Liveright, Inc., 1932), pp. 202-210.

always be difficult for him to practice. The faithful and heroic performance of meek and patient actions will usually not undo in the slightest the forces that make them painful and difficult. Indeed, it is possible in some situations for the performance of a virtuous action to exacerbate an unconscious conflict and produce a very stable increase in the difficulty with which it is performed.

Obviously, the fact that performing a good act would increase a man's aversion to it will not ipso facto relieve him of the obligation to perform it. Likewise, the fact that performing a morally evil act would increase the facility in another good act does nothing toward justifying the evil act. The paradoxes that appear here serve only to highlight the necessity of separating virtue from facility.

The concept of virtue as facility in a good act leads to inconsistency at another point. It is commonly taught that the moral virtues are so connected that they increase and decrease not singly in isolation but all together. Theoretical justification for this is generally presented in the argument that there is no virtue without prudence, which estimates what is the moral good in each case, and through this prudence all the virtues must be connected. The position is commonly supported by citing cases in which the practice of one virtue necessarily involves the practice of another. Thus restitution is cited as an act of justice that "will not be placed easily and therefore will sometimes fail, unless the person has the disposition of temperance."[16]

If all the acquired moral virtues are thus connected, this is one more reason why facility can be neither an essential component nor a necessary consequent of virtue. There are countless cases in which facility is attained in one virtue without any corresponding increase in the facility with which other virtues are practiced. Indeed, the disparity between the facility with which men practice different virtues is far more striking than any parity. There are many who find acts of fortitude easy but acts of humility difficult, who find it easy to be generous but difficult to be patient. Such disparities would be impossible if virtue entailed facility in the manner traditionally taught.

[16] George P. Klubertanz, *op. cit.*, p. 191. It should be clear at this point that it does not follow that *because* a virtuous act is "not . . . placed easily" *therefore* it "will sometimes fail." The possibility of failure, as well as that of perfect constancy, is a necessary consequent of freedom. It cannot be tied in this manner to difficulty or ease in the performance of the act.

This difficulty cannot be circumvented by the distinction that is often made between perfect and imperfect moral virtue. Imperfect moral virtues are defined as dispositions to good acts that are easy to change and perfect moral virtues as dispositions to good acts that are difficult to change. This qualification "difficult to change" has been accepted since Aristotle as one of the essential notes of habit, and hence of virtue, distinguishing it from mere dispositions and tendencies to good which do not promise any great constancy.

In treating of the connection of the virtues Lumbreras adverts to this distinction and notes that this connection does not exist between the imperfect moral virtues. "Some men have an inclination or disposition, innate or acquired, to the act of one virtue, for example, justice," he writes, "and have no disposition or inclination to the act of another virtue, such as temperance."[17] When we are dealing solely with innate inclinations, Lumbreras admits that a person who is disposed to one virtue, for example fortitude, may tend by that fact to be indisposed to another, for example meekness.[18]

Thus it may be argued that the disparity between the facility with which different virtuous acts are performed exists only where we have imperfect moral virtue. When we pass from mere good disposition to habit and perfect virtue it is no longer possible for different tendencies to different good acts to produce differing experiences of facility in their performance. Still less would it be possible for a tendency to favor certain good acts and oppose others at the same time.

Such a position conflicts with many of the empirical findings of psychology. It may be pointed out in the first place that the dispositions to good which exist prior to the development of virtue and constancy are not necessarily easily changeable. Tendencies that predispose to certain good acts may spring from unconscious causes and these are for the most part extremely stable and difficult to change. They are certainly far more immovable by any definition of the term than the inclinations to good produced by the formation of habit.

Accordingly, it is erroneous to assume that as a man develops perfect virtue his initial set of dispositions, favoring certain good acts above others and sometimes at the expense of others, will give

[17] Peter Lumbreras, "Notes on the Connection of the Virtues," *The Thomist*, Vol. XI, 1948, No. 2, p. 220.
[18] *Ibid.*, p. 221.

way to a set of tendencies that accord throughout with his virtuous conduct. If we pressed for a step by step analysis of the psychological process by which the disposition that favors fortitude and hinders meekness is transformed into one that is not only more stable but favors both virtues equally, we would soon discover its illusory character. The aggressiveness, for example, that makes fortitude easy and meekness difficult is often not eradicated by virtuous conduct. It only appears to be because the man practices both virtues with constancy. As the forces that favor certain good acts above others or at the expense of others may remain after all the changes effected by habit formation, so also may there remain a disparity in the facility with which different virtuous acts are performed.

It should be pointed out that the view of acquired moral virtue presented here does not in any way depend upon the doctrine of the connection of the virtues. The parity doctrine is not put forward as further proof that acquired moral virtue does not entail facility. The arguments on which it is based appear to me incapable of meeting rigorous standards of proof. However, the parity doctrine is held by those who teach that virtue entails facility and it is relevant to point out the inconsistency.[19]

A few remarks may be added upon some circumstances accounting in some measure for the long acceptance of the facility doctrine

---

[19] The doctrine of the connection of the virtues has had a checkered history. It was taught by the Stoics and, among the Romans, by Seneca and Cicero. "Inter omnes philosophos constat . . . qui unum haberet omnes habere virtutes." Cicero, *De Officiis*, lib. 2, c. 10. The doctrine was accepted by nearly all the early Christian thinkers, among them Jerome, Augustine and Gregory. However, they made no distinction between infused moral virtue and acquired moral virtue, and such arguments as they advanced could apply only to infused virtue. In 1213 the distinction between infused and acquired moral virtue was clearly articulated by Godfrey of Poitiers and the two were henceforth treated separately. For a time, a majority of medieval thinkers, including Albert the Great and Bonaventure, denied that the acquired moral virtues were connected, rejecting the ancient argument of the Stoics. The question took another turn with the introduction of the *Ethics* of Aristotle to the West. According to Aristotle, all the virtues (and with him this obviously meant acquired moral virtues) were connected, and he advanced new arguments for the position, the most significant of which was the one based on the role of prudence in all the virtues. His arguments and conclusion were taken over by St. Thomas Aquinas and, after brief resistance, the parity doctrine began the long reign it has enjoyed until the present day. *Cf.* Odon Lottin, "La connexion des vertus chez saint Thomas d'Aquin et ses prédécesseurs," *Psychologie et morale aux XIIe et XIIIe siècles*, Tome III (Louvain: Abbaye du Mont César, 1949), pp. 197-252.

and for the reluctance that some may feel toward accepting the views set forth here.

First, the facility doctrine has nearly always been expounded by men very much concerned with persuading others to perform good acts. Obviously the doctrine that doing good eventually leads to facility in doing good supplies another inducement that may be offered for the doing of particular good acts. Similarly, the doctrine that the performance of every morally evil action tends to attach us to a habit of vice serves as an added deterrent from doing evil. Even the most technical literature on virtue assumes at times a distinctly hortatory tone and, to the degree that this mood prevails, there will be a tendency to resist the view set forth here.

It may be answered that even if the view here expounded entirely destroyed one motive for doing good, this would have nothing to do with its truth or falsity. History exhibits countless instances of exaggerated claims being made for good institutions and of bad reasons being added to the good ones that already exist for commendable causes. Indeed, the utilitarian character of a doctrine should ordinarily put us on our guard respecting its validity.[20]

A second consideration requires greater attention. The traditional doctrine of virtue as facility in good has generally formed a part of a larger view of morality that regards this life as a period of trial during which free agents are called upon to reject evil and do good. Choosing the good merits reward and choosing evil deserves punishment. This view begets a strong tendency to regard it a fitting work of natural justice that men who persevere in good should in time be rewarded by finding it easier to do good. If a man sets out on the path of virtue by heroically denying the impulses to evil that beset him, it seems necessary to suppose that he will eventually be freed from them. Likewise, it is regarded a

---

[20] Purely to avoid a false impression, it may be noted that the view of virtue presented here still allows great motive for doing good to be drawn from the influence of particular good actions on future behavior. In the first place, the formation of habit and its usual effects will occur in the great majority of cases. Secondly, the performance of good acts can result in a tendency to persevere in them for reasons that have nothing to do with habit formation. Unconscious needs and problems can often be worked out or find expression in any of several different ways. Following a life of virtue can take on an unconscious significance resulting in a disposition to persevere in it incomparably more powerful than any tendencies that can arise out of habit formation.

fitting and inevitable work of natural justice that men obstinate in evil should suffer the misfortune of becoming even more strongly chained to their vice, especially since they often suffer nothing else.

To those who hold such a view it will perhaps seem unintelligible that a man should persevere in good and yet find his good actions becoming increasingly difficult. Still more repugnant will it be to admit that a man could find a good act more difficult precisely because of his past performance of the act. Equally uncongenial will be the possibility that after years of vice a man might be able to break off and begin at once to perform the contrary virtuous acts with less difficulty than another who has long followed the way of virtue.

I submit, however, that in these apparent anomalies, and in the concept of virtue put forward here, there is nothing that is incompatible with the larger view of morality just described.

If this life is a period of trial in which free agents are called to do good in the face of evil, to be tested as gold in the fire, there is nothing unintelligible about its being a trial to the end. If a man suffers difficulty and pain in doing good, this is a physical, not a moral, evil. No physical evil of any sort can be excluded from the range of possible sufferings that a man may have to endure despite his perseverance in good. Whether the pain occasioned by virtuous conduct be due to the more usual macroscopic forces from without or whether it be generated by the myriad subtle complex forces and feelings determined by the unique neural state of the individual with his peculiar store of memories and unconscious dynamisms is entirely accidental so far as concerns the moral character of an act. What is tested in moral trial is the free self that is called upon to overcome every tendency that opposes it in its choice of good, not the complex of psychological characteristics and conditions that constitute the determined side of man.

It could scarcely be maintained that the more virtue a man has the less difficulty and pain he will experience. Yet the facility doctrine is but a step removed in holding just such an inverse proportion to exist between virtue and a certain kind of pain and difficulty, namely that involved in the performance of the virtuous act. Such a correlation is not necessary to uphold the intelligibility of the moral order, not essential to the concept of continuous moral progress in an individual, and not borne out by empirical observation.

No genuine problem is created even in those rare cases where the performance of a good act itself makes the future performance of that act more difficult or where the performance of a morally evil act makes it possible to perform the contrary good act with greater facility. Such cases are not essentially different from those in which moral acts are followed by similarly incongruous effects as a result of forces operating on the macroscopic level. A man may refuse to connive at dishonesty and thereby provoke a retaliatory harassment that impoverishes him and makes it more difficult for him to live honestly in the future. Another may steal an enormous sum of money and then, lacking nothing, find that refraining from stealing is easier than ever before.

It will be objected that these cases are not parallel because in them the incongruous result is due, not to the effect of the action upon the agent's own disposition, but to the fact that it sets in motion hostile forces outside himself. Refusing to connive at dishonesty can only increase a man's interior disposition to justice. If as a result of a just act it becomes more difficult for a man to live justly in the future, this is simply because his increased disposition to justice is more severely tested by trials placed on him from without. Similarly, if a particular theft seems to diminish a man's temptation to steal, this does not mean that he has lost any of his disposition to steal. It means rather that after the theft there is less in his surrounding circumstances to activate his increased disposition to steal.

However, the objection will not stand. It proceeds as if impulses opposing the performance of a good act were compatible with the moral perfection of the act when they arise from external causes but incompatible with it when they arise from relatively internal or psychological causes. This would indeed be the case if such internal causes were themselves the principles of free actions and the subject of moral progress. However, the distinction between external and internal, or psychological, forces bearing on an act is not the same as the distinction between the free and the determined in human behavior. In its choice of good the free self must overcome all the forces that oppose it, including those arising from interior dispositions determined by the laws of psychology and the peculiar history of the agent.

Finally, no difficulty is raised by the thesis that every morally good and evil act increases the tendency of the will in the same direction. Facility in the performance of an action depends on harmony among all the forces bearing on the action and not solely upon the will. The moral progress of the will, or of the man as evidenced by his volitional acts, may follow a course that finds no parallel matching progress in the inclination of the determined side of his nature to those acts. The effects of those acts in the material order of the determined may be opposite to their effect on the will and thus contradict the doctrine that every virtuous act conduces to facility in that act. The doctrine that every act of acquired moral virtue increases the tendency of the will in the same direction is not, of course, presupposed by the present argument for separating the notion of facility from virtue. It is simply pointed out that those who hold the doctrine will have no special grounds for objecting to the view of acquired moral virtue put forward here.

6

ANCIENTS AND MODERNS: NOTES ON INTERPRETING HUME

by

Thomas Prufer

We must, . . . having set forth the phenomena and having first not known our way about, show the ordinary views of the passions, and if not all of these views, then most of them and the most dominant, and if the difficulties can be resolved and the ordinary views left as they were, the showing shall have been sufficient.[1]

There is no common sense answer to a philosophical problem. One can defend common sense against the attacks of philosophers only by solving their puzzles, i.e., by curing them of the temptation to attack common sense; not by restating the views of common sense.[2]

We could not talk to one another about the private if we could not talk to one another about the public. We could not talk unless we could talk to one another.[3]

1. ". . . 'tis almost impossible for the mind of man to rest . . . in that narrow circle of objects, which are the subject of daily conversation and action. . . ."[4] Nature leads (some, at least) toward *theōria*; *theōria* is self-destructive; nature by making the self-destruction of *theōria* manifest, manifests itself as antitheoretical; nature leads back from the solitude of *theōria* to the ordinary and shared, having discredited any noncommon measure of the common. Natural belief is an *Ueberbau* on irreducible passion (uneasiness and ease), not an assent to abstruse argument and refined or elaborate reasoning, which end in suspension of the vulgar attitude.

---

[1] Aristotle, 1145b2-7.
[2] Ludwig Wittgenstein, *The Blue and Brown Books*, Harper Torchbook, New York: Harper and Row, 1965, pp. 58-59.
[3] P. F. Strawson, *Individuals*, Anchor Book, Garden City, New York: Doubleday and Company, 1963, p. 60.
[4] Hume, *A Treatise of Human Nature*, ed. Selby-Bigge, Oxford at the Clarendon Press, 1888, p. 271.

"Nature is obstinate, and will not quit the field, however strongly attack'd by reason. . . . Not being able to reconcile these two enemies. . . ."[5] "Nature is always too strong for principle."[6] "Nature will always maintain her rights, and prevail in the end over any abstract reasoning whatsoever."[7]

2. A blind and powerful propensity of nature throws to the surface that which from the point of view of *theōria* is unmasked as fictitious and illusory[8] but which makes the common life of action possible. The public self-destruction of *theōria* protects natural belief against the deformations and attacks of the extraordinary and extravagant: ridiculous and airy sciences and dangerous superstition and enthusiasm.

3. *Natura (humana) naturans* has the propensity to feign a *natura naturata,* the continuous and independent world, as a remedy for the isolation of reason, although the natural attitude precedes the unmasking of it as an artifice and fiction to which the philosopher in blind and easeful submission to the current of nature returns, fleeing the subversion of reason, which undermines both the belief of the vulgar and itself as speculation without the sphere of common life. The fundamental function of philosophy is to establish by reasoning from a nonnatural perspective the priority of the natural and to defend theoretically the ultimacy of the ordinary: ". . . this absurdity, that it at once denies and establishes the vulgar supposition."[9]

4. Convention and industry against the niggardliness of nature ("the selfishness and confin'd generosity of men, along with the scanty provision nature has made for his wants")[10] is itself the work of a nature which has discredited *theōria*[11] as a measure of the desire

---

[5] *Treatise,* 215.

[6] Hume, *Enquiries,* ed. Selby-Bigge, Oxford at the Clarendon Press, 1902, p. 160.

[7] *Enquiries,* 41; cf. *Treatise,* 213; Machiavelli, *Discourses* I, 37; Sextus Empiricus, *Outlines of Pyrrhonism* I, 20; Reid, *An Inquiry into the Human Mind* I, vi.

[8] Robert Sokolowski, "Fiction and Illusion in David Hume's Philosophy," *The Modern Schoolman,* XLV (March, 1968), 189-225.

[9] *Treatise,* 218.

[10] *Treatise,* 495; cf. *Enquiries,* 188, 193-194; *Essays,* Oxford University Press, 1963, pp. 259-288. Cf. Epicurus, Gnomologium Vaticanum LXIX; Aristotle, 1278b29-30; Hobbes, *Leviathan* XIII, "The passions that incline men to peace."

[11] Contemplation of eternal and necessary nonhuman order, not deliberation about whether or not a human act or product is to be. Aristotle, 1143b18ff., 1177b26-1178a8.

to have more of the humanly useful and pleasant.[12] Nature ends in *Selbstaufhebung:* ". . . we can better satisfy our appetites in an oblique and artificial manner, than by their headlong and impetuous motion."[13] Artifice saves interested passion from "the misery of the condition, which precedes this restraint";[14] private property limits the desire to have more and expanding production of commodity promises to satisfy the desire to have more.

5. Ancient scepticism came close to this position ("necessitation by the passions," "the arts . . . whereby we are not inactive")[15] and drew back. It is important for an understanding of the specificity of modernity to understand why the ancients drew back;[16] compare Hobbes with Epicurean tranquillity, hiddenness, overcoming of fear of death, piety, and praise of generous nature: "thanks be to blessed nature for having made the necessary easy to obtain and the difficult unnecessary"; "whatever is natural is easily obtained and only the vain and worthless is difficult."[17]

6. "Throw any considerable goods among men, they instantly fall a quarrelling, while each strives to get possession of what pleases him. . . ."[18] But the sharing of knowledge as of the highest natural good, a good not lessened but increased in the sharing,[19] is an act of plenty and generosity, an act having the most of what is simply good. Although "to apportion too much to oneself of the simply

---

[12] Aristotle, 981b17-25.
[13] *Treatise,* 521.
[14] *Treatise,* 505.
[15] Sextus Empiricus, *Outlines of Pyrrhonism* I, 23-24.
[16] Plutarch, *Life of Marcellus,* 14-17.
[17] Usener, *Epicurea,* fr. 469; Diogenes Laertius X, 130; see Usener, fr. 446 & 468; Ratae Sententiae XV & XXI; Gnomologium Vaticanum XLVII (Metrodorus); Plutarch, *Moralia* 1124D, 1128B-1130E, esp. 1129B; Usener, fr. 530; cf. fr. 555 with Diogenes Oenoandensis, fr. 41 (Chilton); Lucretius, *De rerum natura* V, 1146-1147; Cicero, *De oratore* III, 17, 63-64; Seneca, *De otio* III, 3, 2; Philodemus, *Volumina Rhetorica,* Sudhaus I, 253-261; II, 28-33; Usener, fr. 13* & 387; Hermarchus, fr. 24; Diogenes Laertius X, 123-124; Oxyrhynchus Papyrus 215; Philodemus, *On the Gods* III; Philodemus, *On Piety* II; Papyri Herculanenses 1232 & 168, col. I; Lucretius, *De rerum natura* II, 646-651; III, 1-30; VI, 43-79; Cicero, *De natura deorum* I, 16, 43-21, 56; Seneca, *De beneficiis* IV, 19; Diogenes Oenoandensis (Epicurus?), fr. 52, col. III & IV (Chilton); Gassendi, *De vita et moribus Epicuri* IV, 3. Cf. Hobbes, *Leviathan* XXXI, "The right of God's sovereignty. . . ."; *Human Nature,* ep. ded.; *De homine,* XI, 15. See Wolfgang Schmid, "Epikur," RAC V.
[18] *Treatise,* 540.
[19] Cicero, *De amicitia,* 88; Seneca, *De brevitate vitae* XV, 3; Boethius, *Consolatio* II pr. 5, Divitiaene; Augustine, *De civitate dei* XV, 4-5.

good and too little of the simply bad"[20] is unjust, if contemplation is a good not diminished by the sharing of it, then justice and injustice have no place in contemplation. Friends need no justice[21] because friends have in common,[22] the best friendship being the sharing of speech[23] about what is best.

7. The priority of act over potency and of rest over motion is the Aristotelian form of the goodness of nature; the political form of this goodness is the priority of leisure over work, of peace over war, and of citizenship over foreign policy.[24]

8. Without shared but not thereby divided contemplation of an actuality eternal and necessary and therefore independent of human construction and choice, the natural desire to have more (*pleonexia*) leads to the natural priority of war and out of such an inimical naturalness into the convention of property and the artifice of production. If the natural state is the state in which all is common and in which there is therefore no justice or injustice, and if nature is antitheoretical, not toward contemplation as what is best, then the natural state is a state of violence and fear; but if contemplation is most natural, then the most natural state will be a state of quietude beyond penury, production, and property, even though the rarity of this state makes it least ordinary and obvious.

9. The importance of cosmology for politics is based on the importance of this question: is there a nonhuman but accessible analogue for the anticipation of excellence and for generous self-communication? Is nature minded by nonhuman mind?[25] ". . . the mind has a great propensity to spread itself on external objects. . ."[26]

10. The clear Aristotelian distinction between science and prudence would make the similarity of roles played in the Aristotelian and the Humean analyses of the excellences of the life of action by pleasure and pain, praise and blame, appearance and need,

---

[20] Aristotle, 1134a33-34; cf. 1137a26-30 (Michael of Ephesus ad loc., CAG XXII/3, 65-66), 1154b15-16, 1267a10-12, b1-8; Plato, *Phaedo* 66b-69, *Gorgias* 490-494; Cicero, *De finibus* I, 1, 2; *Enquiries*, 283-284; Michael ad 1170b5, CAG XX, 518-519; Hobbes, *De corpore politico* I, iv, 2.

[21] Aristotle, 1155a26-27.

[22] Aristotle, *Politics* II, 5; Hobbes, *De cive*, ep. ded.

[23] Aristotle, *Nicomachean Ethics* IX, 9, esp. 1170b10-12.

[24] Aristotle, *Metaphysics* IX, 6 & 8; 1325b14-32; *Nicomachean Ethics* VI, 7; 1010a25-35; *De anima* III, 4.

[25] Ernst Grumach, *Physis und Agathon in der alten Stoa*, 2. Aufl., Berlin: Wiedmann, 1966, pp. 44-71; Paul Moraux, "Quinta Essentia," PWRE XXIV, 1963, 1196-1203.

[26] *Treatise*, 167.

convention and legality, property and moderation, passion and choice, striking except for those few indices in the Aristotelian analysis of another, better, and more natural form of life:[27] contemplation of eternal and necessary nonhuman order overarches human affairs; the nature of man is in bondage in many ways,[28] but there are things more divine according to nature than man, the most manifest of which are those which make up the cosmos;[29] compare Hume: "There is no question of importance, whose decision is not compriz'd in the science of man...."[30] The human goods about which we deliberate because they can be or not be, as we choose, are sought in the context of an eternal and necessary good, which is not the good of man as agent and citizen, which is the principle of contemplative friendship, a community beyond justice, and the attainment of which gives joy astonishing in its purity and permanence;[31] but this good plays no role in the analysis of the life of action in its own terms.

11. What distinguishes Hume's analysis of the political as political from Aristotle's analysis can perhaps be traced to Hume's use of the principle of separate reason, a principle which Aristotle uses for his analysis of the divine contemplative life in its difference from the political life.[32] Aristotelian *nous* is beyond city, soul, and cosmos. The Humean analysis of mind ends in the solipsism of the actuality of the present perception ("nothing is ever really present to the mind, besides its own perceptions");[33] this analysis denies both the *ego cogitans* as a theater where perceptions appear and the continuous existence of bodies independent of our interrupted perception of them, and thus it denies *a fortiori* soul and cosmos ("suppos'd ... neither to be annihilated by our absence, nor to be brought into existence by our presence").[34] A dream, if not a delirium, and laughable to the vulgar, philosophy runs wide of common life: a caricature of the *noēsis noēseōs*. The rejection of this solipsism and the return to the shared and ordinary nevertheless carries back into the

---

[27] Aristotle, *Nicomachean Ethics* III, 3; VI, 7 & 13; X, 7-8; *Metaphysics* XII, 7 & 9; Ptolemy, *Almagest* XIII, 2; *Palatine Anthology* IX, 577.
[28] Aristotle, 982b29-30.
[29] Aristotle, 1141a34-b2.
[30] *Treatise*, xx.
[31] Aristotle, 1177a25-26.
[32] Aristotle, 1177b12-15, 1178a22.
[33] *Treatise*, 197; cf. 212.
[34] *Treatise*, 207; cf. *Enquiries*, 152.

analysis of the common a solipsism not found in Aristotle's analysis of human affairs.

12. Hume in his analysis of the disinterested, calm, and tender passions covers over the role of the separate in so far as he considers irrelevant the Hobbesian and Lockeian[35] reduction of benevolence, generosity, and friendship to an epiphenomenon. Such unmasking of private interest depends on the contrast of subtle and intricate reflection with the common and obvious point of view of the careless observer: "a natural unforced interpretation of the phenomena of human life."[36] "Truths which are *pernicious* to society, if any such there be, will yield to errors which are salutary and *advantageous*."[37]

13. Hume's critique of knowledge of all future matters of fact is similar to Aristotle's critique of knowledge of one kind of future matters of fact: events dependent on chance and choice, possible events the contradictories of which are also possible.[38] Indeed, Hume's position follows if Aristotelian science is absorbed by Aristotelian prudence.

14. Aristotle inquires "what it is that holds events together so that the coming-to-be now occurring follows upon a past event" and considers the position that "one cannot infer from an event which occurred in the past that a future event will occur" because "there cannot be a middle term homogeneous with extremes respectively past and future."[39] Nevertheless in so far as we can argue from what has happened to what must have happened before that happened and in so far as in nature there is cyclic coming-to-be,[40] the middle and extreme terms being reciprocal, we can argue from the past to the future.

15. Present certainty about future events which depend on chance or choice is possible only by artifice or fiction. For Aristotle this artifice or fiction is the imitation by a well-made story of surprising turns of events. That which from a point of view within the imitated action is an indeterminate future is from the point of view of the imitation itself determinate: the whole of the story is already known

---

[35] Richard H. Cox, *Locke on War and Peace*, Oxford at the Clarendon Press, 1960, pp. 6, 88-94, 186-189.
[36] *Enquiries*, 244.
[37] *Enquiries*, 279.
[38] *Enquiries*, 25, 164; Aristotle, *On Interpretation* IX.
[39] Aristotle, *Posterior Analytics* II, 12.
[40] Aristotle, *On Generation and Corruption* II, 10-11; *Physics* II, 8-9.

to the poet, the future ends at the end of the story, the connection between the elements of the story is necessary (or at least probable).[41] But Hume reverses the Aristotelian *para tēn doxan di'allēla*:[42] in accordance with *doxa*, but not *di'allēla*.

16. For Hume our ignorance of the causes of the course of nature would make nature episodic, like a bad tragedy,[43] if it were not for the "customary transition of the imagination from one object to its usual attendant."[44] Yet the course of nature is not the result of chance or choice; all principles of the sequence of events, chance and choice as well as necessity, are ways of covering over our ignorance of the nonhuman.[45]

17. Hume conflates the privacy of mind (for Aristotle separate mind is neither owned by . . . , nor mindful of . . .) and the privacy of body (each's body is just his own alone and not another's) and then argues from the passivity of body against the privacy of mind: "Ourself, independent of the perception of every other object, is in reality nothing. . . ."[46]

18. The private and the public are bound together by the passion of pride in "self, or that succession of related ideas and impressions, of which we have an intimate memory or consciousness,"[47] a passion implying the presence of the self to other selves present to the self: sympathy. The delight and uneasiness of pride and humility depend on the presence to me of the presence to others of what is (or is not) mine or owned: comparison. Hobbes: ". . . all the pleasure and jollity of the mind consists in this, even to get some, with whom comparing, it may find somewhat where'n to triumph and vaunt itsef. . . ." ". . . glory is like honour, if all men have it, no man hath it, for they consist in comparison and precellence."[48] And Aristotle: "We may define what aims at appearance as what a man will not choose if nobody is to know of his having it." "What a man wants to be is better than what a man wants to seem."[49] Hume: "An evil may be real . . . without shewing itself to others." ". . . perhaps the most real and the most solid evils of life will be

---

[41] Aristotle, 1451a16-19, 1454b2-6, 1460b13-14.
[42] Aristotle, 1452a4.
[43] Aristotle, 1090b19; *Enquiries*, 74.
[44] *Enquiries*, 75.
[45] *Treatise*, 13, 84, 164-171, 188-192, 275-276, 404-407; *Enquiries*, 30-31, 94-96.
[46] *Treatise*, 340; 253.
[47] *Treatise*, 277.
[48] Hobbes, *De cive* I, 5 & 2.
[49] Aristotle, 1365b1-8, 1168b3; *Rhetoric* II, 6.

found of this nature."⁵⁰ "A perfect solitude is, perhaps, the greatest punishment we can suffer. Every pleasure languishes when enjoy'd a-part from company, and every pain becomes cruel and intolerable. Whatever other passions we may be actuated by; pride, ambition, avarice, curiosity, revenge or lust; the soul or animating principle of them all is sympathy; nor wou'd they have any force, were we to abstract entirely from the thoughts and sentiments of others. . . ." ". . . the minds of men are mirrors to one another . . ."⁵¹ "Reduce a person to solitude, and he loses all enjoyment, except either of the sensual or speculative kind; and that because the movements of his heart are not forwarded by correspondent movements in his fellow-creatures."⁵²

19. The availability of Aristotelian nontechnical and nonpractical mind is "the science being sought," inquiry together into the eternal and necessary nonhuman order over against human production and action; Humean nontechnical and nonpractical mind is available only in the negative mode of self-destruction. "Every man's interest is peculiar to himself," but the need for common world and discourse "makes us form some general unalterable standard."⁵³

20. The ancients considered the issue between self-sufficient solitude and generous communication on the level of contemplation. Hume's *theōria* is dreary and forlorn solitude; thus his analysis of the political is deprived of the quiet context of a community beyond the political and a joy beyond community.⁵⁴

---

⁵⁰ *Treatise*, 294.
⁵¹ *Treatise*, 363, 365.
⁵² *Enquiries*, 220; Aristotle, 1253a3-6.
⁵³ *Enquiries*, 228-229; cf. *Treatise*, 20-21, 581-584, 602-603; Locke, *An Essay Concerning Human Understanding* III, v & vi.
⁵⁴ Plato, *Apology* 32a2-3 & 33b6-8; *Republic* 519b-521c; *Timaeus* 29e-30a; *Laws* 739cde & 803bc.

7

THE CONCEPT OF TIME IN ST. AUGUSTINE

by

JOHN M. QUINN, O.S.A.

The scientific revolution has imprinted a virtually indelible mark on the Weştern mind.[1] The technology it has begotten has changed the face of the earth, but the glamorous things of applied science reflect deeper, brilliant theoretical insights; radio and TV have grown from Clerk Maxwell's electromagnetic field equations. Modern physics especially has conquered vast specialized regions of natural knowledge. No comparable body of specialized theoretical knowledge can match the soundness and abundance of its wealth. Yet, strangely, this heady affluence is ridden by an insecurity and bafflement before the all-pervasive features of nature. Common mechanical notions like force and mass continue to be indefinable. More elusive and bewildering still has been the more fundamental concept of time. Here our all-conquering contemporaries stand helpless upon a terrain unmapped by the specialized sciences. In his introduction to a recent reissue of a work significantly entitled *Time and Its Mysteries,* a distinguished astro-

[1] This article contains the substance of a paper originally delivered at an Augustine Colloquium that was held by the School of Philosophy of The Catholic University of America, March 29 and 30, 1963. A word should be said about its scope and limits. It does not pretend to be a summary dissertation on or an exhaustive presentation of every aspect of St. Augusine's notion, but aims at nothing more than an analysis of the text, a few explanatory comments along with some critical remarks on other interpretations, plus comparisons with two still influential theories of time. Nothing is said about the connection of time with eternity or the status of eternity. In confining discussion to Book XI of the *Confessions,* we have omitted practically all mention of the purely physical account of time expounded in *De civitate Dei.* Except in one section where it becomes necessary to dispel certain misconceptions about Augustine's relation to Plotinus' concept, we have kept away from tricky questions of doctrinal legacies. It goes without saying also that we have not set out to survey the whole spectrum of opinions about St. Auugstine's concept. We have appraised a few opinions among those deemed more authoritative or more plausible or currently more fashionable.

physicist goes farther: Time is one of the "Unknowables which keep us humble."[2] Effortlessness in handling the parameter t in differential equations furnishes no easy access to what the t measures, and telling time with a precision the ancients never dreamed of fails to tell precisely what time is.

The quandary of the physicist is only a special case of an experience common to man. We are at once completely acquainted with time and totally ignorant of time. Our sense of time we carry with us everywhere; conversations are so threaded with it that no word is "more familiar and well-known." Casual reflection, however, is enough to raise doubt about the sure grasp of time. Every man who wrestles with the problem must make his own the initial perplexity of St. Augustine: "What, then, is time? If no one asks me, I know. If I want to explain it to a questioner, I do not know."[3] Common-sense awareness of time is practical and unsophisticated, adequate for running lives by clock and organizing speech by tense. From the standpoint of meaning, the physicist's technically developed measurement of time also remains vague and inexact. Helplessness in discussion indicates this; when questioning makes us mute and elicits only blank looks, we expose our ignorance rather than the meaning of time.

The astrophysicist's *ignorabimus* teaches a second lesson. Much of the mystery or, more precisely, mystification arises because a scientist tries to solve a pseudo-problem, i.e., because he proposes to settle a nonmetrical question with a metrical answer that presupposes the nonmetrical solution. His confession of failure underlines the truth that the general question of time is explicable by a general noetic strategy no less rigorously analytic, which was employed by the ancients. Indeed we cannot solve the question unless we attack it with the help offered to us by the ancients. Some may write off such a declaration as one further bold but foredoomed try to update the archaic excursions of an early fifth-century thinker. For such critics it must be stressed that Augustine's concept grows out of a legitimate scientific analysis prior and presupposed to

[2] Harlow Shapley, Introduction, *Time and Its Mysteries*, Eight Lectures Given at New York University (Reprint; New York: Collier Books, 1962), p. 6.

[3] *Confessions*, XI, 14, 17. We use the text of M. Skutella in *Les Confessions*, Introd. et Notes par. A. Solignac; traduction de E. Tréhorel et G. Bouissou. Vols. 13 and 14 of *Oeuvres de saint Augustin* (Bruges: Desclée de Brouwer, 1962). Cf. also *The Confessions of St. Augustine*. Translated, with an Introduction and Notes, by John K. Ryan (Garden City, N. Y.: Image Books, Doubleday & Co., 1960).

what savants in the English-speaking countries ordinarily label science. If general knowledge precedes specialized researches in a limited subject matter,[4] then Augustine's scientific analysis of time, one undertaken on the level of general natural philosophy, is plainly antecedent to more specialized natural inquiries that capture the attention of modern natural sciences. Strictly speaking, we cannot scientifically measure time unless we first define, i.e., determine scientifically, what it is we measure or measure with. Later in his treatise Augustine in fact formulates in this way the initial perplexity of not knowing while yet knowing time: we do measure time, but because we do not know what time is, we seem logically barred from measuring it.[5] There follows this necessary corollary: what is cognitively prior and prerequisite cannot be made obsolete by posterior and dependent doctrines. Thus Augustine's definition cannot be toppled by a new hypothesis concerning the specialized mode of time-measurement like Einstein's special theory of relativity. In discussing St. Augustine's doctrine of time, then, we are not reporting with filial piety on the exhumation of philosophic remains.[6] His answer is as alive today as it was over fifteen and one-half centuries ago. A general philosophy of the universe does not run downhill with the universe; nor can time devour what remains viable and valid in a general doctrine of time.

[4] Cf. Vincent Edward Smith, *The General Science of Nature* (Milwaukee: Bruce, 1958).

[5] *Conf.*, XI, 21, 27.

[6] In his *The Idea of Reform* (Cambridge, Mass.: Harvard University Press, 1959), pp. 451-54, Professor Gerhart Ladner hazards "tentative suggestions" that certain "Augustinian insights" play a considerable role in modern science and philosophy "though in a different way and clearly without direct dependence on Augustine." Among these anticipatory insights is Augustine's view of the irreversibility of time. As a perusal of our article will reveal, Augustine implicitly recognizes the irreversibility of time but accords it not the slightest bit of express concern and explication. Whatever its value, Augustine's bare recognition of irreversibility does not raise, let alone solve, the problem of the ground of irreversibility. Nothing in Augustine's treatment even scantily suggests entropy; nothing in his general approach could have faintly prefigured the specialized research out of which the notion of entropy arose. Incidentally, contrary to Ladner's hypothesis, the "psycho-biological" arrow of time, i.e., the one-way direction of time, cannot hinge an entropy, for entropy presupposes the unidirectional path of time: entropy is the measure of the unavailable energy in a system during an interval of time. If entropy presupposes an irreversible time going on, it is viciously circular to invoke entropy to explain the unique direction of time. On this point cf. L. Susan Stebbing, *Philosophy and the Physicists* (New York: Dover Publications, 1958), pp.

The following pages purport to expound his abidingly sound concept. The first section of the essay breaks down the text into a three-stage dialectic. A second section aims at throwing some light on the terminus of inquiry, that time is a distension of the soul. A final section summarily notes correspondences and contrasts with the conceptions of Henri Bergson and Aristotle.

An Analysis of the Text

Analogies and disanalogies detected between Augustine's concept and those of ancient and modern thinkers possess little point and less value unless the multiple comparisons are grounded in a detailed inspection of the text itself. Unfortunately, a close analytical restatement is not customarily favored by interpreters, and its lack may account for a tendency to draw overneat parallels between Augustine and Kant or Heidegger. In one or two cases where commentators do embark on a minute exposition, we have found they are usually satisfied to reword Augustine in a running paraphrase that often tends to obscure and lose the leading strings and the pivotal turns in the discourse. When bestowing more than a casual nod on the text, we try to highlight each significant stage in the development of the definition, the treatise stands out as a compactly and delicately wrought opuscule, a diamond dazzling the mind, a joy to behold.

An outline prefaces the analysis proper. Far from being a maladroit gesture of condescension, this preliminary sketch is meant simply to serve as a guide to forewarn the preoccupied man, who reads as he runs, of the confounding dialectical twists and turns ahead. After outlining the text and retracing the introduction, we will examine the three arguments that terminate the three parts of the treatise: first, real time must be always in some sense present time; second, time is not dependent on bodily movement; third, time is a distension of the soul.

The outline follows.

Introduction: The perplexity and the problem (Ch. 14).

The perplexity: common knowledge of time leaves us analytically ignorant of what time is.

253-64; and Richard Schlegel, *Time and the Physical World* (Lansing, Mich.: Michigan State University Press, 1961), pp. 17-30.

Concept of Time in St. Augustine 79

The problem: how can past, present and future exist if they are either nonexistent or unknowable?

Part I: Real time as present time (Ch. 15-21).

1. Whereas the physical present is pointlike (Ch. 15), the present that we sensibly observe can be measured (Ch. 16).

2. Past and future exist (Ch. 17), but only in so far as they are known as present (Ch. 18).

3. Though incapable of explaining how men prophesy (Ch. 19), we can see that all three times, past, present and future, are in some way present times (Ch. 20).

4. One difficulty remains unresolved: how can we truly measure the present interval if the extentless present has no interval (Ch. 21)?

First Interlude: A prayer for light (Ch. 22).

Part II: Time not dependent on motion (Ch. 23-24).

1. Time is not identical with the motions of celestial bodies (Ch. 23).

2. Nor is it dependent on the motion of the sun (Ch. 23).

3. It is not dependent on any bodily motion (Ch. 24). Positively put, time is an independent distension or measure of motion.

Second Interlude: Another prayer for light (Ch. 25).

Part III: Time as a distension of the soul (Ch. 26-27).

1. We cannot measure times in their very passing (Ch. 26 and Ch. 27, 34).

2. Inductive analysis of *Deus creator omnium* proves that time is a distension of the soul (Ch. 27, 35).

3. Measurement of silent intervals establishes the same point (Ch. 27, 36).

4. Silent rehearsal before speaking also proves that time is a psychic distension (Ch. 27, 36).

These inductions solve the initial perplexity in Ch. 14.

Resolution of the Problem (Ch. 28).

1. Future, past and present exist in the soul by virtue of expectation, memory and attention. This insight solves the initial problem stated in Ch. 14.

2. The distension in the soul during the recitation of a psalm exemplifies shorter intervals of time and longer spans like the life of a man and the history of man.

Introduction

The seeming paradox of at once knowing but not knowing time evokes the wonder propaedeutic to knowledge. The polarity of knowledge and ignorance is not due to an opposition between percept and concept. Augustine is not piqued by any disparity of the perceptually plain and the conceptually murky. The perplexity, along with its problematic statement, is posed on the conceptual level. When specified, the perplexity about what time is becomes the problem: in what sense can the past, present and future times be said to exist? When not queried, we confidently assert that the existence of the three times is beyond question. But when driven to question ourselves, we quickly learn that the three dialectically dissolve. Each of these times seems bereft of any sort of firm existence. Both past and future are by definition nonexistent, past meaning what no longer exists, future what does not yet exist. The present does exist but only in a precarious fashion. If the present did not pass, it would not be time but eternity. Since time is distinct from eternity, since the present unceasingly passes, it suffers the inconvenience of existing only by immediately ceasing to exist. The present exists, we seem to be saying, for the precise reason that it will not exist; real time, it is implied, has being only because it tends to nonbeing. Thus all three times apparently harbor contradictory notes. The existence of the past means that it no longer exists; the existence of the future means that it does not now exist; and the present exists only in order not to exist.[7]

[7] *Conf.*, XI, 14, 17.

Part I

A limited attack on this question restores meaningful existence to the three times, but cannot explain in what precise respect time is knowable. The distinction between the punctiform physical present and the spread out present which we observe marks the first step forward in the inquiry. Next, we see that past and future can exist only in remembrance or prognosis, i.e., in present cognition. Thirdly, each of the three times is, strictly speaking, a present time. But, fourthly, this answer raises another question to go unanswered till the outset of Part III: how can the extentless present be measured if what is unextended cannot be measured?

1. A dialectical examination of language frees past and future from the stigma of illusion. It should be remarked that Augustine accepts the deliverance of experience ingrained in language as a reliable point of departure for constructing definitions. Though rudimentary analysis disposes of an existent past and future, they do form part and parcel of ordinary language. We commonly refer to a hundred years past as a long or short time, depending on the time-scale. Too, we note that a century in retrospect or prospect is spoken of as a long time and, alongside it, ten days as a short time. But again it seems no less plain that what was and what will be, by their very terms, do not and cannot exist.[8] Perhaps, comes the next suggestion, in saying "Any century is a long time," we are positing the time-interval as present. This suggestion also turns out to be sterile. For no century exists all at once, and no part of a century, whether day, hour, minute, second, or infinitesimal portion of these, endures as strictly present. No segment of time as such exists in nature; were the present extended, it would include past and future parts. The physical present is punctiform and indivisible; as already mentioned, what has only a kind of fluent position cannot have length predicated of it.[9] However, fact still stubbornly collides with analysis. It is plain that we do compare one time-interval with another, as, let us say, in the statement that an hour is sixty times longer than the conventional minute. What we measure is of course not the past or future but time's actual transit, the present in its passage.[10]

---

[8] *Ibid.*, 15, 18.
[9] *Ibid.*, 15, 19-20.
[10] *Ibid.*, 16, 21.

2. But recourse to fact again rehabilitates the real status of past and future. If they were wholly nonexistent, past and future would be wholly unknowable. But parts of secular and sacred literature predict the future or retail the past. Prophets have foretold things to come and annalists recount past events. If future and past do not exist, then prophecy is a delusion and history myth. Conversely, if, as is undeniably the case, prophecies have proved reliable and various historical reports veracious, then future and past surely do exist. For it is impossible that future and past be at once nonexistent and known.[11] This reaffirmation of the existence of past and future makes sense only when allied with another truth, that past and future exist precisely as present. Just where past and future exist remains at the moment undecipherable, but there is no doubt that wherever they may be, they exist not as past nor as future but as present. A true chronicle narrating past happenings does not resurrect in their own flesh and blood heroes and scoundrels of yesteryear. What each individual draws up from memory is not the personal experiences themselves but verbalized accounts of the images that are, as it were, the footprints stamped on the memory by events that once travelled through the senses. The images an Augustine summons up of boyhood are reviewed and relived in present memory. The future pre-exists its eventuation in current projects. Rational determination of human action involves a predetermination; we deliberately describe beforehand the lines of the action that, when it does occur, will be no longer future but present.[12] Similarly, we confidently forecast future events in nature not because they unintelligibly already exist, but because we recognize their predetermination in their causes or signs. Present observation of the natural run of things carries with it a foreconception of the future contingencies which the present process signifies or to which it is causally preordained. The break of day, e.g., heralds the rising of the sun. Neither the dawn seen nor the sunrise imagined constitutes an actual sunrise, but their co-presence mediates the foreknowledge of the sunrise to come. Like things of the past, then, those of the future cannot be known in themselves; but unlike things of the past, they are known and thus are in things that now are and are known.[13]

[11] *Ibid.*, 17, 22.
[12] *Ibid.*, 18, 23.
[13] *Ibid.*, 18, 24.

3. Exactly how the prophets infused with divine light infallibly forecast the future remains inscrutable; for what lacks existence seems incommunicable.[14] In spite of this vexing opacity, the fact just established stands out: present retrospect reviews what has ensued and present prospect previews what will ensue. It is, therefore, technically incorrect to speak of past, present and future times, as if past and future enjoy existence in absolute independence of the present. There are undoubtedly three times, but all three are undoubtedly in some sense present times. Since past and future do not exist on their own, it is scientifically precise to name the three times "the present of the past, the present of the present, and the present of the future." The time we know, i.e., the time we measure, is always present time: time as present, time as re-present, time as pre-present. Particular acts of the soul underlie these aspects of the triple present. Direct observation of change focuses on the present of the present; memory engenders the present of the past; expectation contains the present of the future. We need not arch our eyebrows at technically imprecise references to past, present and future times. Such expressions pass muster as *façons de parler,* popular ways of speaking, provided we realize what we are talking about, provided we do not install part and future in a realm of time apart from the present.[15] Here, it may be noted, Augustine sows the seed of the definition soon to be developed. But before this hint can safely flower and fructify, he will have to deny the dependence of our measurement of time on a particular physical motion.

4. At the close of this first stage of inquiry, Augustine restates the knotty problem of how we measure present time, then once more leaves it unresolved. While it is plain that we cannot measure things past and future and that we do measure passing durations, it is plain also that we cannot measure what lacks duration. The fact and logic of our measuring are at loggerheads; we experience and measure the present passing but we cannot strictly experience and measure the physical present. The time we measure courses from the not yet existent through the extensionless present into the no longer existent. We have seen that we cannot measure the nonexistent whence and whither of time, and now, it seems, the physical time observed must be, because dimensionless, unobserv-

---

[14] *Ibid.,* 19, 25.
[15] *Ibid.,* 20, 26.

able. No one, it is implied, seriously assigns numbers denoting length and depth to a mathematical point; it seems equally hopeless to speak seriously of measuring the lengthless instant that is the physical present. This impasse does not retroactively nullify the earlier inductively won truths, that we measure the observed present and that all three times are in some way present times. Nor, on the other hand, does their perspicuity shed light on the puzzle: how measure a physical present devoid of measurable magnitude?[16]

First Interlude

Augustine finishes the first part without hitting upon the cardinal idea that will break the deadlock between our measurement of time and the nonmeasurable character of physical time. He signalizes a transition in the inquiry by appealing, as he makes a fresh start, to the Father of mercies for light on this dark, "highly intricate" riddle masked in the clearest and commonest of expressions.[17]

Part II

The second part searches for a basis of time in celestial and terrestrial motions. If the time we measure is outside the soul, it must reside in the collective motions of the heavens, or in the motions of a particular heavenly body, or in the motion of any one particular body. Dialectical critique and empirical checks establish that we cannot identify time with a privileged motion of any bodies or body in the heavens or on earth. Time as measure is neither found in nor dependent on any particular motion. Understood here is the positive insight that time is a kind of distension with which we measure bodily motions.

1. A hypothetical recourse to natural data quickly does away with the naïve opinion of a certain savant that time essentially consists of the movements of sun, moon and stars. "Were the lights of heaven to halt while the potter's wheel still turned," we would still retain the times of its faster and slower wheelings. In addition, simply verbalizing this refutation exposes the fatal weakness of the view refuted, for words containing syllables uttered for shorter or

---

[16] *Ibid.*, 21, 27.
[17] *Ibid.*, 22, 28.

longer times exhibit the existence and measurement of times apart from the stars in their courses. To be sure, we use the regular motions of the heavenly bodies to divide time into days, months and years. But on occasion, in the hypothetical absence of these motions, another motion near to hand, like the rotation of the potter's wheel, also would conveniently serve to mark intervals of time. It would be a crude error to call one rotation of the wheel a day or a part of time. It is no less gross a blunder to hold that the wheel's turning involves no time, i.e., to hold that the heavenly motions alone are essentially the whole of time.[18]

2. Next, in exploring the nexus between a day and the aspects of the sun's motion, Augustine is not drifting off on a sidetrack. A day is a specific division of time; and to determine whether the motion of the sun in any sense constitutes a day means to ascertain whether time is identified with the revolutions of the sun. Three avenues open up, each with its respective consequences: a day may signify the sun's movement, the twenty-four-hour period usually occupied by this movement, or both movement and period together. If we take day to mean any one full circuit, then the conceivable motion of the sun going twenty-four times faster than its present velocity would make one hour equal to one day. Secondly, if by day we mean a twenty-four-hour period, then a sun also travelling twenty-four times faster than its usual rate would need twenty-four round trips to make one day. Thirdly, if we accept both these alternatives, i.e., if we maintain that one complete run of the sun within twenty-four hours constitutes a day, no day at all would exist either in the event that the sun came full circle in one hour or in the event that the sun stood still. Thus all three avenues turn out to be dead ends. The first supposition requires that one hour be equal to twenty-four hours. The second entails a like absurdity, that twenty-four days be equal to one day. On the third hypothesis, a day ceases to exist altogether at certain junctures. In fine, if we identify time with solar motion, then we irrationally equate a part with a whole of time; or we lump a plurality of wholes with one whole of time; or we posit a time that unintelligibly stops and goes under the same respect during one and the same period.[19]

The truth of the matter is just the other way around. It is not, as these senseless hypotheses suppose, solar motion that measures

[18] *Ibid.*, 23, 29.
[19] *Ibid.*, 23, 20.

time; rather, it is time that measures solar motion. If the sun's present velocity were doubled, we would employ time in relating the old rate to the new. If we assume that the sun makes one round trip constituting a day, d_1, in twelve hours, the present circuit, d_2, obviously takes twice as long as d_1; in other words, d_1 covers the distance in one-half the time usually taken by d_2. Notice that we are comparing a day occupying a single or twelve-hour circuit with one occupying a double or twenty-four-hour circuit by reference to a common standard independent of both motions. This common measure in virtue of which we gauge the comparative quantities of the sun's motion is of course time.[20]

Again, according to the Bible, the sun not only apparently but really stood still during Josue's battle. This fact corroborates the independence of time from the sun. The battle pursued its course and lasted a certain length of time undisturbed by the motionlessness of the sun. At this point the meaning of time becomes a bit clearer. The evidence examined suggests that the measure is a measuring-stick; time is a sort of distension applied to the duration of battles and other events to determine their varying lengths.[21]

3. Two arguments similar to those just used generalize the two previous conclusions to read: time is not dependent on any particular bodily motion. We have to face the question posed earlier, why not identify time with the motion of every body? So long as the potter's wheel keeps turning, time goes on, for time does not exist without motion and no body is moved save in time. However, concomitance in occurrence does not unfailingly argue identity of nature. Although time coexists with motion and no motion eventuates outside time, time does not essentially consist of the motion of a body. As with the sun, so with any particular body: its motion in time is measured by time. We learned in the preceding paragraph that time is a distension or temporal extension, a kind of ruler that measures motion as a meter-stick measures space. In spatial measurement we determine how long a segment is by fixing one locus as the starting point and another as the

---

[20] *Ibid.* In exploring the relation between time and the sun and, previously, between time and celestial movements, Augustine resorts to dialectical-empirical technique today widely called thought-experiment. The bases of the arguments, dialetical suspensions of heavily motions and variations in solar velocity, could but never do occur. The procedure is empirical inasmuch as the hypothetical experiments conducted in the imagination prove that the alleged dependence of time on solar and other celestial movements is not verifiable in natural events.
[21] *Ibid.*

terminus. So in temporal measurement we determine how long it took a body to traverse a path from its point of departure to its terminal point. Perception of a particular motion does not tell exactly how long this motion took. Only by comparison with another motion do we specify its time as equal to or twice that of the other. Because no motion can exactly measure itself, time, the measure in virtue of which we assign each motion a time-length, has to be distinct from each individual motion. Once more, as with the sun, so with any particular body: its lack of motion in time is measured by time. We reckon an amount of time for its period of rest correlated with its period of motion. Because a motionless body does not become timeless, time cannot be equated with the movement of an individual body.[22]

The main thrust of the arguments in this second part has been a logically negative one—to submit to a dialectical test and to reject candidates from physical motion as unfit to serve as the definition of time. Time is not the movements of the heavenly bodies; time is not the movement of the sun; time is not the movement of any one body. All three sorts of motion are either conventional standards or indissociable correlates of time, but all three fall by the wayside because they fail to yield "the meaning and the nature of time."[23] This dialectical elimination is primarily precursive; it clears the way for a positive induction, the proper definition of time. But it would be careless to overlook the second positive insight, still a sketchy and inadequate glimpse, accorded us in this second part. If the time we perceive tells how long a motion lasts, it is a distension or temporal extension whereby we measure every particular bodily motion. But precisely what kind of distension? The third and concluding part will introduce fresh data to specify the meaning of this distension and to unsnarl the enigmas that mocked us at the beginning and end of the first part.

Second Interlude

The paradox of known time without knowing what it is continues to haunt Augustine. He marks a second transition in his

---

[22] *Ibid.*, 24, 31.
[23] "Ego scire cupio uim naturamque temporis, quo metimur corporum motus. . . ." *Ibid.*, 23, 30.

inquiry by pleading once more for divine light to banish the darkness enveloping the concept.[24]

Part III

Rethinking already pondered points, Augustine shows that we cannot measure time in its physical passage, while he ventures the surmise that time is a distension of the soul. A searching analysis of auditory data then empirically verifies this surmise. Again, silence also testifies that this distension lies within the soul. Fourthly, speechless rehearsal of a speech supports the same insight.

1. After vetoing proposals that hold time essentially one with motion, Augustine fastens his eyes on the only reasonable hypothesis still available. If, as just seen in Part II, we measure physical motion by time, then we measure time also; we cannot determine the length of the motion measured without in some way first determining the length of our measure, in this case time. The resemblance of time to space comes more strongly to the fore: we measure distension or temporal extension in the way we measure magnitude or spatial extension. We measure a rod by counting; so do we measure a poem by counting its verses. So, too, we name a line long or short according to the number of its measurational units, its feet; we assign a length to a foot according to its syllables; and we measure the length of a long syllable by reference to a short syllable. One important qualification restricts the correspondence of time with space. Spoken words, like all extents of time, pass away, whereas written words, like all parts of space, remain fixed. The first difference gives rise to a second disparity. Lack of natural fixity leaves the measuring units of time-lengths open to variation. An ordinarily short syllable cannot always function as a definite measure of a long syllable. On certain occasions we may alter the lengths of long and short syllables by rapidly barking out the long syllable and protractedly drawling the short syllable. This substitution of measured for measure happens also when we modify the customary lengths of a foot, line or whole poem.[25]

Here Augustine catches the first glimmerings of the truth: time, he tentatively suggests, has to be a distension of the soul. The divergence of temporal from spatial traits lends support to the

[24] *Ibid.*, 25, 32.
[25] *Ibid.*, 26, 33.

hypothesis. The physical basis of time, the instant, and particular bodily motion, the concomitant of time, were earlier discarded as unsatisfactory foundations for a definition. Our inquiry only a moment ago disclosed that time-lengths are transitive and indefinite measures. The soul is the only habitat left, it seems, able to afford a place whereon to stand to a time that lacks fixity and measurational invariance in the physical world. But Augustine's hesitancy cautions that his answer wants empirical warranty. He has established that the distension called time is not outside the soul; it would be wondrous, he muses, if time were anywhere save in the soul.[26] But he still has to furnish the hard data to turn a dialectical conjecture into the positive induction that time is a distension of the soul.

The temporal measuring-stick cannot measure a physically nonexistent past and future nor a physically unextended present. But we do apparently measure current short-lived intervals, transient timesegments, in their very physical transit. But does time measured really consist of times passing but not yet past? The data of experience answer no, for we cannot measure what lacks discernible limits. Suppose that someone utters a sound, say a long "a," then continues to utter this same tone without stopping. As settled earlier, to measure a length of time means to mark its outer boundaries, both beginning and end. The sounding of the one unbroken tone has no beginning here and now observable; it had a starting-point, now past. Moreover, we cannot designate the end-point of what has not ended; the fact that the sound is passing rules out its having passed. True, we will ascertain its terminus when the tone stops, but then the tone will be over and gone, no longer a passing present but an unchanging past. Plainly we can measure times because we do, but plainly we do not measure these in their physical existence because we cannot. Times just departed and those still to arrive cannot now exist; an extended sound cannot last through an unextended instant; and passing sounds or times, because deprived of observable limits, defy measurement. The truth is now adawning, with a full sunrise just beneath the horizon.[27]

2. Inductive proofs let the daylight of certitude in on the opinion that times measured are distensions held in psychic existence. The

---

[26] "Inde mihi uisum est nihil est aliud tempus quam distensionem: sed cuius rei, nescio, et mirum, si non ipsius animi." *Ibid.*
[27] *Ibid.*, 27, 34.

first of these seizes the meaning of time latent in the voicing of the eight syllables of the Ambrosian line, *Deus creator omnium*. The practised ear is unmistakably sure that it is comparing the short to the alternately long syllables. However, reason seems to run counter to the report of the senses. The short syllable must be laid against the long to determine the length of the latter, but neither short nor long syllable so lasts that one may be applied to the other. The long syllable is designated long only by ending, only by ceasing to exist and, apparently, ceasing to be measurable. Yet the witness of sensory evidence remains unchallengeable: we do match one against the other. We cannot measure syllables unless they have passed on, but we cannot measure them unless they are somehow kept in existence. A new insight, by now inescapable, makes the "somehow" precise and lets us break out of the impasse: we measure not the physically nonexistent syllables but their images stamped on and retained in memory; not the physical sounds now past but their psychic impresses still present.[28] Augustine clinches this point with an exhaustive disjunction: "Either these very [impresses] are the time-intervals [measured] or I do not measure time-intervals."[29] Either time is a distension of the soul or our sense of time, anchored in natural experience, reduces to an unexplainable illusion.

3. A second induction bolsters this position. Just as we measure the times in which bodies are at rest, so we ascribe attributes of time to periods of silence. "A ten-second pause for station identification" exemplifies this measurement, but what Augustine has mainly in mind as measure is not the exterior visible movement of a clock hand across a dial, but an imagined, an interior auditory interval that is applied to and measures the pause. Although no sound is emitted, the span of silence, we determine, occupies the same interval as a spoken verse or poem. In making the comparison, "we extend our cogitation": we run over in imagination and thought a verse or poem equal in length to the period of silence. Reviewing a distension previously heard, we sound out within the soul the whole sequence of its syllables, then lay this temporal measuring-stick against the interval of silence to mentally compute its length. We legitimately predicate long or short of stretches of silence, we set the length of one pause against another only because we imaginatively put a time or time-length of sound alongside the

---

[28] *Ibid.*, 27, 35.
[29] ". . . aut ipsa sunt tempora, aut non tempora metior." *Ibid.*, 27, 36.

pauses to be measured, only because time is a distension of the soul.[30]

4. Silence, now taken prior to speaking, provides another empirical proof. Not only does the soul retain sounds uttered; not only does a distension of sounds within the soul measure a silent interval without; but also a silent interval of inner preparation measures, by fixing beforehand, the length of the speaking to follow. Before voicing a single syllable, a speaker may rehearse interiorly and silently the utterance yet to come and thus measure its time-length within the soul. According to the second induction, a distension of sound measures a period of silence after it has passed. In this third induction a period of silence spent in interiorly practicing a memorized piece measures a duration of sound before it is spoken. The exteriorized continuum of sound lasts the length of time measured, for it is measured by an interior distension unfolded in silence. Traversing the temporal course charted by the imaginative model within, the speaker gradually passes through the earlier parts of his speech, so that what were first future parts become past; his onward passage changes still later parts, formerly future, into past. Finally, at the end of his discourse, the whole of what was originally projected as future has become wholly past; there is completed another extent of time, another distension, whose measure lies within the soul.[31]

Resolution of the Problem

The definition of time dissolves the original paradox of knowing while not knowing time and empowers Augustine to explain what time is to a doggedly insistent and most exacting questioner—himself. The resolution of his original problem follows necessarily from the answer to the initial perplexity. If time measured is a distension of the soul, it takes only one step to explain how physically nonexistent times exist and coexist. Future, extended present and past owe their continuity and continuance in existence to acts of the soul. Expecting, attending and recalling, the soul confers psychic fixity on the extents of motion to be measured, so that what the soul expects passes through what the soul attends to into what the soul remembers. In each particular distension or

[30] *Ibid.*
[31] *Ibid.*

time-line expectation projects the psychic extent of what is to come; memory stably duplicates events already gone; attention perdures to grasp the passing present. The time-line is centered in attention. Whereas the sensibly unattainable physical instant is everlastingly alternating, attention endures and lays down, as it were, an expanse in the soul, the pivotal strand that binds and bridges past and future: ". . . attention perdures, and through it that which will be present passes on its way to being no longer present."[32]

1. At the same stroke Augustine fells also an earlier corollary difficulty concerning the ascription of attributes to nonexistent times. The attribute long is predicated of future extents of time presently expected and past extents presently remembered. "A long future is a long expectation of the future, . . . a long past . . . a long memory of the past." The acts themselves need not of course be prolonged. Expectation or memory may consume less than a minute, but rummaging through our store of imagined distensions, we can intellectually recapitulate the last one hundred years or prognosticate a whole century ahead. We imaginatively trace a line that epitomizes the unimaginable but thinkable length of one hundred years. This memorially drawn line and the concept it represents merit the predicate long. Again, when we imaginatively depict a line drawn from the present into the future, this projected distension and the conceptualized span it illustrates are said to be long.[33]

---

[32] ". . . perdurat attentio, per quam pergat abesse quod aderit." *Ibid.*, 28, 37. The memory that makes possible the primitive cognition of a given succession of sounds is what recent psychologists name primary or immediate memory. Cf. William James, *The Principles of Psychology* (New York: Henry Holt, 1890), I, pp. 643-48; and Paul Fraisse, *The Psychology of Time*, trans. Jennifer Leith (New York: Harper, 1963), pp. 81-89. In this sense of memory, no distance, no intervening gap, severs the connection between earlier and later events. What has been primarily remembered has been just perceived, and forms with the posterior data an unbroken perceptual whole. This use of immediate memory enables Augustine to escape the crude errors of certain nineteenth-century psychologists who try to reconstruct time from memory proper, in which strictly remembered items are not immediately joined with what is here and now being observed.

[33] *Ibid.* As intimated in the preceding note, St. Augustine imposes the term memory analogously here and elsewhere. The word refers, first of all, we have just noted, to the elementary present retention, or primary memory, of sense-data, a function that realistic psychologists now ascribe to imagination; the word *Deus* is so memorially imaged prior to one's hearing *omnium*. It signifies also a sensory recall of the absent past as such; Augustine re-

2. Furthermore, the soul is triply active during the recitation of a psalm known by heart. At the outset, when expectation embraces the entire psalm, the time-line symbolically stretches futurewards. Once we actually start reciting, the duration is distended in two directions: memory takes in the parts now spoken and expectation includes the verses yet unspoken, while attention focuses on the phrase being spoken. The more the recitation goes on, the longer the memory becomes and the shorter the expectation, until expectation ceases and what was first wholly expected is at last wholly remembered. Thus we experience roughly three sorts of time-line. The distension may be a segment entirely oriented toward the future; it may arise from confluent acts of expectation, attention, and memory; it may issue from memory alone.[34]

The triple psychic activity results in a threefold time-line on a smaller scale in every verse and in every syllable of the psalm. What occurs in the psalm holds true also for a longer prayer of which the psalm itself may be but a small part. Miniaturized or magnified, the time-line is first a distension of expectation alone; then, a linking of future and past across the present of attention; finally, a distension pointed toward the past alone. This threefold schema can be broadened to embrace also the entire life of an individual or the complete history of the human race. We can imagine the life of a child about to exist as stretching forward for the next sixty years. Or each one of us can reflect on his present condition, while surveying his entire past and estimating the years ahead. Again, we can range over in one memorial span the forty-six-odd years of John Fitzgerald Kennedy. On the plane of uni-

---

membered in this way the dated image of Monica's last words. Thirdly, the word may mean intellectual memory, as in the statement, "A hundred years is a long time"; one can conceptually review, but not sensorily recollect in one image, one hundred years. It is worth remarking that imagination-memory or immediate memory is primordial in our cognition of time; all three inductions certifying the psychic distension hinge on a quasi-perceived, imagined succession of sounds. The distensions due to recall-memory and intellectual memory are rooted in this primary imaginative distension bearing on what is presently perceived.

[34] *Ibid.*, 28, 38. These three ways of forming time-lines seem to correspond roughly with the three sorts of inductive data in 27, 35-36. The speaker silently rehearsing his piece beforehand—raw material for the third induction—projects a distension of expectation. The uttering of *Deus creator omnium*, treated in the first induction, exhibits a distension jointly wrought by expectation, attention, and memory. In the second induction an observer estimates the length of a pause by laying against it a verse recalled from memory.

versal history, we can imaginatively plant ourselves at the dawn of man and from there draw a line to the end of history. Or from the vantage point of contemporary man, we can summarily review man's past and dimly peer into the distension of years till the Day of the Lord. Finally, we can picture ourselves at the Last Judgment, encompassing in one sweep the vast distension stretching from the instant of the creation of Adam down to the last stroke of doom.[35]

Though staggering episcopal duties denied Augustine the leisure indispensable for fully professional scientific pursuits, it argues contemporary shortsightedness to believe him insensitive to logical rigor or unschooled in scientific methodology.[36] Indeed we can briefly summarize this first section by seeing his treatise asking and answering the three questions to be faced in scientific inquiry: does a thing exist? what is it? what are its attributes?[37] Throughout

---

[35] *Ibid.*

[36] "As a philosopher he had depended on collections made in second-class textbooks, on Cicero, on translations like the one by Marius Victorinus of Plotinus' *Enneads,* and, ultimately, on himself. Thus a sober scholar like Marrou, despite his tremendous admiration for Augustine, is not afraid to call him, incomparable though he is, a typical rhetor, a philosophical dilettante, by modern standards a very wise but still relatively uneducated person. Fundamentally, what he knew was his own language and his Bible; Varro, Cicero, Ambrose and Cyprian at first hand; the rest, like almost all the people of his day, from collections. The general framework which his great mind burst, but without completely escaping from it, seems to us today, after some fifteen hundred years, to have been remarkably narrow and one-sided in a literary sort of way. But he did indeed burst it." F. van der Meer, *Augustine the Bishop,* trans. Brian Battershaw and G. R. Lamb (New York: Sheed and Ward, 1961), pp. 561-62. This judgment on the cramped cultural conditions of St. Augustine ironically betrays a particular academic narrowness that now and then infects certain contemporary scholars whose sensitive minds have enriched our civilization with works generally marked by impartial and objective insights. Confusing at times their abundant erudition and textual research skills with true scientific understanding and philosophic comprehension, they sometimes tend to assume a superior attitude to earlier thinkers who have been blessed only with genius of the highest order and whose magnificent discoveries have captured Western minds for only well over one thousand years. By the same academically biased "modern standards," we would be bound also to rate Plato a dilettante a notch below Augustine, since being born several hundred years too soon denied him access to books available to Augustine. Moreover, a careful reading of Augustine's analysis of time is alone enough to cast doubt on the charge of dilettantism. Again, it is inconceivable that "a typical rhetor" could burst asunder the intellectual framework of his age, then brilliantly reshape it with ideas whose force and depth have not been exhausted in our own day.

[37] ". . . cum audio tria genera esse quaestionum, an sit, quid sit, quale sit. . . ." *Ibid.,* X, 10, 17. We have received help in understanding this passage

his discussion Augustine considers the existence of time evident to the senses. This removes any need to build up a dialectical defense and mount a counterattack against those who might relegate time to a limbo of illusion or abandon the problem as an insoluble mass of antinomies. He contents himself with reaffirming the existence of something we indubitably measure. A datum part and parcel of science and human life, a datum woven into grammar, prophecy, history, biography and literature, a datum ingrained in every oral expression of thought bearing on natural experience—such a naturally omnipresent object cannot be reasonably banished to a never-never land. Time plainly does exist, but its multi-exidenced existence does not become a dogmatic instrument of iteration for evading issues. Rather, our common experience serves as a touchstone for rationally determining the meaning of time. Against it we sift and check, discard or verify solutions proffered. The definition of time and the existential status of past and future grow out of our contact with a real time; they are finally validated because they square with the real time we really know. The question concerning the what of time is posed in Chapter 14 and fully answered in Chapter 27. The first two inductions, achieving a partial vision of the nature of time, smooth the way to a complete definition. First, measured time always exists as present time in some way. Second, time is a distension independent of bodily motion. Times past and future seem to be present in the soul; a distension apart from physical motion seems to be a psychic distension. These dialectical indicators in the first two parts are empirically proved in the third part, where time is defined as a distension of the soul. Faithful to his methodological program, Augustine raises in Chapters 14 and 15 and resolves in Chapter 28 the problem of the attributes of time. A physically nonexistent past and future and a noninstantaneous present acquire a stable existence through their psychic vicars. Expectation projects, memory reproduces and attention observes processes so as to form a threefold psychic timeline. Furthermore, we predicate long and short not of future and past as such but of expectation and memory. A psychically drawn time-line may symbolize future and past periods of one century or one week. Thus are the three questions of scientific inquiry posed and answered: We do measure time; empirical inquiry demands

---

from the excellent translation of John K. Ryan, *The Confessions of St. Augustine* (New York: Image Books, 1960).

that we define time as a distension of the soul; these distensions of the soul, whether composing a single psalm, an individual lifetime or the unique history of man, are the proper subjects for the attributes of time.

Time as a Distension of the Soul

St. Augustine resolves his problem, but a rapid reheasal of a text struck off by genius calls for commentary and comparisons to make it perspicuous to our more plebeian minds. Perhaps the most direct route to what he means lies in clarifying the conclusion that time is a distension of the soul. First, time said to be of the soul is not a precursor of Kant nor the offspring of a derivative Platonism; on the contrary time is objectively discovered in natural experience. Secondly, time specified as a distension is a continuum begotten from pastward and futureward segments emerging from the focus of attention. Thirdly, the theoretical character of this definition renders nugatory various moralistic nuances that some profess to find in it.

1. An unprejudiced reader carries away one unforgettable impression. At every stage Augustine strives for a transcript scrupulously faithful to sensory data. Far from dictating an answer by fiat from on high, he is evidently checking and squaring his generalizations with the deliverances of natural experience. This belaboring of the obvious is excusable, perhaps obligatory, because of recent overdrawn analogies between Augustinist and Kantian time and because of a persistent misreading of St. Augustine's general philosophy. One scholar alleges that time in Augustine mediates between the intelligible and the sensible world in much the same way as in Kant.[38] Another writer propounds the curious hypothesis that Augustine fashion a theory of perception identical in spirit with that of Kant.[39] Memory functions like the transcendental unity of apperception. Its unifying activity molds time, then in virtue of

[38] Robert Catesby Taliaferro in a note to his translation of *De musica*, The Fathers of the Church Series, Vol. 2 of the writings of St. Augustine (New York: Cima Publ. Co., 1947), p. 378, n. 22.

[39] P. Lachièze-Rey, "Saint Augustin précurseur de Kant dans la théorie de la perception," *Augustinus Magister* (Paris: Études Augustiniennes, 1954), I, pp. 425-28. See also Catherine Rau, "Theories of Time in Ancient Philosophy," *The Philosophical Review*, 62 (1953), p. 525; and Johannes Hirschberger, *The History of Philosophy*, trans. Anthony N. Fuerst. (Milwaukee: Bruce, 1958), I, p. 324.

the time-synthesis gathers together pieces of spatial experience into a whole. So, we are told, the drift of Augustine's doctrine is unmistakably Kantian: the perceiving subject synthesizes time, organizes space, imposes these on the raw manifold.

a. No doubt painstaking scrutiny cannot fail to ferret out some parallels in the two approaches, but to take such resemblances seriously seems no less questionable than trying to capitalize on remote similarities discernible between the stream of consciousness and the flow of electric current. To read Kantian themes into Augustine turns accidental likenesses into essential points of agreement and in addition risks disfiguring his realism, for it is hard to put one's finger on one piece of solid evidence to support Kant's theory. Kantian perception presupposes Hume's naïve and dogmatic description of thingless, causeless sequence, whereas things, centers of activity striving for congruent goods, people the universe measured by Augustinist time. Furthermore, it is well known that Kant's time is simply the absolute time of Newton relocated in human sensibility; unlike that proposed by Augustine, absolute time is empirically unverifiable and internally inconsistent. Thirdly, the Kantian position rests in part on the groundless assertion that one is aware of time without motion. The experiential and introspective way of Augustine assures one, however, that here the cart is pulling the horse about, for it is in fact acquaintance with motion that precedes awareness of time.[40]

Fourthly, space and time are, for Kant, pure forms of sensibility casting what is materially given into empirically real but transcendentally ideal spatial and temporal objects called phenomena. But even the subtle genius of a Kant cannot bar recognition that here he apparently tries to have his cake and eat it too. In truth, what is transcendentally ideal cannot be empirically real. Kant's tortuous disclaimers are not enough to dissociate his idealized phenomenon from being essentially one with the reified percept of Berkeley. The monstrous absolute idealisms in nineteenth-century Germany did not pop out by happenstance from the creative bosom of Kant's transcendental ego.[41] Relying too confidently on corrupted data inherited from rationalistic and empiricistic predecessors, the great devotee of reason neglects to train his

[40] Immanuel Kant, *Critique of Pure Reason*, trans. Norman Kemp Smith (London: Macmillan, 1929), pp. 74-82.
[41] Cf. Morris R. Cohen, *Reason and Nature*, 2nd ed. (Glencoe, Ill.: The Free Press, 1953), pp. 62-66.

critical powers on what the transcendental unity of apperception entails. Dispassionately considered, this unity compels one to embrace the self-stultifying view that the vast spatial and temporal frames of the universe are created by a tiny mind whose proprietor touches only a fraction of the magnitude of nature and survives for only a pitiably brief span. But the cosmological anthropocentrism to which certain modern philosophers are driven is unthinkable in the less academically sophisticated but more robust realism of St. Augustine. In his outlook, space is wholly objective and time fundamentally objective. Spatial magnitudes in various configurations are perceived by the soul as patterns embedded in natural entities. Intervals of time are also impressed on the receiving soul by physical movements. One difference sets time received within apart from the time ingredient in events without; time as measured, time as cognized, enjoys a psychic fixity not found in nature. Therefore, the psychically stable time of Augustine clearly cannot adumbrate the Kantian construction of time.

The soul does not manufacture time, for supplemental work is poles apart from transcendental idealization: memory, doubling within the sequence of sounds without, fuses and holds in stable images what passes and vanishes in nature. The misunderstood text from *De musica,* upon which the case for an affinity with Kant mistakenly rests, makes this very point with shrewd psychological penetration. Just as natural light enables the eye to embrace in one glance a complex of spatially distributed objects, so auditory memory, "the light of temporal extents," enables one to hear as one complex a transient succession of sounds.[42] The light from auditory memory creates or constitutes time no more than the light necessary for seeing creates the quantitative structure of things. The parallel between space and time can mean only that

[42] "In audienda itaque vel brevissima syllaba, nisi memoria adjuvet, ut eo momento temporis quo jam non initium, sed finis syllabae sonat, maneat ille motus in animo, qui factus est cum initium ipsum sonuit, nihil nos audisse possumus dicere. . . . Quod si de una syllaba brevi minus sequitur mens tardior quod invenit ratio, de duabus certe nemo dubitat, quin eas simul nulla anima possit audire. Non enim sonat secunda, nisi prima destiterit: quod autem simul sonare non potest, simul audiri qui potest? Ut igitur nos ad capienda spatia locorum diffusio radiorum juvat, qui e brevibus pupulis in aperta emicant, et adec sunt nostri corporis, ut quanquam in procul positis rebus quas videmus, a nostra anima vegetentur; ut ergo eorum effusione adjuvamur ad capienda spatia locorum, ita memoria, quod quasi lumen est temporalium spatiorum, quantum in suo genere quodammodo extrudi potest, tantum eorumdem spatiorum capit." *De musica,* VI, 8, 21; *PL,* 32, 1174.

both are essentially objective, both essentially independent of eye, ear, and auditory memory. Still, the mode of perceiving space differs from the mode of perceiving time. Because spatial extents are fixed, they can be visualized as they lie before us; but because temporal extents or sounds succeed one another, it requires auditory memory to fix and join the fleeting sounds into one perceptual whole.[43] Hence, like the light of the eye vis-à-vis space, the light of auditory memory is an indispensable condition for perceiving time, far removed from a fantastic transcendental form that manufactures the time we perceive.

b. More dangerous over the long pull than this coarse Kantian misreading is the overview of Augustine's thought propagated chiefly by the eminent historian of medieval philosophy, Etienne Gilson. Arbitrarily arranging various texts and inaccurately rendering certain key words, Gilson neatly chops Augustine to the Platonist frame and makes him over into an essentialist for whom being is an inert structure empty of efficacy.[44] This Platonizing

[43] Recent research solidly confirms St. Augustine's keen psychological discernment and indirectly further undercuts the possibility of a kinship with Kant or mentalizing psychologists. According to P. Fraisse, *op. cit.*, pp. 72-74, in perceiving a sequence of tick-tocks, after we have heard the second sound, "the first is no longer present and only memory, an immediate memory, permits me to know that this 'tick-tock' was preceded by another. . . . It is important to note that the order of succession is *perceived*. It is not the result of an organization imposed on stimuli which are independent of each other, as if we were threading beads. In the organization of perception (spatial or temporal), the activity of our minds does not impose a form on dissimilar elements, for in every field of our knowledge, order has its own laws and cannot be forced. . . . The order is inherent in the stimuli themselves and in the case of rhythm it is practically impossible to reproduce the individual elements in any other order." Other portions of the chapter, "The Psychological Present," pp. 67-98, also tend to corroborate Auugstine's account of the auditory perception of time.

[44] Gilson labels St. Augustine an essentialist in his *The Christian Philosophy of St. Thomas Aquinas* (New York: Random House, 1956), pp. 49-50 and p. 449, nn. 15-19; and in *The Christian Philosophy of Saint Auugstine* (London: Victor Collancz, 1961), pp. 21-24 and p. 285, nn. 45-49. Since these two discussions overlap, all further references will be to the latter work. According to Gilson, St. Augustine conceives God as a pure essence; essence refers to a strictly nonexistential description of being inherited from Plato. God is the supreme being or supreme essence because he is wholly immutable. Two texts are adduced to document the charge of essentialism. The first is from *De Trinitate*, 5, 2, 3; *PL*, 42, 912: "Est tamen sine dubitatione substantia, vel si melius hoc appellatur, essentia, quam graeci óusían vocant. Sicut enim ab eo quod est sapere dicta est scientia; ita ab eo quod est esse dicta est essentia. Et quis est magis, quam ille qui dixit famulo suo Moysi: *ego sum qui sum*; et, *Dices filiis Israel: Qui est, misit me ad vos?* Sed aliae

interpretation would obscure or wipe out the realistic stress in the *Confessions* by judging the text in the light of the psychological

> quae dicuntur essentiae, sive substantiae, capiunt accidentia, quibus in eis fiat vel magna, vel quantacumque mutatio; Deo autem aliquid ejusmodi accidere non potest; et ideo sola est incommutabilis substantia vel essentia; qui Deus est, cui profecto ipsum esse, unde essentia nominata est, maxime ac verissime competit." The second text is from *De civitate Dei,* 12, 2; *PL,* 41, 350: "Cujus erroris impietate tanto quisque carebit expeditius et facilius, quanto perspicacius intelligere potuerit, quod per angelum dixit Deus, quando Moysen mittebat ad filios Israel: *Ego sum qui sum.* Cum enim Deus summa essentia sit, hoc est summe sit, et immutabilis sit; rebus quas ex nihilo creavit, esse dedit, sed non summe esse, sicut ipse est; et aliis dedit esse amplius, aliis minus; atque ita naturas essentiarum gradibus ordinavit." It is not cheap rhetoric to note that, surprisingly, these texts undermine rather than uphold Gilson's position; their meaning runs flatly counter to what Gilson purports to extract from them. Clearly Augustine maintains that an essence is a being; clearly in his conceptual lexicon *essentia* signifies being or substance. Probably misled by the Thomistic signification of *essentia,* Gilson converts the terms of the proposition as if Augustine is saying: a being is an essence, i.e., every entity is devoid of what Thomists call existence or existential act. Unfortunately, this crucial error warps the entire sense of the passages under consideration.
> (i) In *De Trin.* Augustine derives the noun *essentia* from the verb *esse.* Just as "wisdom" takes its name from the verb "to be wise," so "essence" takes its name from the verb "to be." The man who is wise is said to have wisdom; so the man who exists is said to have being. But since wisdom and essence are categorically distinct, a man not only has being or essence, but he is a being or essence. In other words, an essence is something that exists; the term essence, as Augustine explicitly remarks, is interchangeable with substance. As already noted, Gilson turns the sense completely around; his misreading has Augustine oddly saying that being means a de-existentialized essence, as if *esse* or to-be takes its name from an abtsract essence. Moreover, Augustine holds, essences or substances below God support accidents, and because of these accidents, the real beings called essences undergo change. If, following Gilson, we take *essentia* to mean a Platonic essence, Augustine's lucid derivation of the name essence becomes a dark clutch of paradoxes: essences, the text now reads, admit of accidental attributes and thereby change while remaining the same. It is unthinkable that a genius of the highest rank would blindly plunge into such a quagmire of irrationalities. Surely St. Augustine never maintains that essences as such exhibit nonessential traits. Surely he never so stultifies himself as to assert that changeless essences do change in virtue of their changeable accidents. Individual things of a certain grade of being may be born and die; new natural species may arise and others become extinct in the course of a hypothetical evolution; but essences as such cannot change. If essences change, there are no essences, and all rational knowledge reduces to a conventional academic delusion. To saddle St. Augustine with such unbecoming absurdities seriously damages the plausibility of the essentialistic thesis. (ii) In *De civ. Dei,* Augustine holds, "Since God is the Supreme Being, i.e., He exists supremely, and therefore he is immutable; He created beings from nothing, He gave them being, but not supreme being as He Himself is. . . ." Here Gilson switches reason and consequent, making the text now read: since God is immutable, therefore he is the supreme being. True, in certain other texts, Augustine argues

CONCEPT OF TIME IN ST. AUGUSTINE   101

and epistemological contentions, borrowed in small part from Platonism, that are advanced in the earlier *De musica;* thus the scheme of time would descend from the higher numbers within the soul.[45] Unfortunately, the virtuosity of a superbly gifted historian

---

that God is the supreme being because he is immutable (this seems to be implied in *De Trin.* quoted above). These texts see the formal dependence of the supreme *esse* of God on his immutability according to our mode of knowing, whereas the text from *De civ. Dei*, misconstrued by Gilson, sees supreme *esse* and immutability according to the ways they are actually related in the thing known, i.e., according to the nature of God. The reasoning in *De Trin.* runs: since God has no accidents, he cannot change; since he alone is immutable, we know that he exists in the highest and most real sense. As we come to know him, he is first known without accidents; then, without change; then, without trace of imperfection, as the supreme being. From the standpoint of the divine nature, however, God is first of all the supreme being; hence immutable, hence without accidents. Moreover, identification of the *esse* of God with immutability (as in *Sermo* 7, 7; *PL* 38, 66) is not a formidable obstacle, for Augustine assigns to mutability and immutability roughly the same tasks taken care of by potency and pure act in Thomism. The words, "*Esse, nomen est incommutabilitatis*," do not reveal an essentialistic bias; they simply mean that the one supreme being is free of all imperfection, a statement no more essentialistic than the unassailable Thomistic view that *ipsum esse*, the essence of God, is pure act. (iii) The passage from *De civitate Dei* also informs us that in creating, God "gave being to things," and in giving some more, some less being, he "ordered the natures of beings according to the grades of beings." Here an essentialistic translation of *essentia* once more weaves nonsense into the text so that the argument becomes a tissue of barbarous inconsistencies: Because God supremely exists, he makes nonexistential essences; to put things in existence means to create existenceless essences; and variety in creation involves giving some essences more of essence, some less of essence.

It must be mentioned that I owe the Augustinist sense of *essentia* to a lecture delivered at Villanova University in March, 1963, by Dr. Vernon Bourke. He is not responsible, however, for any of the texts cited above or below, for their explanation, or for the explicit criticism of the Gilson thesis of essentialism in St. Augustine. Bourke's lecture has since appeared under the title, *Augustine's View of Reality* (Villanova, Pa.: Villanova University Press, 1964). More recently James F. Anderson, in *St. Augustine on Being* (Martinus Nijhoff: The Hague, 1965), has pursued further reaches of Bourke's illuminating rendering of Augustine's *essentia*. Acknowledging a large debt to the original research of Fr. Roger Hanouille, O.S.A., Anderson uncovers such striking correspondences between Augustine and Aquinas in the meanings of being, creation, participation, and analogy, that in addition to discarding the label of essentialism, he repeatedly portrays Augustine as a kind of existentialist in the Thomist sense. Given a wide scholarly circulation, these studies, one may hope, will soon bury the ahistorical essentialist caricature of Augustine that has indirectly blocked understanding of his realistic-empirical analysis of time.

45 In surveying the role of memory in retaining duration, Gilson comments that the soul "not only passes judgment on sense knowledge, it creates it." *Ibid.*, p. 64. The Augustinist theory of knowledge, we are told also, is notable for its "pronounced *mentalism*." *Ibid.*, p. 281, n. 21. This mentalism takes

of ideas in marshalling sources to fall in with a sweeping preconception is not enough to spare this interpretation from fatal flaws. Its tidiness is achieved only by skipping over text after text in which Augustine unequivocally sets down the main lines of an authentic realism.[46] But its fundamental paralogism consists in exactly reversing the order of learning presumed for valid interpretation. Outside a subjectivistic framework, a philosophy of natural things comes first. The primary conclusions of a general philosophy of the universe are arrived at independently of and prior to the articulation of the special psychological and epistemological conditions of discovery and learning. Those who fit Augustine into an essentialist pigeonhole invert the true order of understanding. They accord primacy to alleged semi-Platonic psychological and epistemological conditions for the awareness of objects and assign a derivative role to the naturally real objects that Augustine strives to define and expain.[47] This vicious disorder actually precipitated the malignancy within Descartes and Kant that has metastasized throughout the body of modern philosophy. In fact, Gilson in-

---

on a Bergsonian accent in Gilson's interpretation of *Conf.*, XI, 28, 38, where memory "appears as the aptitude of an indivisible, vital activity to expand, so to speak, . . . in two directions. . . ." *Ibid.*, p. 195, p. 339, n. 33. A check of the text itself (cf. the third part of the first section above), however, shows that memory expands in only one direction, toward the past; that it is the lived span of the speaking or action, not the vital activity, that is expanded in both directions; that neither vital activities of memory and expectation are aptitudes of the lived span. And whatever may be the "analogies uniting Bergsonism to this psychology of duration," Augustine refuses to predicate a discontinuous attribute of what is continuous. No expanding activity or distension can be called indivisible; what is undivided may expand, but what is indivisible cannot possess parts that spread out into larger non-parts. This significant element of disanalogy alone divorces Augustine's notion of duration from Bergson's. The third and concluding section below will instance several other points of contrast between Augustine and Bergson.

[46] The two preceding notes touched on the large discrepancies between Gilson's essentialistic and psychologistic interpretations and the actual texts of St. Augustine. Notes 47 and 48, to follow, deal with an interioristic misreading that inverts the framework of Augustine's doctrine. These four notes are sufficient, I believe, to raise grave doubts about the soundness and reliability of some of Gilson's main theses on St. Augustine. We hope to prepare a short article that will try to examine in a more systematic and more detailed way some of the major misconceptions widely broadcast about Augustine's teaching on God, the relation between body and soul, the theory of knowledge, and causation.

[47] As evidence for what some observers might deem an extravagantly interioristic rendering of Augustine's outlook, Gilson leans heavily upon a

sinuates the reduction of Augustine's thought to the subjectivistic pattern where he boldly makes him a progenitor of the Cartesian proofs for God.[48] Applied to the problem of time, these critical remarks mean that if the matter in Book XI of the *Confessions* is burdened with the sins of omission and commission in the theories of illumination and the soul, then the incontestably realistic doctrine of time is adulterated or destroyed. But in the right order of things known, the realist terminus of the *Confessions* stands: the time-line is excerpted from experience, then held in a fixed state by triple psychic activity. The detailed psychological factors and

---

famous expression that apparently epitomizes the proper Augustinian method of inquiry, "*ab exterioribus ad interiora, ab inferioribus ad superiora.*" *Enarr. in Ps. 145*, 5; *PL* 37, 1887. "These are Augustine's exact words: 'from the outer to the inner and from the lower to the higher,' but his method lifts us up from what is lower in the inner to the higher." *Ibid.*, pp. 19-20; p. 256, n. 38. But Gilson radically alters the clear import of what Augustine supposedly lays down as his characteristic procedure of inquiry. According to Augustine, we are to begin with the outer, i.e., first explore the structure of the natural universe; then, we go on to look into the make-up of the inner life of man; then, we ascend from inferior natures to the superior, finally attaining some knowledge of the invisible things of God from the things He has made. A glance through its table of contents shows that Gilson's work deviates in spirit and direction from the order that he accredits to Augustine. Gilson begins with the proofs for the existence of God, next deals with the human soul and cognition, and last of all (after a second part concerned with morality) examines natural beings like time, matter and form, and causation. Thus he reverses the order in St. Augustine; he goes from the higher to the lower, then from the inner to the outer. Gilson, in effect, fits Augustine's doctrine into an order of learning similar to what the first modern metaphysic of inner experience proffers. According to Cartesian rationalism, epistemological and psychological problems receive top priority; only after settling these interior issues may we move on to study the general structure of the physical world without.

48 ". . . an Augustinian proof is essentially an act of submission on the part of the mind to the intrinsic necessity of the Divine Essence. We do not prove that God should exist but that He does exist, just as we do not prove that seven plus three should make ten, but that they do make ten. Therefore, the mere presence in man's mind of a datum which obviously transcends man implies the existence of its object. This deep-seated tendency to find in God alone sufficient reason for the idea we have of Him, is the bond which links the metaphysics of St. Bonaventure, Duns Scotus, and Descartes to Augustinian metaphysics." *Ibid.*, p. 23; p. 258, n. 48. In support Gilson cites *Epist. 162*, 2; *PL* 33, 75, part of a letter to Evodius. In an earlier letter Evodius advances a curious argument: if reason discovers that God exists, it follows, he holds, that God's existence hangs on the power of reason. Augustine's reply dissipates the alleged inconvenience. Our reason of itself does not make God be; that God should exist does not flow from the power of human reasoning. We do not preside in judgment over God or mathematical structures; no a priori fiat of a reason inferior to truth dic-

the episteemic texture of judgments on time are logically posterior, analytically secondary concerns. Defects in detailed and specialized matters do not enfeeble prior cognitive acquisitions. A mistake in calculus does not obliterate one's knowledge of the multiplication table. Any conceivable faults in Aristotle's *De anima* do not contaminate his *Physics*. So supposedly questionable features of the theories of the soul or knowledge in *De musica* and other works do not corrupt or taint the straightforwardly realistic doctrine of time in the *Confessions*.

c. A more credible interpretation notes a kinship, that betokens a dependence, of Augustine's definition with respect to a formula of Plotinus. If *distentio* is an approximate Latin rendering of the Greek *diastasis*, "time is a distension of the soul" seems to translate on a related conceptual plan the Plotinian statement that "the distension of the life of the soul occupies time."[49] Emphasis on the soul's spirituality, according to another interpreter, prompted Augustine to elect the Plotinian psychological perspective in preference to the Stoic cosmological outlook.[50] It would be the height of folly to deny that the theory of Plotinus worked some lasting influence on the analysis of Augustine. But it is also foolhardy to swell a limited influence into a relationship suggestive of a fundamental dependence in content and strategy. First of all, the term

---

tates the nature of God or the laws of numbers. Hence, for Augustine, it is more accurate to speak of discovering that God is rather than technically judging that he should be. In short, in repudiating what may be called Evodius' crude anticipation of the ontological argument, Augustine, in effect, dissociates himself from the less naive ontological proofs later worked out by St. Anselm and others. This letter to Evodius and other texts reach conclusions diametrically opposed to the affinities Gilson claims to find there. Because we cannot judge God, we cannot see "the intrinsic necessity of the Divine Essence." In Augustine, the mere mental detum, the idea itself of God, does not bring with it "the existence of its object." We do prove, but do not ordain from on high, that seven and three make ten; so not as judges superior to God but as discoverers do we prove that God exists. The human mind confronts a realm of immutable truth immune to human control. Beyond human devising, this world lies beyond human judgment in the Augustinist sense. The "mere presence" of certain human ideas, then, cannot cause their objects to be; the fixed inferiority of human judgment makes it impossible here to pass from the ideal to the real order. Thus the supposed "deep-seated tendency" to leap from the human idea to the existence of God lies not in St. Augustine but in misunderstanding what he means.

[49] A. Solignac, Notes complémentaires for *Les Confessions*, Vol. 14, p. 588. He slightly amends Bréhier's translation of the *Enneads*, III, 7, 11, 41, to point up the affinity of Augustine's distension with the expression of Plotinus.

[50] Ladner, *op. cit.*, pp. 206-207.

diastasis in reference to time did not originate with Plotinus. Its long career can be traced back through the Stoics to the Aristotelian school; it originally signified the analogical participation of time and motion in the spatial continuum.[51] The extensity or quasi-spatial character of time is practically taken for granted in ancient physical philosophy after Aristotle. Secondly, this preliminary remark admittedly leaves untouched the point at issue—the nature of the resemblance between "distension of the soul" and "distension of the life of the soul." Though a leading German existentialist has exploited, with surprising success, contrived philological linkages to justify certain dubious philosophical claims,[52] the philological fallacy of running together verbal agreement with conceptual correspondence ordinarily detours minds into profitless thoughtways. For Augustine, the soul steadily retains a succession of auditory intervals to form one natural psychic time-line. For Plotinus, on the other hand, the soul does not receive impressions from natural events. A succession of immaterial acts generates and upholds the lower world of material forms, and in generating nature, the soul produces time. Because the making of time involves its life, its life alone is truly time.[53] Thus a verbal resemblance disguises an essential disparity of content. One distension consists of the psychically stabilized impressions of a natural interval received in the soul of a being subject to time. The other, its supposed forebear, consists of the operations of an extra-natural soul, a god that produces a time properly outside nature.

Thirdly, the fallacy of verbalism apparently enters again with the inference that the use of the word soul puts Plotinus' theory in a psychological framework. The Plotinian argument is strictly metaphysical. Not the course of natural motion but matterless patterns from on high prescribe the meaning of time. Plotinus does not distill his definition from natural experience but constructs it in an a priori manner to accord with the necessities in his architectonic emanationism, in which mind, soul and nature descend from and ascend to the ineffable One. Indeed, Plotinus explicitly

---

[51] *Ibid.*, pp. 205-206.

[52] Rudolf Allers, "The Meaning of Heidegger," *The New Scholasticism*, 36 (1962), pp. 445-74.

[53] Plotinus, *The Enneads*, trans. by Stephen MacKenna; revised by B. S. Page (London: Faber and Faber, 1956), III, 7, 11. For an excellent exposition of Plotinus' view, see Gordon H. Clark, "The Theory of Time in Plotinus," *The Philosophical Review*, 53 (1944), pp. 337-58.

offers his view as a modified reconstruction of the metaphysical definition of Plato.[54] Plotinus' account is of course plagued by all the ills which even the metaphysicism of a magnificent mind is heir to. Whereas in Augustine the distension of the soul is a psychic rendering and counterpart of natural intervals, the metaphysical definition of time in Plotinus splits the soul off from nature. Consequently, a certain metaphysical aloofness from natural fact entangles him in insuperable paradoxes: nature is within a time that is outside nature; time is within, or is, the life of a soul that is outside time.[55]

Fourthly, the second part of Augustine's treatise unquestionably mirrors a portion of Plotinus' critique of previous theories. Against the view that time is identical with motion, he argues, after Plotinus, that motion is in time and that while motion is punctuated by periods of rest, time goes on unbrokenly. The hypothesis concerning a full circuit of the sun in twelve hours is a novel adaptation of the Plotinian argument, derived from Aristotle, that one-half the revolution of the universe also involves time.[56] However, the determinative sequel to these partially similar dialectical approaches simply aggravates the opposition between Plotinus and Augustine. It is instructive to mark the differences of subject matter and technique between Plotinus' problematic and his definition. His dialectical introduction deals with time as a physical entity, but once he has run over the preliminary polemic, he suddenly switches to the supraphysical level to deduce a definition of time that springs from an unalterable metaphysical precommitment. His dialectical preamble does not prepare the way for his solution; the physical prelude is divorced from the metaphysical resolution. Lacking organic connection with what follows, Plotinus' dialectical preface could have perhaps been tacked on as a postscript or dispensed with altogether. Again Plotinus uses a double standard of science. In his critique he appeals to physical induction to censure various flaws;[57] yet in reaching his own definition, he abandons physical tests and relies solely on a metaphysical deduc-

---

[54] *Ibid.*
[55] *Ibid.*, 13, 30-47.
[56] *Conf.*, XI, 23, 30. Compare this with Plotinus, *op. cit.*, III, 7, 8; and with Aristotle, *Physics*, trans. by R. P. Hardie and R. K. Gaye, IV, 10, 218b1-4, in Richard McKeon (ed.), *The Basic Works of Aristotle* (New York: Random House, 1941).
[57] Plotinus, *op. cit.*, III, 8, 8-10.

tion from the nature of the soul. In contrast, Augustine's dialectical reflections mesh smoothly with the final determination that follows. As already seen, the predominantly negative course of the second part does issue in one positive insight, that time is a distensive measure of motion, an insight fully specified in the third and definitive part. Again, no violent shift in method mars Augustine's discussion. He inductively certifies in three empirical arguments what the extrusion of other physical alternatives has tentatively indicated: time is a distension of a natural soul measuring motion in the natural universe.

d. The elimination of these Kantian and semi-Platonic analogies does not allay a doubt that may be lingering in some minds: in what sense, some may ask, are we to deem this distension and its nonpresent components objective? In the sense that neither past nor future exist in themselves, neither is objective in one iota. But in the sense that both are cognitively present, signified in images that either renew or forecast their occurrence, both are given a share of objectivity. Memory-images presently noted faithfully point backward to what once actually was. These cognitive impresses are footprints stamped on the paths of the mind, witnessing to the career of the past. Moreover, were the past not objectively recorded in and reviewed through memory, the *Confessions* would have to be relegated to the fiction shelf, with the consequence that for an Augustine unable to truly relive his odyssey the problem of time could not arise. In one respect, the future proves more nettlesome than the past. Because it can leave behind no relics, foresight is more precarious than hindsight. Nevertheless, the future also receives a secondary and derivative objectivity from present cognition. Anticipation mirrors the orientation of events in nature, as, e.g., in seeing the break of day, we foresee the rising of the sun. Too, the prefiguring of the future in the present event betokens a predetermination. The constellation of factors making up the dawn is a causal complex ordered to what will be observed as a sunrise.[58] Thus past and future are objective insofar as foregone and forthcoming are linked significantly and causally to events presently cognized. Thus its past and future components do not sink the distension of the soul into the pit of the nonobjective.

2. But there is more: what the mentally sustained times compose is a distension. Here we note briefly that the word seems qualified

---

[58] *Conf.*, XI, 18, 23-24.

for its job; that in denoting a measure, its meaning bears a resemblance to physical extension; and that its notion involves a totality.

a. The word itself causes little trouble. Its oddness, we may suggest, is not wholly unintentioned; a peculiar term is selected to designate a peculiar, not to say unique, phenomenon. It is not a bizarre piece of preciosity; rather for this highly cultivated rhetorician sensitive to nuances, it may be *le mot juste*, the right word to mark off clearly a psychic extent from its physical counterpart. One need not be a Latinist to detect how felicitously its proper signification grows out of its etymological sense. *Distentio* is literally a tending away from. A distension of the soul is fashioned when the mind tends away from its present attention in two directions or, literally, in two "tendencies," backward to the memorial impress, forward to the presentiment of what is to come. There is an express allusion to this careful coupling of the literal and proper senses toward the close of the short treatise. Before beginning a psalm known by heart, we are told, expectation ranges over the whole psalm. The recitation once begun, memory then is extended *(tenditur)* over what has already been said: ". . . as a result, the lived span of this activity of mine is distended *(distenditur)*."[59] The attention-concerned present sends out its extensions along two paths; two psychic extents tend away from or branch out from an extended present to make up a distension of the soul. If past and future be taken as extensions of the one line, distension conveys a closely related notion, that of a full stretch or relatively complete expanse. This meaning immediately implies that time is a totality resulting from the joint psychic activity that underlies the extents of time. Even when according to some, the discussion shifts from the theoretical to the moral domain, *distentio* keeps its sense of psychic expanse; its continuity is not scattered in a moral dispersion or disarray.[60] For those who believe that the Augustinist intellect always telescopes the first and second operations of the mind, it is not idle to append the remark that

[59] ". . . atque distenditur uita huius actionis meae . . ." *Ibid.*, 28, 38. On this passage see the fine comment of A. Solignac, *op. cit.*, p. 589.

[60] According to John F. Callahan, *Four Views of Time in Ancient Philosophy* (Cambridge, Mass.: Harvard University Press, 1948), pp. 184-85, distension in *Conf.*, XI, 29, 39 means a moral distraction or disarray experienced by the soul tossed about in the welter of this life. For a refutation of this opinion, see part 3a below in the present section, to which nn. 70-72 below pertain.

the word distension does signify the formal terminus of a definition; here at least the Augustinist intellect does not straightway judge but defines what the sensory data report.

Physical length is the primary reference of distinction, but this fact alone does not make the word a metaphor.[61] To call it metaphorical clashes with Augustine's resolve to track down "the meaning and nature of time."[62] Recourse to figures would be tacit admission that the mind has not yet captured its prey. Distension is essentially no more metaphorical than stock terms like deliberation and discourse, both of which first referred to weighing and running. Long use has worn away the threads of their physical origins, and today their signification of mental operations alone evokes no associates with hucksters and milers. One main difference between distension and these common counters is an historically incidental one. Distension in Augustine's day had not been used so constantly as to harden into a fixed, exclusive reference. What was lacking was the familiarity to breed oblivion of its sensory source. But a summoning up of images affiliated with physical extent does not deprive extension of essential reference to psychic activity. Augustine, it seems, had in mind what logic calls analogical naming, but his avowed desire to grasp the nature of time is satisfied in the use of distension: it properly signifies the pattern or state of soul exhibited in or identified with the time we measure.[63]

Our analytic summary of the text made clear the foundation for the transfer of meaning from the physical to the psychic realm. Since measure includes extension or continuity, time as measure has to be an extension in some respect. In repeatedly asserting an initial resemblance between the spaces of time and strictly spatial continua,

---

[61] Callahan calls distension a metaphor in *ibid.*, p. 176.

[62] *Conf.*, XI, 23, 30. See n. 23 above.

[63] So far as I know, Augustine never set forth a full-blown theory of analogical naming. But considerable rhetorical experience and hard philosophic thinking surely schooled him in the differences between vulgar and technical usages (cf. *Conf.*, XI, 20, 26) and attuned him to the multiple related senses that branch out from an original signification. He chooses the term distension because it is best suited (cf. n. 59 above) to convey the meaning of the timeline as measure and measured. The first use of distension is physical, but within the context of time, its foremost use is psychical. In short, the term distension is not metaphorical but properly analogical; and its original physical reference does not prevent its being a scientific instrument for laying hold of the nature of time, any more than the original use of quantity to mean magnitude bars us from speaking scientifically of a spiritual quantity of power manifested by the soul (*De quantitate animae*, 32, 69; *PL* 32, 1073).

Augustine's thought is, almost inevitably, carried to assessing time as an extension of the spirit, a distension of the soul. Unlike change, the physical background of time, physical space is a permanent continuum, its parts being coexistent, statically juxtaposed and fused to form one whole line. But to no stretch of change, where time physically resides, can we assign the attributes proper to a measure, fixity, integrity, and uniformity. Thus the time-continuum must be located in the soul, for the soul is capable, so to speak, of standing with head and shoulders above the flux. Its quasi-independence assures the past and future of a psychic existence apart from but representative or indicative of ever-fleeting physical factors. The fact that the acts of memory, attention and anticipation spring from a common source gives this psychic measure its integrity or union of parts and also a feature of uniformity.

b. From another standpoint, if time is a measure it must be a totality. It is in virtue of time that we estimate times; it is a virtue of the whole line that we determine the short and long of the time-segments. It would be of course inept to characterize this distensive whole as a psychic now. Not even the Pickwickian sense can suffer designating a time composed of times by what properly names the discontinuous. Still, according to one commentator, ". . . the now which is the boundary of time is the present attention of the soul, for time itself exists only in the activity of the soul."[64] Present attention, it is held, is a psychic now; like the Aristotelian now in the physical domain, it divides and continues future and past. But unlike the physical now, it is a psychologically indivisible; it is "a vital activity . . . without quantity."[65] This correspondence of the psychic with the physical present, though initially appealing, appears to be exaggerated and unwarrantable. One key passage that this interpretation evidently leans on for support substantiates the opposite view.[66] True, if every feature of time involves extent, then the spaceless and dimensionless physical present disappears from time —and its departure virtually banishes time itself. The physical present cannot be a substretch of time. Its punctiform nature, however, makes it elusive and endlessly varying and bars its founding the measurement of time. A psychic now that doubles the physical instant does not slough off unsuitable traits by entering the psycho-

[64] Callahan, *op. cit.*, 179.
[65] *Ibid.*, p. 180.
[66] *Conf.*, XI, 28, 37. See n. 32 above.

logical order; if pointlike, it is equally unreliable. According to Augustine, the difference between the two presents—one is unextended, the other extended—furnishes one reason why we can intelligibly measure time.[67] The act of attention supplies the abidingness that limited human perception cannot grasp in the never-abiding physical now. The present of attention functions as a nucleus of constancy; it is a span over which march future events incessantly becoming past. In perduring, the psychic present serves to bound future and past, not, however, as midpoint but as a midpart dividing the other two parts. Again, the act of attention is of course an indivisible, nonquantitative vital activity. It is no less true that all cognitive activities in the soul, including expectation and memory, are likewise indivisible. It is, then, fallacious to go from the indivisibility of attention to the exclusive indivisibility of what is attended to. Otherwise, if expectation and memory are indivisible activities, what they signify must be also indivisible, and time measured would paradoxically reduce to a nondistension of the soul. But expectation and memory, for Augustine, bear not on the discontinuous but on the distensive. Now, like expectation and memory, attention is an indivisible activity; therefore, like the future and past extents signified by memory and expectation, the present signified by attention must be not discontinuous but distensive. In brief, attention, like expectation and memory, is a nonquantitative act of the soul that points to a distension or continuous quantity. The omission of this distinction between act and object traps one in express absurdity. ". . . the continuity possessed by time for St. Augustine," we are told, "must, strictly speaking, be without quantity, although the duration of any motion which is measured by time is thus represented as quantitative."[68] If time is strictly without quantity, it is misleading to call it a distension and to speak of its continuity. If time is a measure without quantity, it cannot measure durations or represent them as quantitative. Thus the commingling of attention and the present attended to turns a clear definition into a meaningless conjunction of conflicting terms.

It is no mistake, consequently, to put the present on the same footing with future and past. If the present is not an extent, the structure of time can unaccountably comprise only future and past. Or if one insists on inserting the present as an unextended factor

[67] *Ibid.*; also, 27, 34 and 36.
[68] Callahan, *op. cit.*, p. 180.

in the psychic distension, the present resides therein only by simultaneously dwelling in some weird sanctuary apart from distensive time. But the present is a part within time, so much so that it is from the present that future and past come to be within time. As a component, it is the central determinant or constitutive ingredient in the making of the triadic continuum. To deem the present a part does not entail fusing future and past. In the absence of a partless present in nature, it is true, the parts of future and past would overlap in some fantastic midland. The physical instant is the indivisible divisor that distinguishes but continues measured motion, taken in nature. But it is not necessary—it is inconceivable—that we observe, expect or remember concretely, a precise instant of time. An enduring attention suffices to set apart roughly but adequately the remembered from the anticipated. Only the instant can distinguish temporal parts in nature. But since the psychic counterpart of the instant is not its duplicate, only a noninstantaneous present can distinguish temporal parts psychically measured. An earlier semantical bit watched Augustine spelling out the etymological connections of his key word: distension is formed by two tending away from's generated by acts of anticipation and memory. These diverse stretches are possible only because they arise from a present that is itself extensive. From the present springs the whole distension, because we attend to a present object or event that is extended; that is, the fact underlying the present and primordial in time attends to an ongoing interval unthinkable without extension.

A crude illustration, doing duty as a concrete summary, may make some of this clearer.

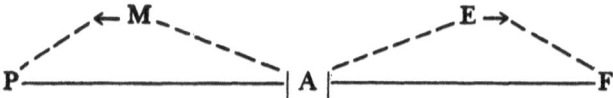

Let M, E, and A stand for the respective acts of memory, expectation and attention, and A P, to the left, and A F, to the right, represent past and future respectively, and A the present maintained through attention. Small arrows next to M and E indicate that acts of memory and expectation mentally reinstate the past and foresee the future event. This simple diagram sums up symbolically the drift of a passage analyzed earlier: ". . . atque distenditur vita hujus actionis meae ... (as a result, the lived span of this action of mine is distended)."[69] The current grasp of, or attention to, what is occurring spreads out in two directions, retrospectively by retentive acts of memory, prospectively by provisional acts of expectation. The upshot is a time-line, a bilateral distension of past and future line-segments from the centrally distended present. This dual psychic prolongation originates in a noninstantaneous present; the opposite arms of the distension are bounded and joined by the distended present rooted in and one with attention. So is formed the measure called time, so is impressed the distension of the soul.

3. A commendable but misguided zeal for detecting moralistic strains in St. Augustine's concept has stimulated certain commentators to offer interpretations that link his definition with certain religious and existentialist themes. In one view, the definition is pregnant with salvific values. According to another opinion, the negatively oriented distension is overcome by a positive *intentio*. From another angle to the same observer, distension looks like a human time of the Heideggerian sort.

a. According to Gerhart Ladner, psychological time in St. Augustine is hooked up with the notion of religious reform. The instability and insecurity associated with time are mastered when the soul recognizes that "time is part of its own life"; the true concept of time carries with it the conquest of time. Rightly ordered, a full awareness of time unlocks doors opening out on eternity.[70] Unhappily, the main text cited as proof furnishes no substantial backing for this position. Stripped of its literary power, this passage contrasts the temporal frame of human life with the vertical aspiration toward eternity through grace. His life is a distension, a time-pinioned natural existence, Augustine says, but through divine mercy he can extend toward a supratemporal goal by dint of a supernatural intention.[71] Nothing in this passage joins Augustine's theoretical definition with the idea of reform. The distension called time makes its abode indifferently in unbeliever and Christian, in sinner and saint. An atheist, fully conscious of the role of the soul in measuring time, would not necessarily feel bound to commit himself to a religious conversion. On the other hand, moralists who know nothing of time as distension have pondered the grandeur

---

[69] *Conf.*, XI, 28, 38.
[70] Ladner, *op. cit.*, pp. 209-12.
[71] *Conf.*, XI, 29, 39.

and misery of man and have cried out, before and after Augustine, for human dedication to imperishable values beyond the seductive, gossamer goods of time. At the root of this moralistic interpretation lies a confusion between psychological time and ethical or human time. Augustine's definition expresses the nature of the time we measure: an inner time-line reproduces the outer flow of events. As a natural structure accessible to every man, this psychic distension embodies no more per se moral implication than the truth that man is equipped with five external senses. What is naturally common to all men cannot necessarily imply a special spiritual reform for only some men. Granted that change is a raging torrent sweeping all things away, granted that man whirled about by vicissitudes yearns for redemption,[72] it simply does not follow that distension, time as such, properly makes man a subject of reform. Thus the connection between time and reform is not essential and intimate, but at most incidental and remote.

b. According to another interpreter, distension and intention are negative and positive poles synthesized in the complete definition. In apprehending time, the mind is at one and the same moment temporalizing and temporalized. It temporalizes, "effects and surmounts" time in virtue of intention or attention; it is temporalized by distension. This dual rhythm weds two aspects of time: time is "a distended intention and an intentionalized distention."[73] The time we measure may contain polar opposites, but a patient search through the text uncovers not one firm piece of evidence to justify the inference of a distension-intention polarity. One hunts in vain here for an intelligible sense in which distension is negative. If time is a distension, it cannot be negative. For a measure is not negative; a triadic continuum is not a past-present-future vacuum; a psychic time-line is hardly the source or paradigm of physical or human nonbeing. It is puzzling also how intention positively "surmounts and corrects" the negativity of distension.[74] For if we grant that intentional activity constitutes the time-line, the resulting distension can be scarcely less positive and dynamic. In other words, a polarity of distension and intention entails the contradiction that the positive engenders its contrary. The absurdity evaporates of course when we dissolve the contrived antithesis between so-called

---

[72] *Enarr. in Ps. 38*, cited by Ladner, *op. cit.*, p. 209, n. 26.
[73] Solignac, *loc. cit.*, p. 590.
[74] *Ibid.*

positive and negative aspects so as to see objectively what Augustine saw, that time is positively a distension of the soul. Apart from the violence done to the text by a quasi-Hegelian technique, no cognitive grip on time warrants the claim that the human mind "effects and surmounts" time.[75] The tree of theoretical knowledge does not of itself bear practical and technical fruits. Surely, no one really believes that in defining the time he measures, he somehow masters and produces time and thereby liberates himself from the unalterable frame of time.

c. According to a corollary opinion of the same interpreter, Augustine has anticipated the human time of Heidegger. To reduce time to bodily movement, it is held, signals the loss of presence and the human present and, in addition, shrinks man's knowledge to an inauthentic curiosity condemned to seeing time without rather than livingly observing it from within the self. The inner awareness of time empowers man to temporalize, i.e., to "effect and thus surmount" time.[76] Two powerful minds can hardly work the same field without sharing some common harvest of aperçus and conclusions, but it is extremely doubtful that an accommodated reading in the Heideggerian sense leads one anywhere but astray in the understanding of St. Augustine's text. First of all, the two lines of attack radically differ. Heidegger's quest for the structure and function of authentic human existence involves, despite the heavy battery of ontological terms, a novel endeavor to build a moral philosophy alive to concrete needs. In this view, man must humanize time, i.e., must properly integrate within his own being a temporal scheme for which an individual's death marks the real limit.[77] Augustine,

---

[75] *Ibid.*

[76] *Ibid.* Other interpreters have worked out somewhat similar readings of other parts of the text to accommodate Augustine's theory to the humanized time now the vogue among certain continental literary philosophers. Cf. Rudolph Berlinger, "Le temps et l'homme chez saint Augustin," *L'Année théologique augustinienne* 13 (1953), Fasc. iii-iv, pp. 260-79; and Erich Lampey, *Das Zeitproblem nach den Bekenntnissen Augustins* (Regensburg: Verlag Habbel, 1960), especially pp. 57-65.

[77] Martin Heidegger, *Being and Time*, trans. John Macquarrie and Edward Robinson (New York: Harper, 1962), pp. 281-311, 477-80. Heidegger makes only one explicit attempt to link Augustine's doctrine with his own. Along with an elliptical passage from Aristotle, he cites Augustine's dialectical conjecture, ". . . it would be wondrous were [time] not [a distension] of the soul itself" (*Conf.*, XI, 26, 33), to suggest that the objective perspective of time, in which world-time is considered primary, does include a connection with soul and spirit, "even if this is still a far cry from a philosophical inquiry oriented explicitly and primarily toward the 'subject' "; *ibid.*, pp. 479-80.

on the other hand, examines the past-present-future scheme from a strictly theoretical viewpoint. To be sure, in other passages Augustine alerts us to time humanly considered, to the important truth that the human use of time is big with supratemporal valuational consequences.[78] But his dialectic and strict definition of time exert no direct, per se impact on shaping one's moral personality.

Again, Heidegger seems to propound the romantic thesis that the man who temporalizes, the authentic man correctly apprehending himself as a time-bound being oriented toward death, molds his own authenticity and, in effect, creates his own system of values. Like American pragmatism, this naive moralism oddly omits—or arbitrarily assumes—the primary moral question, the meaning of the good. It illicitly presupposes that only a good-willed man—a John F. Kennedy rather than a Joseph Stalin—will capitalize on its elaborate practical techniques. However, Augustine never locates the source of human values in time as such; according to his definition, both Peter and Judas fashioned their diverse moral natures according to the same distensive nature of time.[79] Finally, different stands on world time forbid all but the most superficial resemblance between the two. Those attracted to Heidegger should not turn a blind eye to the fact that in defiance of the Western tradition, Heidegger explicitly embraces the paradoxical view that time is primarily man-made, because world time stems from human time.[80] This bold claim affronts man's sense of being a fragile vessel of clay and his awe in the face of a cosmos no man has made. It seems sophistical to make world-time, which clearly antedates and keeps rolling on after billions upon billions of individual human existences, essentially dependent for its being on your or my narrow individual imagination and practical intellect. Augustine's conflict with

---

Evidently Heidegger classifies Augustine's theory as an objectivized account, no more than a distant prefigurement of the subjective time that issues in authentic being.

[78] "Denique ubi venit plenitudo temporis, venit et ille qui nos liberaret a tempore." *In Johannis evang. tr. 31*, 5, cited in Ladner, *op. cit.*, p. 212, n. 39. Also, cf. n. 72 above.

[79] *Conf.*, XI, 28, 38.

[80] ". . . astronomical and calendrical *time-reckoning* . . . does not occur by accident, but has its existential-ontological necessity in the basic state of Dasein as care. Because it is essential to Dasein that it exists fallingly as something thrown, it interprets its time concernfully by way of time-reckoning. *In this*, the 'real' *making-public* of time gets temporalized, so that we must say that *Dasein's throwness is the reason why 'there is' time publicly.*" Heidegger, *op. cit.*, p. 464.

Heidegger on this point follows from his views that time is con-created;[81] that it exists in nature coextensively with matter in motion;[82] and that, as measured, time is not made but received and held fast on the sensory and intellectual levels in man.[83]

Comparison with Bergson and Aristotle

Comparisons with the theoretical accounts of Henri Bergson and Aristotle promise to throw more light on the import of St. Augustine's definition. Bergson's celebrated polemic at the turn of the century against the mechanistic immobilizing of time stirred thinkers to take a fresh look at physical time. The distinction between lived time and measured time, which he so eloquently dwells on, has become for many common philosophical currency, so officially adopted in certain quarters that its denial would seem temerarious. Augustine's "lived span" seems to be a relative of the lived time or duration of Bergson. Expositions akin in mode of analysis and inductive examples, it seems, lend credence to the reflection that essentially similar doctrines on time unite two minds over a gulf of fifteen centuries. It will come as a surprise to some that Augustine's definition bears a closer resemblance to that of Aristotle. Indeed, Augustine and Aristotle substantially agree on certain essential points, whereas in spite of verbal likenesses, Bergson's conception of time radically diverges from that of St. Augustine.

1. The distinction between measured and lived time dominates and pervades the whole of Bergson's treatment.[84] In measuring time, a task characteristic of modern physics, we tend to arrest the flow of time by depicting it as a series of dots or an immobile curve. Such a representation, a conceptual device useful for controlling nature, has helped work the marvelous practical results that physical science has lavished on the modern world. However, it is a grotesque error, Bergson holds, to leap to the conclusion that this physicistic construct truly corresponds to the concrete process we experience. Spatialized or clock time is simply a mental contrivance invented to handle practically the undivided flow which is something alto-

---

[81] *Conf.*, XI, 13, 16 and 30, 40; also, XIII, 33, 48.
[82] *Ibid.*, XII, 11, 14.
[83] *Ibid.*, XI, 27, 35-36.
[84] Henri Bergson, *Time and Free Will*, trans. F. L. Pogson (London: Allen and Unwin, 1910), pp. 98-99.

gether outside the order of space.[85] Real or lived time is not the frozen residue of what has passed but time in its very passing, the unbreakable surge of pure duration.[86] Hence, present, past and future arise from arbitrary cuts in processes; not hard-and-fast physical lines but subjective preferences carve them out of experience.[87] Moreover, the present is, in a real sense, perpetual; the preservation of the so-called past in the present is nothing else than the indivisibility of change verifiable "for the past of any change whatsoever."[88] Attention controls the shifting borders between present and past. An individual may restrict the present to the sentence now being spoken, may enlarge it to include an entire lecture, may further stretch it to gather up great portions of the past, and, in moments of personal crisis, may elongate it to envelop the beginning and near-end of one's life. "The present occupies exactly as much space as this effort" of attention.[89] Too, the unified awareness of a canticle or melody whose successive phrases the mind enjoys as parts of one harmonious theme reflects the indivisible continuity of time-experience in *le moi profond*.[90]

2. Only a critic in blinders could miss the marked correspondences here that pique and startle the mind. As sponsors of Augustinist interiorism and others have noted,[91] Augustine's lived span and Bergson's lived time seem to have sprung from the same stock; they look like blood-brothers born and reared in different environments. A kindred mode of attack, similar language, and similar illustrations apparently corroborate the close relationship in content. In both analyses we track down and seize the meaning of time within the mind; time is made whole and endures as a unified scheme of past relived and future prelived in the cognitively lived present. It is attention, too, that demarcates the boundaries of the present. Again, the perception of auditory intervals, sung or spoken, best exemplifies for both the meaning of time; the psychically undivided grasp of the fluent parts of a psalm or song constitutes a particular temporal whole.

[85] *Ibid.*
[86] Henri Bergson, *Creative Evolution*, trans. Arthur Mitchell (New York: The Modern Library, 1944), pp. 5-6, 369-71.
[87] Henri Bergson, *The Creative Mind*, trans. Mabelle L. Andison (New York: Philosophical Library, 1946), p. 179.
[88] *Ibid.*, p. 183.
[89] *Ibid.*, p. 179.
[90] Bergson, *Time and Free Will*, pp. 126-27.
[91] Gilson, *op. cit.*, p. 339, n. 33. Cf. n. 45 above.

3. The striking quality of these similarities, however, should not divert the eye from less superficial, indeed radical dissimilarities that a closer inspection reveals concerning duration, the nature of the physical world, and the spatial character of time.

a. Bergson's conclusion that the past entitatively lives on in the snowballing present is simply a paradox,[92] which, had it not been subtly and appealingly argued by so powerful a mind, would probably have been accorded a much less serious hearing. The past as past can be revived in present knowledge, but it seems absurd to jumble the memorial survival of the past with what is physically and actually persisting in present events. In iterating over and over the nonactuality of the past, Augustine implicitly brands incongruous any continuance or re-enactment of the past outside present memory. Apart from its impossibility, the thesis of Bergsonian duration invites each one to enjoy an incommunicable experience.[93] The only change whose inner life anyone penetrates and resonates with is that of his own reflectively known self. If intuition in depth is limited to oneself, this metaphysicsal experience in its concretion has to be scientifically ineffable. Jones can sympathetically palpitate to the qualitative duration of Jones, and Smith can metaphysically exult in the intuition of the individual change that is his own glorious being, but neither can communicate to the other in a scientific or nonintuitive manner what each personally intuits. An intuited duration that is the private preserve of an individual subject cannot be objectively discussed or proved; at most those specially favored by the vision can fervently exhort the less privileged to seek this quasi-mystical experience. In contrast, Augustine refuses to fix a gulf between intuition and intellect. Slow, patient labor of intellect, refining the coarse perceptions enshrined in common-sense language, achieves a definition intended to communicate to a questioner what time is.

b. The paralleling of Bergson's with Augustine's account of time meets new obstacles when we juxtapose their views on the natural associates of time. The fluxism extolled by Bergson cannot pass the tests of simple observation and logic. A summons to throw off narrow ingrained ways of knowing cannot overthrow the fact

[92] Jacques Maritain, *Bergsonian Philosophy and Thomism*, trans. Mabelle L. Andison (New York: Philosophical Library, 1955), pp. 219-23.
[93] Bergson, *Time and Free Will*, pp. 126-27. Cf. Arthur O. Lovejoy, *The Reason, Understanding, and Time* (Baltimore: The Johns Hopkins Press, 1961), pp. 68-73.

that no one can truly know a flow wholly purified of quantitative differentiation and succession. Tones of a melody come one after another; they are clearly distinct and successive. Otherwise, the plurality would be folded up into one solitary note, and, if plurality goes, the melody goes with it. If quantitative differentiation is artificially superimposed on an undifferentiated flux, then the pure flow must be absolutely homogeneous, i.e., change has to be an everlastingly unchanging slab of duration. For Augustine, on the other hand, the first and last syllables of a verse are simultaneously held in compresent memory images, yet remain diversified along the psychic distension, their different positions along the time-line representing the natural occurrence of one syllable before the other. Nor are the limits marking off past from present and future drawn sheerly by subjective interest. When we pronounce the word *Creator*, it is objectively true that the two syllables of *Deus* are immediately past and that the three syllables of *omnium* are immediately future.[94] To be sure, we can employ the same time-line to symbolize longer and shorter intervals, but this change in our mode of representation does not disturb the boundaries in the objective course of time itself. Secondly, Bergson's vicious distinction between intuition and intellect demands a gratuitous pre-established harmony between a speculatively illusory spatial construct of time and the physical order explained by classical differential equations. Outside an irrationally postulated miraculism or an unbroken run of flukes, gross theoretical errors cannot be successfully applied to explain or control natural phenomena. The impregnable conviction that straw is ten times stronger than steel does not ordinarily insure an indestructible bridge. Since Augustine does not deprecate intellect, his general philosophy does not have to grapple with the insuperable problem of supplying reasons why the splendid scientific triumphs of modern physics rest upon a theoretical illusion.

c. It is no exaggeration to remark that Bergson's obsessive horror of quantity causes him to war continually against the habitual modern tendency to spatialize time.[95] The inclusion of quantitative features, he believes, contaminates and denatures time, transmogrifying the pulsating qualitative multiplicity of lived time into its dead, inert rectilinear caricature, measured time. Now, Augustine sharply distinguishes, without compartmentalizing, space and time.

---

[94] *Conf.*, XI, 27, 36; 28, 37.
[95] Bergson, *Creative Evolution*, pp. 360-74.

Temporally measured entities are fluid, while the spatially measured are static; words that pass when spoken are subject to time, while their printed counterparts that do not pass are measured by space.[96] Moreover, since distinction does not denote divorce or connote absolute independence, Augustine situates time, rather sees it situated, against a spatial backdrop. The fact that the word *spatium*, in one case or another, appears thirty-odd times in a few chapters furnishes a significant clue to the spatial residence of time.[97] Too, in its office of measure, time requires the divisible parts proper to quantity. Distension is the definite name selected to specify the sort of measure time is; and distension is simply the temporal analogue of extension. As with spatial extents, we also assign quantitative predicates like long and short to various time-lines. From beginning to end Augustine's treatise repudiates a total segregation of space apart from time. Furthermore, Augustine disproves a strained opposition between lived and measured time. A continually sounded tone bereft of discernible limits cannot be rightly said to be in time or to have time. We live time by knowing time, and we know time only by delimiting its boundaries, i.e., we live time by measuring time.[98] A duration is not qualitatively multiple but quantitatively determined; it is a length of time measured or measurable. It is meaningless, then, to separate lived time from measured time. We lay hold of the nature of time not by being elevated to a privileged intuition of pure duration but by analytically examining our actual measuring of time. Each of the three inductions proving that time is a distension of the living soul expressly speaks of our measuring time. At the risk of oversimplifying, we may recommend one sure heuristic rule for unraveling the meaning of certain vexing passages in St. Augustine's treatise; let us imagine ourselves measuring time somewhat as we measure the length of a room.[99] Just as we apply a meter-stick to determine fixed dimensions, so, Augustine argues, we apply time as a measure to determine the dimensions of motion; so we lay our quasi-spatial temporal stick against syllables, feet, verses, psalms, and human lives to discover their time-lengths. The distension of the soul is nothing but a temporal linear magnitude, a length of a syllable or a verse received into the soul and retained

[96] *Conf.*, XI, 26, 33.
[97] *Ibid.*, 14-28, 17-38. *Spatium* occurs thirteen times in Chapter 26 and five times in Chapter 27.
[98] *Ibid.*, 27, 34.
[99] *Ibid.*, 26, 33; 27, 34.

as a minimal uniform measure of other temporal extents. Thus Augustine's analysis stands as a coherent refutation of Bergson's case against the linkage of time with space. Without turning time into space, Augustine's definition does spatialize time, and it does so only because the parts of time we perceive and measure originally pass before us in a milieu of space that does not pass, until, held in one whole by the soul, they form a psychic extension, a distension of the soul.

2. A decent respect for Augustine's fidelity to empirical data spurs one to search for more solid correspondences in a more congenial doctrine, that of Aristotle, seen through the commentary of Aquinas. Whereas superficial similarities in Bergson conceal deep irreconcilable oppositions, something of the reverse obtains in this case. Dissimilarities first catch the eye but give way to a substantial concordance on the existence and totality of time. After running over the elements of Aristotelian time, we shall sketchily note that there are genuine formal differences; that their views on the time-continuum coincide; and that the two dovetail, one being the complementary of the other.

a. Perhaps the readiest path to the heart of Aristotle's doctrine is a summary analysis of his classic definition: Time is the number of motion according to before and after. First, our awareness of time springs from motion. Second, time is an extrinsic concomitant of movement: it is of motion according to before and after. Suppose, Aristotle is saying, a leaf is blown from B to A. That motion is distinguished by its before-place and its after-place, neither term nor point of rest being a part of the motion as such ". . . it is only when we have perceived 'before' and 'after' in motion that we say time has elapsed." That is to say, the mind notes the passing of time only by saying now . . . now, only by freeing the nows or instantaneous points of rest from their concrete matrix. There must be two nows, a before and after; one now does not make a time-lapse. This brings us to the third element in the definition. We count off the terminals or nows, and the result of counting the limits or the before and after is the number of motion. A number is a multitude measured by unity. The terminals of the process compose the plurality; they are unified because each is a now: "The 'now' measures time, insofar as time involves the 'before,' and 'after.'" Three more remarks, and our boiled down version will be complete. i. Time is physical number; it is the number of the physical, of motion. Five is the numerable aspect of the fingers of the hand; so two is the aboriginal number of nows embedded in numbered physical becoming. Thus, incidentally, Aristotle forestalls Bergson's charge that time formally regarded as the number of instants is a mathematical idealization. ii. Time, however, is not real in exactly the same way place is. Time outside the soul is actualized in the ever-alternating now. Like motion, time has only imperfect being in nature. Hence, as perfected, as a line or totality, time is partly a being of reason, for no existential bond without unites the successive nows. Held by the internal senses and intellect, the parts of time are psychically related and combined to form a continuum bound by nows through intentional acts. iii. Intrinsic time resides in the simplest and most uniform motion in nature; this is the extrinsic measure of all other numbered motions in the cosmos.[100]

b. It requires little labor to see contrasts between Aristotle and Augustine. An Aristotle constructing a definition neatly coherent with a fundamental natural philosophy bears little affinity with an Augustine engaged in a kind of spot-science. Weightier still than contextual dissimilarity are differences concerning the physical instant on the proper formality of the definition. For Aristotle the instant is sovereign: it is the principle, source, and measure of time. Without the now no time exists, no time is possible. Moreover, we perceive and conceive time in counting two nows. Because the nows are two, time is number; because they delimit the timeline, time is formally number. For Augustine, on the other hand, the continuous occupies the foreground while the physically discontinuous retires to the sidelines. But Augustine is not purblind on this point. What dictates the difference here is the very formulation of his question: what and where is the natural meter-stick that measures and therefore relates immediate past, present and perceptually proximate future? Posed in this fashion, his question indirectly extrudes a discontinuous now as a candidate for the solution; it implicitly stipulates that only a continuum somehow fixed in the soul can embrace intervals no longer or not yet in existence. Augustinist time is formally a continuum primarily resident in the soul, whereas Aristotelian time is formally number,

---

[100] *Physics*, 217b29-224a16. Cf. also St. Thomas' commentary, *In octo libros physicorum Aristotelis expositio*, Ed. Maggiolo (Rome: Marietti, 1954), IV, 15-23.

whose now is primarily located outside the soul. All the other differences branch out from this central one. Addressing himself to a less narrowly framed question, Aristotle inserts time within cosmic causality. Therefore, to use Augustine's example, should the primary cosmic motion cease, the potter's wheel, for Aristotle, would not continue to turn. Should the machine of the world collapse, time, for Aristotle, would stop. Here and elsewhere Augustine reaches a concrete answer that, while at odds with Aristotle's, is nonetheless realistic. The reason for his divergence from Aristotle's answer lies not in any lack of realism but in his restricted setting of the problem. A different mode of attack is the reason why Augustine can faultlessly assess the data, yet achieve a definition different from that attained in the flawless realism of Aristotle.

c. When we adopt the Augustinist standpoint and take time primarily as continuum and *totum,* dissimilarity gives way to a fundamental similarity. For Augustine the primordial schema of past-present-future is extracted from and imitates the parts-outside-parts character of natural motions plotted in celestial wheelings or heard in snatches of divine song. Over and over the theme of temporal magnitude recurs: time is made up of times; it is a tract distinguishable into temporal spaces, and so on. But this psychic distance exists in a way physical motion cannot, for the course of creaturely contingents is irremediably transient. Syllables unroll and suns spin, the old state vanishing with the onset of the new. In Augustine's words, it would be baffling only if time the measure and totality were anything but a distension of the soul. In this perspective, it is not butchering the sense to translate his expression into Aristotelian terms. A distension of the soul is roughly equivalent to a psychic measure according to before and after (broadly taken). Time, for Aristotle, is primarily a being of nature, but the totality of time depends on the soul. The time-line unable to exist all at once is imagined and thought all at once. Its never coexistent parts are psychically combined as if they were coexistent. Therefore, though Augustine parts company with Aristotle over the physical primacy of the now, they join hands on the totality of time: the ordering activity of the soul holds and fuses the fluent divisions of the time-line.[101]

[101] Compare *Conf.,* XI, 27, 36-28, 37, with *Physics,* IV, 223a16-18, along with *In IV phys.,* 23, nn. 1-5. Aristotle deals with the perception of time in *De memoria et reminiscentia,* 450a10-14, trans. J. I. Beare. St. Thomas comments

d. Augustine's answer is true; real time contains no less than he says. But it is not wholly true; real time contains more than he says. His version is correct in what it puts in, imperfect in what it leaves out. Add to psychic distension its relation to the physical now; integrate it with cosmic causation; and the outcome is the full-fledged time of Aristotle. The two views are not only partially correspondent but also complementary. The end of a concrete psychological analysis invites further physical analysis; or, in scholastic language, what is actual for the one is potential for the other.

Augustine never positively excludes the instant but argues that the instant cannot account for certain data. Concrete inspection assigns first place to psychic time without reading cosmic time out of existence. For Aristotle, too, the soul is in a real sense the seat of total time. For both thinkers, then, time extends in one dimension. But distension, we may say, is taken twice over. Where Augustine stresses the whole of the distension, Aristotle marks the discretes that bound the line. What is primary for Aristotle is peripheral for Augustine; what is ultimate for Augustine is provisional for Aristotle. Augustine accents the connectiveness of all three modes in a common presentiality, and it is inevitable, once Augustine sets his sights on analyzing time primarily as measure, that its parts cohere in the soul. This psychic continuum, we may say, Aristotle regards as a potential, a select datum for further physical analysis. The primacy accorded the now underscores the discontinuity and divisiveness formally extrinsic to the continuum. The mind counts off the beats of the melody and, as it were, lifts the discrete rest-points or nows apart from the process. The psychic is a matrix or condition of fact within which the mind lays bare the terminal and divisive nows. Thus does the perspective of Aristotle recast the definition of Augustine.[102] The instant is restored to its primacy; the building-blocks of time are the nows, the terminals of change.

Which of these views is the superior? While permissible to moot

---

on this in his *In Aristotelis librum de memoria et reminiscentia commentarium*, ed. Spiazzi (Rome: Marietti, 1949), nn. 318-322.

[102] Not even the genius of the Stagirite could actually recast a definition that will first see the light seven centuries later! But it is surely permissible to situate comparative views in a kind of extra-temporal context. We have used the present tense throughout the comparisons of Augustine with Bergson and Aristotle, to portray these thinkers engaged, as it were, in a timeless or always-contemporary dialogue on time.

such an issue, it is also somewhat dangerous. The kernel of truth in the adage, "Comparisons are odious," recalls that comparisons often irritate rather than stimulate, and are often suspect of a narrow party spirit if pronounced from a nonabsolute point of view. Value-judgments can claim a reasonable accuracy only when absolute, i.e., only when all pertinent circumstances help balance the evaluation. It is pertinent that Augustine lacked the time for wholly undistracted scientific contemplation and that his milieu barred complete familiarity with each and every philosophic technique. It is most pertinent, moreover, that Augustine set as his horizon a concrete quasi-physical, psychological analysis within whose limited scope he settles the problem of time. It should be clear, then, that an absolute comparison seems practically impossible, since it comes down to comparing incomparables, i.e., placing in opposition views, each of which is sufficient within its own domain, that are not irreconcilable but complementary. It betrays a strange insensitivity to historical differences to explain away or bewail Augustine's failure to achieve a physical analysis that his framework of inquiry makes unthinkable. On the other hand, relatively speaking, from the angle of scientific content, even a devoted Augustinist will not hesitate to admit that the Aristotelian account represents a scientific advance. Time fits nicely into a coherent natural philosophy and knits together the psychic and physical aspects only loosely related in Augustine. These two reasons are rooted in a third factor: without dwarfing or eclipsing the psychic side of time, the Aristotelian takes the Augustinist definition to a deeper level of analysis.

To sum up. A three-stage inquiry reveals, first of all, that real time is always present time. Past and future are present-past and present-future, i.e., always known as present. A second stage yields the interconnected truths: time is not celestial motion, nor can it be equated with any bodily motion. The first two conclusions dialectically insinuate the third. A measure that contains a present enduring beyond the flitting physical instant, one that is also independent of all bodily motion, seems to be present in its totality within. Three inductions verify this surmise: time is a distension of the soul. The time-line of future, present and past is woven by the acts of expectation, attention and memory. A second section developed three interpretative remarks. First, time is neither similar to a Kantian form nor akin to a semi-Platonic product of purely immaterial regions. Second, time is, rather, a psychic magnitude that duplicates in a fixed way the successive continuum in nature. The last section compares Augustine with Bergson and Aristotle. Although distension and Bergsonian duration tally in some superficial respects, Augustine's account collides on essential points with Bergson's theory of time. Dissimilarity between the psychic measure of Augustine and the number of motion in Aristotle is muted by their complementarity. The two thinkers see time from perspectives that eventually dovetail. The psychic continuum is a dimension potential for further analysis; psychic distension is a matrix that yields time as the number of motion.

DUNS SCOTUS AND ST. ANSELM'S ONTOLOGICAL ARGUMENT

by

BERNARDINO M. BONANSEA, O.F.M.

It is customary to dismiss St. Anselm's ontological argument for the existence of God on the ground that it involves a transition from the ideal to the real order, from a concept in our mind to the existence of the being so conceived. This transition, it is asserted, is never permissible, not even in the case of the greatest conceivable being, as the Anselmian argument seems to imply. The fact that many great thinkers, such as Aquinas and Kant, have felt a need to refute the argument is a further proof, so it is claimed, that the *ratio Anselmi* has little more than a historical value. St. Anselm would have fallen victim to an illusion, and no dialectic effort could ever rescue his argument from the attacks of its critics, even though no serious thinker would subscribe today to Schopenhauer's view that the *ratio Anselmi* is merely a charming joke.

Yet, despite the many attacks and "refutations," the argument has a peculiar power of survival and continues to exert its fascination upon philosophers of all casts of mind. There is a growing realization, even among those whose philosophical background is very different from St. Anselm's way of thinking, that the argument is not as simple as it first appears to be and that much of the criticism directed against it is due to a superficial knowledge of its context and the general framework of St. Anselm's thought. As a contemporary author points out, "If Anselm is to be refuted, it should be for what he said, taken in something like the context which he provided, and not for something someone else said he said, or a fragment of what he said, torn wholly out of context."[1] The Anselmian argument, which has been called "one of the boldest creations of man's reason and a credit not only to its inventor, but to human reason itself,"[2] is not to be treated lightly, nor are some of its later formulations, such as that of John Duns Scotus. His attempts to strengthen the *ratio Anselmi* by establishing it on more solid grounds are well worth considering.

It is the purpose of this study to present the essential features of the ontological argument as stated in the *Proslogion* by its author and show Duns Scotus' contribution to a proper understanding and evaluation of it. This is a task which has often been neglected, if not completely ignored, even by some of the best qualified historians of philosophy.

I

The chief objective that St. Anselm proposed to himself in his *Proslogion* was to present an argument that would in itself alone suffice to prove the existence of God. "I began to ask myself whether there might be found a single argument which would require no other for its proof than itself alone, and alone would suffice to demonstrate that God truly exists."[3] This thought had caused him so much trouble that, in the words of Eadmer, his first biographer and disciple, he had for a while lost all desire for food, drink and sleep. Worst of all, the thought had been interfering even with his prayers and devotions.[4] But suddenly one night during matins, his biographer continues, the light was shown to him and his heart was filled with an overwhelming joy. He had finally discovered the argument he was looking for. He wrote it down immediately on tablets, and later, after some

[1] Charles Hartshorne, Introduction to the Second Edition of *Saint Anselm: Basic Writings*, trans. by S. W. Deane (La Salle, Ill.: Open Court Publishing Company, 1962), p. 2.
[2] Richard Taylor, Introduction to *The Ontological Argument from St. Anselm to Contemporary Philosophers*, ed. by Alvin Plantinga (Garden City, N. Y.: Doubleday & Company, 1965), p. xviii.
[3] Preface to the *Proslogion, Patrologia Latina*, Vol. 158, col. 223. (Henceforth to be referred to as PL followed by volume number and column). For the English translation of the *Proslogion* cf. *Saint Anselm: Basic Writings*, above mentioned.
[4] Cf. *The Life of St. Anselm, Archbishop of Canterbury, by Eadmer*, ed. by R. W. Southern (London-New York: Thomas Nelson and Sons, 1962), pp. 29-30.

mysterious happenings which resulted in the loss of the first draft and the partial destruction of the second, Anselm was able to restore the argument to its original form and put it down on parchment for the benefit of future generations.[5] The origin and early history of the argument may well point to its later destiny.

The argument takes the form of a discourse on the existence of God, as the subtitle of the treatise indicates. It was written primarily for the "brethren" of his monastery, and therefore for believers who, like Anselm himself, try to understand the meaning and import of their belief. "I have written the following treatise, in the person of one who strives to lift his mind to the contemplation of God, and seeks to understand what he believes."[6] Anselm does not conceal the limited scope of his argument; on the contrary, he states explicitly that faith is required for its understanding. "I do not seek to understand that I may believe, but I believe in order to understand. For this also I believe, that unless I believed, I should not understand."[7]

This last statement is enlightening. It shows that Anselm clearly distinguishes between the intrinsic value of the argument and conviction of such value. Since this latter depends on many factors extraneous to the argument itself, it is quite possible that the same logical reasoning may appeal to one person and not to another. More precisely, the argument is not meant to convince an atheist or an agnostic—no theistic argument will ever do so—but only those who have been enlightened by faith and are favorably disposed towards it. It is true that in his reply to Gaunilo's objections Anselm writes: "It was a fool against whom the argument of my *Proslogion* was directed."[8] However, this does not mean that the argument was written *for* a fool but rather *against* a fool, i.e., one whom we would today call an unbeliever. Anselm's aim was to show to his fellow monks the truth of the biblical statement that only a fool will say there is no God.[9] To have set the exact limits of the

---

[5] *Ibid.*, pp 30-31.
[6] Preface to the *Proslogion*, PL 158, 224.
[7] *Prosl.*, chap. I; PL 158, 227.
[8] Introduction to *Liber apologeticus*, PL 158, 247.
[9] *Prosl.*, chap. II; PL 158, 227. M. J. Charlesworth does not seem to have given sufficient consideration to Anselm's statement, "This I also believe, that unless I believed, I should not understand" (*Prosl.*, chap. I), when he wrote that Anselm could not mean that "the whole *Proslogion* argument . . . would only be persuasive for those who already believe in God." *St. Anselm's Pros-*

argument according to the mind of its author is already a big step towards the understanding of the argument itself.

Addressing himself to God, Anselm says: "We believe that you are a being than which nothing greater can be conceived." This, he goes on to say, even a fool is able to understand, and yet he cannot convince himself that this being exists in reality. Anselm now tries to prove the inconsistency of such a position by arguing that a being than which no greater is conceivable cannot possibly exist in the understanding alone but must also exist in reality. "For, suppose it exists in the understanding alone, then it can be conceived to exist in reality also, which is greater." Hence, if the notion of the greatest conceivable being has any meaning at all, it must include the actual existence of the being so conceived, since existence is a perfection and the greatest conceivable being must possess all perfections.[10]

Further, existence is so essential to the greatest conceivable being that without it the being in question cannot even be conceived. Indeed, how can one conceive of a being whose nature is to exist—since existence is one of its essential perfections—and deny its existence without denying the very content of his concept? One can form the concept of man and still know nothing about his actual existence, because the nature of man is not such as to demand existence. Man, Anselm would say, can exist in our mind as a mere concept without contradiction. But in the case of the greatest conceivable being this is not possible, since existence enters to form the concept itself of that being. It is not the question of mere possible existence, for that is excluded by the very nature of the greatest conceivable being;[11] it is the question of actual, real existence. In other words, a being than which nothing greater can be conceived either exists in reality or is not

---

logion (Oxford: At the Clarendon Press, 1965), p. 57. As Thomas McPherson states, "Anselm does not suppose that his Ontological Argument will convert the sceptic: it is the person who believes in God already who can profit from it." *The Philosophy of Religion* (London-Toronto-New York: Van Nostrand Company, 1965), p. 28.

10 *Prosl.*, chap. II; PL 158, 227-28.

11 This point has been strongly emphasized by Charles Hartshorne: "A common method of seeking to trivialize Anselm's claim is to hold that 'necessary existing' (to use a non-Anselmian phrase) means only 'existing necessarily if it exists at all'. 'Divinity exists' is perhaps necessary if true; however, it may be false." *Anselm's Discovery. A Re-Examination of the Ontological Argument for God's Existence* (La Salle, Ill.: Open Court Publishing Company, 1965), p. 6.

that kind of being; it is a contradiction, and therefore a nonbeing.[12] Hence Anselm's conclusion: "There is, then, so truly a being than which nothing greater can be conceived, that it cannot even be conceived not to exist; and this being you are, O Lord, our God."[13]

This is the general structure of the Anselmian proof. To understand it better, some observations are in order. The argument rests on the idea that existence is a perfection, a teaching that is not peculiar to Anselm but has been widely accepted by philosophers before and after him. Existence is also called a pure perfection, since its concept, whether simple or complex, direct or indirect, implies no imperfection whatsoever. When Kant challenged the argument on the ground that existence is not a predicate, since it does not add anything to the concept of a thing, he failed to see—perhaps one should say that his antimetaphysical approach to philosophy prevented him from seeing—the difference between the beings of our experience, whose nature is indifferent to existence and nonexistence, and the greatest conceivable being, whose nature is to exist. In this latter case, and in this case alone, existence is so much of a perfection that without it the being in question cannot even be conceived. This does not mean that we can form a simple and direct concept of such a being, for we have no immediate knowledge of it; nor does it mean that we can attain to the knowledge of the existence of such a being merely through a concept. Nowhere in Anselm's writing can we find support for this view. It is only by reasoning and inferential judgment that we can attain to such a knowledge, and reason will tell us that not only in the case of the greatest conceivable being but in the case of any being whatsoever existence is a perfection.[14]

---

[12] Alexandre Koyré pertinently observes: ". . . *l'ens quo maius cogitari nequit* ne peut pas être envisagé comme n'existant pas, et cela non seulement parce que c'est une impossibilité *quoad rem*, mais aussi et surtout parce que c'est une pensée impossible à penser, une pensée qui contredit les lois immanentes de la pensée elle-même." *L'idée de Dieu dans la philosophie de St. Anselme* (Paris: Éditions Ernest Leroux, 1923), p. 202.

[13] *Prosl.*, chap. III; PL 158, 228.

[14] In his short but penetrating analysis of the Anselmian argument, P. Franciscus Spedalieri, S.J., makes the following remark: "Igitur, potius ad artem studiumque attendas, quibus sanctus Doctor ad opusculum istud conscribendum processit, atque animadvertas illum plane dicere omnique vi asserere se non ex mero conceptu, verum ex iudicio argumentum deducere: et hoc quidem non . . . quia mens nostra Deum quodammodo intueatur, sed quia omne, quod intelligitur vel iudicatur, cum sit in intellectu quia et sicut

As such, it *can* be predicated of any being that is not in a purely potential state, and *must* be predicated of a being that cannot be conceived otherwise than as existing.

Another presupposition of the Anselmian argument is that we already have a notion of God as a supremely perfect being. This is evident from the very nature of the *Proslogion* as an attempt to understand the God known by faith, and from Anselm's explicit statement that anyone can arrive at such a notion from the degrees of goodness of the beings of our experience. "It is therefore evident to any rational mind, that by ascending from the lesser good to the greater, we can form a considerable notion of a being than which a greater is inconceivable."[15] Anselm does not imply in any way that the proposition "God exists" is self-evident, as Aquinas seems to suggest. On the contrary, the knowledge of God's existence is the result of a complex process of reasoning which extends to at least two chapters of the *Proslogion* and the whole *Liber apologeticus,* and which even a trained philosopher has difficulty in following. The argument is definitely not for the ordinary man but for the intellectual elite, such as Anselm's fellow monks for whom it was originally written.

Again—and this is the most crucial point of the entire issue— the Anselmian proof does not involve an illegitimate transition from the ideal to the real order, as though Anselm would attempt to prove the existence of God from a purely abstract concept or the notion of a supreme conceivable being in the logical order.[16] Rather, Anselm wants to show that the notion of the supreme conceivable being, which according to the Augustinian ideological realism has an objective intelligibility of its own and is not therefore a pure abstraction, implies of its very nature the existence of the being in question. It is the ontological value of the idea that forces the mind to accept the existence of that being as its

---

intelligitur, independenter a mentis cogitatione, quadantenus saltem, ordinem ad esse dicit." *Selectae et breviores philosophiae ac theologiae controversiae* (Rome: Officium Libri Catholici, 1950), pp. 22-23.

[15] *Lib. apol.,* chap. VIII; PL 158, 258.

[16] Charlesworth writes in this connection: "The objection that St. Anselm argues directly from the conceptual or logical order to the real order, that is, from the idea of God to the actual existence of God, is simply a vulgar travesty of his argument." *St. Anselm's Proslogion,* p. 63. The same observation had already been made by Spedalieri, *op. cit.,* p. 38: "Et longe a recta eius mentis interpretatione aberrant quotquot Anselmum de transitu ab ordine logico ad ordinem ontologicum, nostris etiam diebus, arguere volunt."

necessary implication.¹⁷ Briefly, the *ratio Anselmi* is an attempt to show that it is impossible for the human mind to fully understand the meaning and ideological content of the notion of a being than which nothing greater is conceivable and simultaneously deny the existence of that being. This goes to prove, Anselm would insist, the truth of the biblical statement that only a fool can say, there is no God. "For God is that than which a greater cannot be conceived. And he who thoroughly understands this, assuredly understands that this being so truly exists, that not even in concept can it be non-existent. Therefore, he who understands that God so exists, cannot conceive that he does not exist."¹⁸ Anselm is so convinced of the value of his discovery, that he concludes the argument by thanking God for his enlightenment and does not hesitate to say that, as a result of it, it would now be impossible for him to deny his existence. "What I formerly believed by your bounty I now so understand by your illumination, that if I were unwilling to believe that you exist, I should not be able not to understand this to be true."¹⁹

The limits of this study do not allow me to go into the debate between Gaunilo and Anselm. Important as the debate may be for a thorough grasp of the argument's intricacies, it is not absolutely necessary for a general understanding of the subject. I will turn instead to Duns Scotus and examine his view of the Anselmian proof.

II

Duns Scotus, whose attempts to work out a most complete and thorough proof for the existence of God have perhaps never

---

¹⁷ The objective nature of the concept that serves as a starting point for the Anselmian argument is clearly stated by Cardinal José Saenz Aguirre, an eminent scholar and recognized authority on Anselmian studies. He writes: "Itaque Anselmus ex mente omnium *supponit* conceptum obiectivum, significatum hoc nomine *Deus,* esse id quo nihil melius aut excellentius cogitari potest. Eiusmodi autem conceptus, si recte intelligatur aut penetretur, habet immediatam connexionem cum existentia. Qui enim recte concipit optimum cogitabilium omnium, eo ipso concipit ipsum ut simpliciter existens, et existens necessario." Quoted in Josephus M. Piccirelli, S.J., "De mente S. Anselmi in Proslogio," *De Deo: disputationes metaphysicae* (Paris: Lecoffre, 1885), pp. 521-22. It is wrong, therefore, to interpret the Anselmian argument in the light of Aristotelian-Thomistic philosophy according to which the objective value of our ideas can only be derived from sensible experience through the process of abstraction.

¹⁸ *Prosl.*, chap. IV; PL 229.
¹⁹ *Ibid.*

been matched in the history of human thought, could not remain indifferent to Anselm's argument. In addition to its highly stimulating nature, the argument had a special appeal to him because of the spiritual kinship of Anselm and the Franciscan school in which he had been raised. The fact that St. Bonaventure and other Franciscan masters had adopted a different view from Aquinas's and sponsored the Anselmian argument made it all the more necessary for him to examine the issue and, setting aside all school prejudices, see whether the argument could be put to use for his own approach to God.

Scotus discusses the argument in several works. His most complete treatment of it is found in the *Ordinatio,* otherwise known as the *Opus Oxoniense,* and in *De primo principio,* a short tract whose striking similarities to the Anselmian work have led some historians to call it the thirteenth-century *Proslogion.*[20] Since the treatment of *De primo principio* follows along the general lines of that of the *Ordinatio,* from which the greater part of the tract has been taken,[21] the text of the *Ordinatio* will be used in this study. However, references to *De primo principio* will be given whenever they are relevant.

Scotus' first approach to the Anselmian argument takes the form of an objection to the question whether the existence of an infinite being—the aim of his theistic proof—is a self-evident truth. It is logical for him to discuss such a question at the very outset of his demonstration, for if a positive answer is given to it, all demonstrations will be superfluous. One does not have to prove what is obvious. As an alleged indication of the self-evidence of God's existence, he quotes Anselm's statement that a being than

---

[20] Cf. Etienne Gilson, *Jean Duns Scot. Introduction à ses positions fondamentales* (Paris: Vrin, 1952), p. 178: "Cet écrit [*De primo principio*] peut être comparé sans trop d'inexactitude à un *Proslogion* de type anselmien dont l'auteur aurait maîtrisé, outre les resources de la dialectique, celles de la métaphysique de son temps." See also the study of Robert Prentice, O.F.M., "The 'De primo principio' of John Duns Scotus as a Thirteenth-Century Proslogion," *Antonianum,* 39 (1964), 77-109, where the author shows the similarities of Anselm's and Scotus' works as regards their spirit, their purpose, their outline, and their argumentation.

[21] Cf. Charles Balic, "The Life and Works of John Duns Scotus," in *John Duns Scotus, 1265-1965,* ed. by John K. Ryan and Bernardine M. Bonansea (Washington, D. C.: The Catholic University of America Press, 1965), p. 23. While affirming the unquestionable authenticity of *De primo principio,* Father Balic maintains that conceivably Scotus is not the only author of the treatise. *Ibid.*

which nothing greater can be conceived must exist, or else it would not be such a being.[22] Before answering the question, Scotus makes a detailed analysis of what he considers to be a self-evident proposition. Disregarding the distinction between a proposition that is evident in itself (*per se nota*) and one that is evident to us (*nota quoad nos*), which serves as a basis for Aquinas' rejection of the Anselmian proof,[23] he states that a proposition is self-evident if its terms and their relationship are immediately known.[24] Hence if the terms of a proposition are not known as soon as their meaning is understood but a third concept must be introduced to define them, the proposition is not self-evident. Likewise, if the relationship between the subject and the predicate of a proposition is not evident but becomes so only through demonstration, the proposition is not self-evident either. Furthermore, just as there is no distinction between a proposition that is evident in itself and one that is evident to us,[25] so for Scotus there is no distinction between a proposition that is known by itself (*per se nota*) and one that is knowable by itself (*per se noscibilis*), for the evidence of a proposition does not depend on its actual cognition but on the aptitude of its terms to cause self-evident knowledge.[26] More specifically, a proposition is and remains self-evident despite the fact that its terms are not immediately known to us, if the evidence of the proposition can be known by a superior mind, such as the divine intellect and the angelic minds, or even by the blessed in heaven, whose intellect is in direct contact with the divinity.

Having clarified the meaning of a self-evident proposition, Scotus goes on to apply his principles to the question at issue, namely, whether the proposition "God exists" is self-evident. Surprisingly enough, he says "Yes," but he immediately qualifies his

[22] *Ord.* I, dist. 2, pars 1, q. 2; Vatican ed., Vol. II, p. 129.

[23] *Sum. theol.*, I, q. 2, a. 3 c. For a recent study of the subject cf. Anton C. Pegis, "St. Anselm and the Argument of the Proslogion," *Mediaeval Studies*, XXVIII (1966), 228-67.

[24] *Ord.* I, dist. 2, pars 1, q. 2; Vatican ed., Vol. II, p. 131: "Dicitur igitur propositio per se nota, quae per nihil aliud extra terminos proprios, qui sunt aliquid eius, habet veritatem evidentem"; *ibid.*, p. 135: "Est ergo omnis et sola propositio illa per se nota, quae ex conceptis sic conceptis ut sunt eius termini, habet vel nata est habere evidentem veritatem complexionis."

[25] *Ibid.*, p. 136: "Nulla est distinctio de per se nota in se et naturae et nobis, quia quaecumque est in se per se nota, cuicumque intellectui, licet non actu cognita, tamen quantum est ex terminis est evidenter vera et nota si termini concipiantur."

[26] *Ibid.*: "Non est distinguere inter propositionem per se notam et per se noscibilem, quia idem sunt."

answer. Since the terms of the proposition are apt to produce evident truth in the intellect that perceives them, such as the divine intellect and the minds of the blessed in heaven, the proposition must be called self-evident or *per se nota*.[27] Moreover, since there is no distinction between a proposition that is evident in itself and one that is evident to us, it follows that the proposition in question is also known to us as self-evident—or else how could we say it is so in regard to God? However, since in the present state our knowledge of God is only possible through common concepts derived from creatures, we do not have a direct grasp of the terms of the proposition under discussion or any evidence that existence belongs to the divine nature. Hence the proposition "God exists" is not precisely understood by us as self-evident and its truth can and must be demonstrated.[28]

What has been said of the proposition "God exists" is equally true, Scotus argues, of any other statement in which existence is predicated of a concept by which God is known to us, such as "A necessary being exists" or "An infinite being exists." These propositions are not self-evident for three reasons. First, because they can be demonstrated, whereas a self-evident proposition admits of no demonstration; second, because their terms, far from being self-evident, are known to us either by faith or by demonstration; and third, because none of the proper concepts we have of God, such as "infinite being," "necessary being," and the like, are absolutely simple (*simpliciter simplex*) but all are composite. Since they are composite, no proposition about them is self-evident unless it is also evidently known that the components of such concepts go together. If this is true in the quidditative order, it is much more so in the existential order when the being in question

[27] *Ibid.*, pp. 137-38. "Est igitur ista 'Deus est' sive 'haec essentia est' per se nota, quia extrema illa sunt nata facere evidentiam de ista complexione cuilibet apprehendenti perfecte extrema istius complexionis, quia esse nulli perfectius convenit quam huic essentiae." *Ibid.*, p. 138.

[28] *Ibid.*: "Sic igitur intelligendo per nomen Dei aliquid quod nos non perfecte cognoscimus nec concipimus ut hanc essentiam divinam, sic est per se nota 'Deus est'." The apparent ambiguity of Scotus' position is explained by Gilson, *Jean Duns Scot,* p. 123, n. 2, in the following terms: "L'ambiguité apparente de la position de Duns Scot tient à ce que l'on ne distingue pas comme lui les moments du problème. Le fait que la proposition *Deus est* ne nous soit pas, en fait, *per se nota* n'empêche pas qu'elle doive rester pour nous, en droit, la proposition *per se nota* qu'elle est en soi. Autrement dit, une proposition est *per se nota* lorqu'elle est évidente à l'intellect qui en appréhende les termes. C'est le cas de la proposition *Deus est.* Que nous n'en appréhendions pas intuitivement les termes, ne change rien à sa nature."

is not immediately known. Hence, Scotus concludes, the proposition "An infinite being exists" is not self-evident and must be demonstrated.[29]

Turning then to the problem under discussion, Scotus rightly says that Anselm does not assert that "a being than which nothing greater can be conceived exists" is a self-evident proposition. In fact, Anselm's reasoning implies at least two syllogisms. The first is: "A being is greater than a nonbeing; but nothing is greater than the supreme; therefore, the supreme is not nonbeing." The second syllogism is: "What is not a nonbeing is a being; but the supreme is not a nonbeing; therefore, the supreme is a being." That Anselm's proposition is not self-evident is proved by the fact that it is not immediately known to us that the nonexistence of a supreme conceivable being involves a contradiction, or that the components of the concept of a supreme conceivable being do actually go together. The two requirements are necessary for a self-evident proposition.[30]

To say that Anselm's proposition is not self-evident and to say that it is not true are two entirely different things. As a matter of fact, Scotus holds to the truth of the proposition but says that this must be proved. Anselm, it is worth mentioning, never attempts to prove the possibility of a supreme conceivable being in his *Proslogion*. He takes it for granted, or perhaps he holds that if a proof were needed, he has already offered it in his previous work, the *Monologium*, where not only the possibility but the actual existence of a supreme being is demonstrated by a posteriori arguments. If we look then at the *Proslogion* as a mere continuation of the *Monologium*, we have in it an added reason for believing in God based on the analysis of the notion of a supreme conceivable being whose existence is already known to us. However, in such a case the *ratio Anselmi* will lose its specific characteristic and can no longer be called an argument for God's existence, as its author holds it to be. Scotus realizes the weakness of the Anselmian argument and attempts to provide it with a rational foundation that will give it strength and solidity and make it somewhat acceptable.

The *ratio Anselmi*, Scotus says, can be "colored" or reformulated this way. "God is such a being that, if it is possible for it to be

---

[29] *Ord.* I, dist. 2, pars 1, q. 2; Vatican ed., Vol. II, pp. 138-42.
[30] *Ibid.*, pp. 145-46.

conceived without contradiction, no greater being can be conceived without contradiction."[31] The introduction of the principle of contradiction to justify the notion of God on which the argument is based is most important. Indeed, if the *summum cogitabile*—this is Scotus' contracted form of "a being than which nothing greater can be conceived"—were found to be self-contradictory, no argument whatsoever could be built on it; the argument would have failed its preliminary test. But far from being self-contradictory, the *summum cogitable* seems to completely satisfy my intellect which finds in it a certain delight, as though it were confronted with the supreme object of its knowing ability. Moreover, if there were any contradiction in the notion of a *summum cogitabile*—which for Scotus is the same as the infinite being whose existence he purports to prove—my intellect, whose primary and proper object is being, could not fail to notice it, just as my sense of hearing immediately notices discordant sounds.[32] Thus the notion of a *summum cogitabile* is not contradictory, and since whatever implies no contradiction is possible, "a being than which nothing greater can be conceived" is possible.

To have proved the possibility of a supreme conceivable being is already a major and perhaps decisive step in the reformulation of the Anselmian argument. Scotus is able to make such a step because of his theory of being as the proper object of the human intellect and his doctrine of the univocity of the concept of being. No recourse is necessary in his case to the ideological realism in the light of which, as we have shown, the *ratio Anselmi* must be understood.

Once the possibility of a supreme conceivable being has been established, it remains to prove its actual existence. The transition from the essential to the existential order, or, to use Scotus' terminology, from the *esse quiditativum* to the *esse existentiae,* is done by the Subtle Doctor in a way that anticipates Leibniz' reasoning and helps to substantiate the *ratio Anselmi*. Scotus' reasoning is as follows.

The supreme conceivable being cannot be merely in our mind, for

---

[31] *Ibid.,* p. 209. See also *De primo principio,* in John Duns Scotus, *A Treatise on God as First Principle,* trans. and ed. by Allan B. Wolter, O.F.M. (Chicago, Ill.: Franciscan Herald Press, 1966), p. 123. Henceforth the *De primo principio* will be quoted from the Latin text in the above work.

[32] *Ord.* I, dist. 2, pars 1, q. 2; Vatican ed., Vol. II, p. 208; *De primo principio,* pp. 121-23.

then it would be possible, since it can be conceived as existing without contradiction, and at the same time it would not be possible, i.e., it could not exist, since of its very nature it cannot depend on any cause for its existence.[33] Otherwise stated, the supreme conceivable being can only be thought of as self-existing for, on the one hand, it admits of no extrinsic cause for its existence and, on the other hand, it is against its nature not to exist. It is greater, in effect, to exist in reality than to exist merely in the mind.[34] Hence, if our thoughts have any objective value, the very nature of the supreme conceivable being demands its actual existence.

To add further strength to the Anselmian argument, Scotus submits another reason. Whatever exists, he argues, has a greater degree of intelligibility, and therefore a greater degree of perfection, than that which does not exist, since the former can be known intuitively, whereas the latter, not being present or visible, can only be known abstractively. Hence the supreme conceivable being must exist, or else it would lack one of the perfections that go along with supreme intelligibility, namely, the perfection of being apt to be known intuitively.[35] This is in line with Scotus' teaching that intuitive cognition, whereby an object is directly known in its actual existence, is superior to abstractive cognition, which is knowledge either of a nonexisting object or of an object that exists but is not precisely known as existing.[36]

With this, Scotus concludes his "coloration" of the Anselmian argument. Much discussion has been going on among Scotus' interpreters as to whether such a coloration amounts to a conditional approval of the argument—an outright endorsement of it is out of question—or whether it is simply a touching up or reformulation of the argument without ascribing to it any real value as a theistic proof. The two interpretations can perhaps be brought together by saying that the *ratio Anselmi* is integrated, as it were, in Scotus' proof for the existence of an infinite being, not as an

[33] *Ord.* I, dist. 2, pars 1, q. 2; Vatican ed., Vol. II, pp. 209-210; *De primo principio*, p. 123.

[34] *Ord. I*, dist. 2, pars 1, q. 2; Vatican ed., Vol. II, p. 210: "Maius ergo cogitabile est quod est in re quam quod est tantum in intellectu. Non est autem hoc sic intelligendum quod idem si cogitetur, per hoc sit maius cogitabile si exsistat, sed, omni quod est in intellectu tantum, est maius aliquod quod exsistit." See also *De primo principio*, p. 123.

[35] *Ord.* I, dist. 2, pars 1, q. 2; Vatican ed., Vol. II, pp. 210-211; *De primo principio*, pp. 123-25.

[36] *Ord.* I, dist. 1, pars 1, q. 2; Vatican ed., Vol. II, pp. 23-24. See also *ibid.*, dist. 2, pars 2, q. 4; Vatican ed., Vol. II, p. 352.

essential and indispensable element of it—Scotus' proof is self-sufficient and equally valid without it—but as a confirmatory argument to the effect that a supreme conceivable being, or what amounts to the same thing, an infinite being, is not contradictory and hence is at least negatively possible. This seems to be the mind of Scotus himself, who states that, while no a priori demonstration of the existence of an infinite being is possible,[37] some persuasive reasons can be used to support Anselm's reasoning.[38]

Thus Scotus' position shows a balanced judgment that avoids two extremes: the view of those who reject the Anselmian argument altogether because they make little or no effort to understand it in its true perspective, and the view of those who accept it as a theistic proof without any reservation as to its demonstrative value. Scotus' main contribution to the argument consists in providing it with a truly rational basis by showing the noncontradiction, and hence the possibility, of the supreme conceivable being and by pointing out, more effectively than St. Anselm did and long before Descartes and Leibniz were to do in their own way, the real contradiction that would result from accepting such a concept and denying the existence of the being so conceived.

It is the writer's hope that the considerations submitted in this paper may help towards a better understanding of the working of two great minds and lead to a more objective evaluation of their positions on one of the most provocative and controversial issues in the entire history of philosophy.

---

[37] *Ord.* I, dist. 2, pars 1, q. 2; Vatican ed., Vol. II, pp. 206-207: "[Quod] enti non repugnat infinitas . . . non videtur posse a priori ostendi." See also *De primo principio*, p. 121.

[38] *Ord.* I, dist. 2, pars 1, q. 2; Vatican ed., Vol. II, pp. 207-208; *De primo principio*, p. 121. Bettoni holds that although in Scotus' view the *ratio Anselmi* has no cogency of its own as an argument for the existence of God, the Subtle Doctor developed it for the purpose of his own theistic proof and gave it a full demonstrative value. Efrem Bettoni, *Duns Scotus: The Basic Principles of His Philosophy*, trans. and ed. by Bernardine Bonansea (Washington, D. C.: The Catholic University of America Press, 1961), p. 144. Gilson maintains that Scotus' coloration of the Anselmian argument is for the purpose of proving God's infinity rather than his existence. *Jean Duns Scot*, pp. 166-67. This view had already been advanced by Séraphin Belmond, *Dieu: existence et cognoscibilité* (Paris: Beauchesne, 1913), p. 21, n. 1, and Zacharias van de Woestyne, *Cursus philosophicus* (Malines: Typographia S. Francisci, 1925), II, pp. 712-13, n. 2, who base their position on Scotus' statement: "Quomodo autem ratio eius [Anselmi] valeat dicetur in sequenti quaestione, argumento sexto, de infinitate probanda." *Ord.* I, dist. 2, pars 1, q. 2; Vatican ed., Vol. II, p. 146.

9

THE ANACHRONISM OF CERTAIN NEOTHOMISTIC PHYSICAL DOCTRINES

by

MARIUS G. SCHNEIDER, O.F.M.

"The attempts at an explanation of this virtual permanence (of elements in compounds) in general do not contribute to the honor of Scholastic clarity of thought."[1] Thus wrote Virgil Michel two generations ago, characterizing neothomistic interpretations of the traditional hylomorphic conception of material reality. A study of the latest publications of neothomistic thought will convince the reader that the critique and complaint of 1925 are in no way less justified today. Neothomistic views of the constitution of corporeal being conflict not only with one another, but—in spite of their intended faithfulness to Aquinas' philosophy—also with the teaching of St. Thomas itself.

There is, first of all, disagreement between the opinions of those we may call orthodox and progressive neothomists. The orthodox neothomist rejects the insights of modern science as the result of an identification of "the physical with the mental universe," of a "theory, for which quantity is the formal principle of measure," or of the definition of physical reality "exclusively by the framework of instrumental experimentation" to be corrected by a "philosophical experience" which turns out to be a simple pre-philosophical sense experience.[2] He declares the works of St. Thomas as the only legitimate source of Thomism. This in turn is identified with the final truth, and he will thus "naturally combat and refute the born enemies of this doctrine."[3] Among the "born enemies" of the truth

---

[1] Virgil G. Michel, O.S.B., "On the Theory of Matter and Form," *The Ecclesiastical Review*, 73 (1925), p. 252.

[2] L. M. Régis, O.P., *Epistemology*. Trans. by Imelda Choquette Byrne. (New York: The Macmillan Company, 1959), pp. 202 ff.

[3] *Ibid.*, p. 106.

deposited in the writings of Aquinas is anybody who dares to express doubt about the correctness of the basic Aristotelian tenets concerning the constitution of material reality and the psychology of its cognition. The sensible qualities of the scholastic tradition have to be considered as "the specific accidents of material things,"[4] we are informed. Further, the "purely receptive role" of our senses in relation to these physical properties of corporeal substances as conceived in Aristotle's physics must be defended as the necessary condition of "the objectivity of all intellectual knowledge, which, in the final analysis, depends upon the determining realism of our every sensation."[5] No trace of relativity is admissible within a Thomistic understanding of the intentional activity of sensitive life. An explanation of sensation "in terms of the organism's vital reaction to the physical action of things, by virtue of the principle, *quidquid recipitur ad modum recipientis recipitur*," or by way of a "recourse to a *sensus agens* whose function was to produce a sensible species" is maintained to "deprive human knowledge of the only experimental contact possible between it and the physical universe by which it is nourished."[6] Only "by copying . . . more or less faithfully"[7] the physical properties of corporeal beings, or rather by being passively assimilated by and to them, can the senses serve as instruments of this experimental contact allegedly required for all true human knowledge.

According to Thomistic psychology, man's sense endowment is seen to be marvelously adjusted to this necessary service. Not only do our passively operating senses represent their proper object, the physical sensible qualities, in their formal objectivity, but their organic constitution guarantees also an immediate, objective report of all possible material properties of the universe. For the number of our senses "is equal to the possibilities of specific action by the exterior real upon the physiological living being,"[8] and thus "the specific accidents of material things are grasped in their existential individuality by the ensemble of our sensory powers."[9] The physical qualities "constitute the structure of the intentional species itself," and as such represent, together with the sensory copy of the quanti-

---

[4] *Ibid.*, p. 219.
[5] *Ibid.*, p. 216.
[6] *Ibid.*, pp. 215 f.
[7] *Ibid.*, p. 216.
[8] *Ibid.*, p. 208.
[9] *Ibid.*, p. 219.

tative aspects of reality, "the only natural path leading man to a comprehension of the nature of a thing."[10] For the sensible accidents, the qualitative and quantitative aspects of corporeal things, represent "the exterior images of the reality hidden beneath sensible appearances," "as the proper effect of substantial hylomorphism."[11]

The profession of these doctrines, which obviously separate Aquinas' "conception of the physical and our knowledge of it from the whole modern scientific theory,"[12] logically demands also the admission of all the assumptions required for a reasonable account of the assumed formally objective validity of sensation. Not only must we subscribe to the view that the power of physical change is possessed and exercised solely by means of the qualities of the third species, i.e., the sensible qualities, and that consequently "in Thomism the entire field of sensation is given over to the causation of *quality*,"[13] but we must also ascribe to physical reality "a double causal action upon man," a physical and a spiritual immutation.[14] Should anyone suspect that this conception of a spiritual causality exercised by material reality is merely the postulate of a psychology of sensation developed in conformity with the demands of Aristotelian physics, he is assured that the respective teaching is dictated by "St. Thomas' metaphysics of the act, not, as is often believed, the experimental science of his day." For "only act causes, and only form or quality is act, apart from the act of existing that completes it."[15]

Most present-day neothomists reject such an unqualified endorsement of medieval physics. Various professed proponents of Thomistic thought seem to recognize that such mechanistic, unpsychological conceptions of a subject's vital relations to its physical environment, and such ancient notions about the nature of "the specific accidents" of material things are outdated. Both commonsense[16] and the scientific experiences of our electronic, atomic, and space age are not disproved by an arbitrary reference to a Thomistic "metaphysics of the act" ascribing the production of the "spiritual" change of sensation to the exclusive efficiency of physical properties.

[10] *Ibid.*
[11] *Ibid.*
[12] *Ibid.*, p. 206.
[13] *Ibid.*
[14] *Ibid.*, pp. 202 f.
[15] *Ibid.*, p. 206.
[16] Cf. Karl F. Herzfeld, "The Structure of the Atom," *St. John's University Studies*, Philosophical Series 2, pp. 45 f.

So "the whole modern scientific theory," rightly recognized as incompatible with Aquinas' doctrine and therefore scorned by the orthodox Thomist, is at length taken into account. We are presented, for instance, with attempts at "investigating, against the epistemological background provided by Thomism, the reality of . . . elementary particles,"[17] or of "a Thomistic study of the measurement and definition of sensible qualities."[18] This epistemological background assumed to be helpful for such modern investigations seems largely to be identical with Aquinas' "Aristotelian methodology, with its accent on *a posteriori* demonstration" which is rightly considered as "peculiarly well adapted to this task"[19] of determining the mode of existence and the nature of properties of the "unobservable"[20] physical elements.

In a philosophical analysis of related scientific assertions the application of this method is to reveal that the elementary particles, including "such entities as nuclei, atoms, and molecules,"[21] represent extramental realities no less than macroscopical bodies of our everyday experience. As free particles, these elements are found to "exist as subsistent entities"; "as part of a composed body," such an element is determined to be "a real part of such a body, . . . an integral part."[22]

The existence of such actual, elementary parts of physical being finds further confirmation in a neothomistic account of sensory phenomena. A causal analysis of "sensible qualities" as "predicamental accidents" of material substances determines this appropriate "subject or substance,"[23] for instance, in the case of heat, as "aggregates of atomic particles."[24] "The proper subject of sound" is said to be "a medium or entity with parts susceptible to regular vibratory motion," that is, "subjects large enough to include macroscopic domains of molecules that can support such motion. . . . Again, the

[17] William A. Wallace, O.P., "The Reality of Elementary Particles," *Proceedings of the American Catholic Philosophical Association*, Vol. XXXVIII (1964), p. 155. In the following, this paper will be referred to as *Proceedings*.
[18] William A. Wallace, O.P., "The Measurement and Definition of Sensible Qualities," *The New Scholasticism*, Vol. XXXIX (1965), p. 2. Hereafter referred to as *NSCH*.
[19] *Proceedings*, p. 156.
[20] *Ibid.*
[21] *Ibid.*, p. 155.
[22] *Ibid.*, p. 162.
[23] *NSCH*, pp. 14 f.
[24] *Ibid.*, p. 23.

proper subject of color is an entity whose electronic parts are capable of a special type of resonance."[25]

Correspondingly, the "sensible qualities" themselves are discovered to involve the reality of physical elements too. "The precise formal effect which we recognize as sound in a medium is the regular vibratory motion of the medium, at greater or lesser amplitude, with differences of frequency and wavelength dictated by the characteristics of the medium and the driving source," that is, "a regular vibratory movement of relatively large masses of molecules."[26] The formal cause of heat is described as "essentially a random molecular movement," being "either a translational motion of entire molecules or vibratory and rotary motions within molecules themselves on the part of their constituent atoms."[27] Finally, "color seen by the eye in opaque surfaces" is "some particular wavelength distribution" of light rays, selectively scattered or reflected by a surface or volume whose molecules, when subjected to radiation, are in a state of a special vibratory motion or chemical resonance due to a modification of electronic vibration.[28]

Certainly the discoveries of modern science are not considered as abortive or irrelevant for a philosophical understanding of material being in these discussions of the reality of physical properties and elements. However, even the most eloquent endorsement of the scientific view of physical reality of our time by various neothomists does not seem to affect their medieval philosophical conceptions of the corporeal world. According to their opinion, sensible qualities still function as predicamental accidents of material substances; physical elements are merely virtually present in compounds; and the constitution of corporeal being is necessarily hylomorphic.

In spite of the explicit or implicit recognition of the essential difference between physical and mental sensible qualities as it is established in modern physics, physiology, and psychology, sensible qualities are usually defined in neothomistic literature in terms of Aristotelian-Thomistic physics. For instance, the physical phase of sensation, that is, "the object with its material qualities of size, shape, color, odor, temperature," is declared to be the "proper domain of the physicist with his investigation of wavelength and

[25] *Ibid.*
[26] *Ibid.*, p. 18.
[27] *Ibid.*, p. 19.
[28] *Ibid.*, p. 20.

other physical properties."[29] Yet the sensible quality is determined as proper formal object of external sensation or as "that formality in the object which a particular activity reaches directly and by itself (*per se*),"[30] and is described as "the quality of a material object stimulating a receptor organ."[31] This proper sensible object is said to be "of itself and immediately . . . known by one sense; it is the moving and specifying cause of one kind of sensation."[32] The "external sense is a passive power, and must be put into act by a cause." Accordingly, it cannot be in error. For "precisely as acted upon by the external cause, the external sense receives its determination; it adds nothing of its own."[33]

In spite of all the quantitative determinations of the physical correlate of sensation in terms of wavelength, frequency and amplitude, and in spite of the explicit statement concerning "the peculiar quantitative modality that is the formal effect of sound,"[34] it is maintained that "the measurement of sensible qualities . . . when reduced through causal analysis to its ontological foundations . . . in no way implies that qualities are quantities."[35] Sensible qualities constitute "a species of predicamental accidents"[36] which have quantity merely as "their proximate ontological subject,"[37] or which are intimately or "more radically"[38] "associated with quantity," and only in this sense "can be said to be quantified."[39] The "Thomist's traditional assertion of the ontological priority of quantity over quality" is found to be well illustrated by the fact that sensible qualities demand, at least, "aggregates of atomic particles" and thus "certain minimum quantitative dimensions" as material cause or proper subject.[40]

Physical qualities are, then, simply identified with sensible qualities, and characterized and classified in conformity with

[29] James E. Royce, S.J., *Man and His Nature* (New York: McGraw-Hill, 1961), p. 60.
[30] *Ibid.*, p. 52.
[31] *Ibid.*, p. 59.
[32] George P. Klubertanz, S.J., *The Philosophy of Human Nature* (New York: Appleton-Century-Crofts, Inc., 1953), p. 120.
[33] *Ibid.*, p. 428.
[34] *NSCH*, p. 18, Footnote 37.
[35] *Ibid.*, p. 14 and Footnote 25.
[36] *Ibid.*, p. 14.
[37] *Ibid.*, p. 11.
[38] *Ibid.*, p. 14.
[39] *Ibid.*, p. 5.
[40] *Ibid.*, pp. 23 f.

Aquinas' view of the material universe. They are to be divided into "two general categories," we are informed. The first of them "comprises qualities that produce alteration or qualitative change in other bodies or are themselves the result of such alteration." Known "as sensible qualities or more accurately as *qualitates passibiles*," they "in turn are subdivided on the basis of their proximity to sense experience. Some are directly sensible, such as heat, color, sound, odor, and taste, all of which can be sensed immediately by external organs." Others like "electricity, magnetism, chemical affinity, etc." are not directly sensible, but can be known through sensible effect and were, because of this indirect manifestation to sense experience, "known to medievals as 'occult qualities' . . . A second category of sensible quality includes qualities" listed in the Middle Ages as "motive or resistive potencies, or powers, or virtues; an example of motive potency would be gravity, while inertia would be an instance of resistive potency."[41]

Faithfulness to Aquinas' philosophy of nature will also prevent some neothomists from allowing an admission of the reality of physical elements as conceived in our age to interfere with their view of the merely virtual presence of elements in compounds. However, it seems that difficulties are met with in an attempt to dispose of the scientific evidence speaking against this traditional conception. For the neothomistic interpretations of this fundamental doctrine of Aristotelian-Thomistic physics reveal surprising differences and shortcomings.

The most radical cure of a conflict between modern scientific evidence and the medieval understanding of the composition of mixed bodies consists in an identification of the related modern and traditional physical doctrines by simply declaring "virtual existence" to mean "real existence." An elementary particle, it is asserted in a neothomistic study of the problem, is "as part of a composed body . . . a *real* part of such a body, as an integral component. Although *real,* however, it is not fully actual . . . ; rather it has a *virtual* existence." "When incorporated into the nature of the molecules as *integral* parts, the components become *virtual* parts of that nature."[42] In this fashion, the basic Thomistic understanding of the composition of mixed bodies is finally established as a true expression of the constitution of physical reality as known today.

[41] *Ibid.*, pp. 4 f.
[42] *Proceedings.*, p. 162. Underlining is mine. M. Sch.

Certain other present-day proponents of Aquinas' physical doctrines recognize a difference between real and virtual existence, but are unable to agree on the definition of the latter notion. However, their defense of a Thomistic hylomorphic composition of especially organic beings seems to dictate a common procedure for their argument for the merely virtual presence of the seemingly really existing elements in composed corporeal beings: The scientific evidence which is admitted as a fact, as starting point of the discussion, is to be interpreted in a way that finally some kind of "virtual existence" appears to be realized.

According to one such neothomistic interpretation, "virtual presence" is explicitly said to mean the preservation of "most, if not all" characteristic activities of chemical elements and compounds in the organism, while actually it is identified with their full reality as component parts of the living body on the one hand, and with a lack of their supposital existence on the other. The elemental components of the organism "are not substances in the philosophical sense of the term, when they form a part of a living body," because their characteristic activities "are subordinated to the good of the whole, and thus show that the chemical substances do not act as independent beings."[43] As a philosophical reason for denying substantiality to such component parts of the organism, the hylomorphic constitution of corporeal substances, permitting only one substantial form, is introduced.[44]

This Thomistic doctrine of the unicity of the substantial form determines also the interpretation of related empirical and experimental data of other neothomistic authors. According to their understanding, "virtual presence" means the manifestation of some, in no case all, of the original activities of elements when incorporated and transformed into the substance of the body in question. The observations adduced as evidence for the presence of elements in compounds, for example, the fact that the "spectograph of a living thing . . . shows the characteristic spectrum of water, carbon, and so forth," or that " 'tagged' atoms can be followed through the bodily system and located when they are assimilated" are declared to be "really facts."[45] And "the concern of the philosopher is not

---

[43] Henry J. Koren, C.S.Sp., *An Introduction to the Philosophy of Animate Nature* (St. Louis: Herder, 1955), p. 34.
[44] *Ibid.*, p. 42.
[45] Klubertanz, *op. cit.*, pp. 23-25.

to question facts. Rather, it is the interpretation of the facts and the correctness of the ultimate conclusions drawn which fall within his competence." To be avoided is the "failure to consider other pertinent facts."[46] And inasmuch as the present problem is concerned, the whole evidence includes "the demonstrative evidence for the unity of any living thing,"[47] which allows "only one substantial act in a being that is substantially one,"[48] and "also some evidence... with regard to the constituent material parts of man."[49]

In an attempt to decide the question concerning the "formal and actual" presence of chemical substances and elemental particles "as distinct substantial entities" in, for instance, a human body, it is held that "we can go only by a man's activities. Does a man look and act like an electric current? or move about like an alpha ray?"[50] Or again, "do these chemical 'substances' exhibit *all* and *only* the properties they have when not in the body? Nitrogen does not grow, water does not see and hear. They now do things that they were never capable of doing before. But this means they are a different kind of being. They are no longer nitrogen and water, but living human flesh.... Essentially different operation shows different kind of substance; even though elements enter into the composition of man, they do so precisely by being substantially changed into man."[51] So "when man eats food, he actually transforms water, carbohydrates, and other substances into his own substance, so that this same matter which formerly existed by the substantial forms of these molecules... now ceases to be that kind of being and begins to exist by the substantial form which makes matter to be man."[52] To give another example, when "a cat kills and eats a mouse" which is then assimilated by the cat, "something has disappeared and something has persisted" during this process of assimilation. "When digested by the cat, the mouse is no longer a mouse; its 'mouseness,' its substantial form, has disappeared. But its prime matter persists. The prime matter is neither the cat nor the mouse; it is not the dead mouse or the proteins or other chemicals which analysis may discover in it. It is a principle of being which, when

---

[46] Royce, *op. cit.*, p. 264.
[47] Klubertanz, *op. cit.*, p. 24.
[48] *Ibid.*, p. 17.
[49] *Ibid.*, p. 24.
[50] *Ibid.*, pp. 26 f.
[51] Royce, *op. cit.*, p. 265.
[52] *Ibid.*, p. 286.

united to the substantial form of a cat constitutes a cat." A contemporary student may read with relief that to "the modern reader the foregoing explanation may sound naive, typically 'medieval.'" However, before he is even able to observe that it not only sounds but most certainly is naive and medieval, he is warned against this possible mistake. "Hylomorphism—and especially the concept of prime matter—is a profound and difficult doctrine, an essential part of moderate realism."[53] It is the only position able "to repudiate any splitting of man into two beings."[54] At any rate, it helps to interpret the modern scientific evidence against this Aristotelian-Thomistic understanding of the constitution of corporeal being, and thus to maintain the doctrine of the virtual existence of elements, essentially connected with Thomistic hylomorphism. If elemental particles and chemical substances are truly transformed into the substance of an organism so that their prime matter becomes existing under the one substantial form of the organism, they naturally cannot be "present there formally and actually as distinct substantial existents." Since they actually show some of the properties of the distinctly existing elemental parts and compounds after being substantially changed and perfected into parts of the living being, and also were or "will be actually existing as a distinct substance" outside of the organism, they are said to have virtual being.[55]

A last neothomistic position finally solves the problem by subordinating the modern scientific view of the constitution of material reality, as comprising merely hypothetical specialized and detailed assertions, to the evidently certain "general science of nature" of Aristotle's *Physics*. Like other principles of the traditional philosophy of nature, the notions of primary matter and substantial form are declared to be independent of "the specialized experiences" of modern science and to require "only a knowledge of logic and our common experience of change." As perennially true, they are presupposed, and not affected by modern scientific discoveries.[56] It is true that when "commercials of radio and of television join the newspaper headlines in discussing atoms, germicides, interplanetary travel, viruses and other entities that indoctrinate the mind

[53] J. F. Donceel, S.J., *Philosophical Anthropology* (New York: Sheed and Ward, 1967), pp. 10 f.
[54] Royce, *op. cit.*, p. 282.
[55] Klubertanz, *op. cit.*, pp. 26 f.
[56] Vincent Edward Smith, *The General Science of Nature* (Milwaukee: The Bruce Publishing Company, 1958), p. VII.

with modern science before it has a chance to explore that general level of material things which modern science presupposes," it is "difficult to teach and to learn" the ideas of primary matter and substantial form, "when, as a matter of fact, Aristotle could consider them in the very first book of his *Physics*." However, in spite of the fact that "there is surely no ground to deny their reality, . . . it is hardly ever sufficiently emphasized for us that atoms and their parts are hypothetical entities, . . . dialectical constructs or conceptual schemes." Certainly, "it is much more evident that the burning of wood is a substantial change," which on the basis of "general experience" can easily be explained in terms of primary matter as pure potency, functioning as common subject of succeeding substantial forms, "than it is apparent how atoms and their parts exist and behave." Hence if "there is an apparent conflict between the notions of primary matter and substantial form and a popular-science explanation of change, it is the second kind of explanation which must be adjusted to the first and not the first which must be abandoned in favor of the second." For surely "we ought to use what is better known, i.e., the familiar world, to explain what is lesser known, i.e., the dialectical constructs of atomic physics." At any rate, a possible reconciliation of the modern scientific and the Aristotelian view of constitution and change of material reality "involves specialized knowledge which is out of place in the general science of nature." Whatever insights scientific endeavor may reveal, they can represent only "details which can be fitted into our more general framework."[57]

Such conflicting, self-contradictory, and unrealistic statements and arguments concerning the composition of corporeal being cannot be an expression either of the actual conditions of reality or of Aquinas' teaching on the subject. In fact, they manifest lack of understanding of the true meaning of St. Thomas' physical doctrines when they are intended to apply his concepts to modern scientific findings. They likewise indicate disregard of St. Thomas' insights and intentions when simply repeating his physical and psychological conceptions, as the following presentation of related Thomistic doctrines will reveal. It is not only a practical reason, that is, the continuous frustration of a teacher who uses neothomistic textbooks and must therefore struggle to make his students see at least some trace of truth behind such misunderstood and obsolete notions, that

---

[57] *Ibid.*, pp. 99-101.

motivates this discussion of the meaning of the traditional scholastic understanding of physical reality. The following explanations are primarily inspired by the conviction that neoscholastic philosophy cannot fulfill its task of offering a much desired realistic philosophy of nature as it is known in our age, unless it recognizes the radical difference between the Aristotelian-Thomistic and the modern world view.

The traditional Thomistic conception of the constitution of corporeal beings has its foundation in Aristotle's doctrine of sensible qualities. The best approach to an understanding of their meaning in Aristotelian-Thomistic physics is probably found in the first lecture of the third book of Aquinas' commentary on *De Anima*. Following the philosopher, St. Thomas investigates the possible number of senses and establishes the correctness of Aristotle's opinion, according to which there cannot be more than the traditional five sensory powers cognitive of proper sensible qualities.[58] The proof of this opinion reads as follows: "Whoever possesses a sense organ by which some sensible quality can be known, recognizes by such organ all the sensible qualities of that type. But the perfect animals have all sense organs. Consequently, they recognize all sensible qualities."[59] The minor of this argument, which presupposes the possession of the five external human senses by all locomotive animals as a fact of experience, is established by a consideration of the possibilities offered by the constitution of the sublunary bodies for the realization of medium and organs of sensory knowledge. Sublunary physical reality, since it consists of the four elements and of corporeal substances composed of them, allows only the construction of the five sense organs and of their media, when these are conceived to be in physical potency to the proper object of the senses.[60]

The force of the argument evidently rests upon the truth of the traditional scholastic conception concerning the constitution and dynamics of sublunary corporeal beings; its analysis would thus logically lead to an insight into Aquinas' notion of the meaning of the sensible qualities. However, such an investigation would demand an understanding of nature and function of the

[58] Cf. S. Thomae Aquinatis, *In Aristotelis Librum de Anima Commentarium* (Taurini: Marietti, 1948), *Lib.* III, *lect.* 1, *n.* 565. In the following referred to as *Anima*, followed by numbers of book, lecture, and section.
[59] *Anima*, 3, 1, 566.
[60] *Anima*, 3, 1, 570 ff.

four elements in Aristotelian-scholastic physics. This understanding is made easily accessible through Aquinas' proof of the major of the argument. It is this proof which lays bare the cornerstone of the Thomistic theory of both the structure and the sensory cognition of physical reality and of their mutual relations.

Aristotle's view that a sense organ adapted to serve as an instrument for the perception of some sensible qualities is capable of the reception of all qualities of the corresponding genus or species is to be justified. Following the philosopher, Aquinas attempts to achieve his task by way of an examination of the conditions prevailing in the case of the sense of touch. A comparison of our subjective touch experiences with the objectively possible tangible qualities is to reveal the intended potentiality. Both kinds of touch qualities are easily known: the first, since we experience them; the second, because they represent the specific differences of the elements and are thus to some degree necessarily found also in all mixed bodies.[61] The experiment shows that our possible touch sensation truly correspond to the elementary properties, and consequently that our sense of touch is receptive of all objective tangible qualities.[62]

The full meaning of this asserted fitness of our sense of touch and of the tangible qualities themselves in Aristotle's physics becomes evident when the reason for this exact correspondence between subjective and objective sensory qualities is seen. Obviously the value of the comparison in question depends upon the knowledge of the nature and of the number of the elements. We may be certain about the all-comprehensive capability of our sense of touch, it is asserted, because the tangible qualities constitute the specific properties of the elements. But how can we know for certain that the tangible qualities truly are the elementary specific differences, or that we have a knowledge of all the properties of the elements, and of all the possible elements themselves? The text declaring the tangible qualities as properties of corporeal beings refers to *De Generatione et Corruptione* for the desired information.

[61] *Anima*, 2, 23, 546: . . . tangibiles qualitates sunt differentiae corporis, secundum quod est corpus; idest differentiae, quibus elementa distinguuntur ab invicem, scilicet calidi, frigidi, humidi et sicci.
[62] Cf. *Anima*, 3, 1, 568; 569: . . . nos habemus sensum omnis sensibilis, cuis tactus est perceptivus quod ex hoc apparet quod omnes passiones tangibles, inquantum huiusmodi, a nobis sentiuntur.

In conformity with the human mode of arriving at knowledge of the nature of material things, determination of number and nature of the physical elements can be achieved only by an investigation of the accidents of material reality. However, not all physical characteristics can be assigned as elementary properties. Only those material accidents demanded for an explanation of the function of the elements in the constitution of corporeal substances can serve as their specific differences. Since the physical elements are the first principles of all changeable bodies and thus "the cause of generation, corruption, and alteration in all other (terrestrial) bodies,"[63] their properties must necessarily represent "the immediate principles of substantial change."[64] But among all the material accidents, which primarily and directly are the cause of qualitative,[65] and thus ultimately of substantial change,[66] that is, among the qualities of the third species, the sensible qualities,[67] only the tangible qualities fulfill the basic conditions required for properties of primary bodies. The proper object of the distance senses cannot serve as elemental properties of material being because they presuppose the constitution of the body, and consequently the properties of the body as such. Moreover, they are not mutually active and passive, as the proximate dynamic principles of generation and corruption of the elements must be,[68] for experience shows that "light and darkness, odors and sounds have no effect on sensible bodies."[69] The tangible qualities, how-

---

[63] S. Thomae Aquinatis, *In Aristotelis Libros De Generatione et Corruptione Expositio* (Taurini: Marietti, 1952), *proemium, n.* 2. In the following referred to as *Generatio*, followed by numbers of book, lecture, and section.

[64] *Generatio*, 2, 2, 190.

[65] *Generatio*, 1, 10, 74: . . . alteratio primo et per se est in qualitatibus tertiae speciei, mediantibus quibus ex consequenti fit alteratio etiam in aliis.

[66] Cf. S. Thomae Aquinatis, *In Libros Aristotelis De Caelo et Mundo Expositio* (Taurini: Marietti, 1952), *Lib.* 3, *lect.* 8, *n.* 600: . . . generatio et corruptio est per alterationem. In the following, referred to as *Caelum*, followed by numbers of book, lecture, and section.

[67] Cf. *S. Th.*, 1, 78, 3, *ad* 1: . . . non omnia accidentia habent vim immutativam secundum se, sed solae qualitates tertiae speciei, secundum quas contingit aleratio. Et ideo solae huiusmodi qualitates sunt objecta sensuum, quia, ut dicitur in VII *Phys.*, 'secundum eadem alteratur sensus, secundum quae alterantur corpora inanimata'.

[68] Cf. *Generatio*, 2, 2, 190.

[69] *Anima*, 2, 24, 560. Naturally some capability of qualitative change had nevertheless to be ascribed to the sensible qualities of the distance senses in the Aristotelian psychology of sensation; for, as an alteration, sensation demands a qualitative change of medium, organ, and psychic power. However, the defective active force of color, sound, and odor which can influence "only

ever, are not only primary properties of a body, and as such also the cause of all other sensible qualities[70] and of all contrarieties;[71] but it is also only through them, that the necessary condition of physical change, i.e., the contact of the corporeal agent with the subject of change, can be realized.[72] Hence they represent "the active and passive qualities of the elements through which all corporeal alteration takes place."[73] However, not even all seven Aristotelian pairs of contrary qualities of tactile experience can be considered as differentiating characteristics of simple bodies; elementary properties are only those opposed tangible qualities which are irreducible and mutually active and passive. The two pairs of hot-cold and wet-dry are finally selected as the primary dynamic physical accidents of the terrestrial world.[74]

After this discovery of the elementary properties, the problem of the determination of the elements themselves is not difficult to solve. To recognize their constitution and number, one has only to calculate the possible combinations of the primary sensible qualities. Since coexistence of contrary qualities in the same subject is impossible, and since the mutual substantial change of the elements demands the possession of active and passive qualities, the pairs of the active qualities hot-cold and of the passive qualities wet-dry allow only four possible combinations corresponding to the specifying accidents of the traditional four elements. "Thus it is clear that this world around the earth consists of the four bodies."[75]

---

indeterminate and unstable bodies, like air and water" (cf. *Anima*, 2, 24, 562) is sufficient for the achievement of this change required in psychology, since these "rather passible" elements represent the medium of the distance senses and since, for the sake of the corresponding sensation, only a "spiritual immutation" is necessary any way. (cf. *S.Th.*, 1, 78, 3.)

[70] *Anima*, 2, 24, 562: . . . qualitates tangibiles sunt causae aliorum sensibilium.
[71] Cf. *Generatio*, 2, 2, 192.
[72] Cf. S. Thomae Aquinatis, *In Libros Aristotelis Meteorologicorum Expositio* (Taurini: Marietti, 1952), *Lib.* I, *lect.* 2, n. 12. Hereafter referred to as *Meteor.*, followed by numbers of book, lecture, and section.
[73] *Anima*, 2, 24, 561: Si enim corpora insensibilia non paterentur a qualitatibus tangibilibus non esset ponere a quo paterentur et alterarentur corpora inanimata. Nam tangibilia sunt qualitates activae et passivae elementorum secundum quas accidit universaliter alteratio in corporibus.
[74] Cf. *Generatio*, 2, 2, 193 ff.
[75] *Meteor.*, 1, 2, 11: Alia vero principia corporum inferiorum sunt quatuor, propter primas tangibiles qualitates, quae sunt principia agendi et patiendi, scilicet calidum, frigidum, humidum et siccum, quarum sunt tantum quatuor possibiles combinationes . . . Sic igitur patet quod iste mundus qui est circa terram, constat ex quatuor corporibus.

There should not be any doubt about the exact correspondence between subjective and objective tangible qualities, as asserted in Aristotelian-scholastic physics, after this short report about the ancient determination of constitution and number of elements. If the adequacy of our tactile experience is to be established by a comparison with the objective tangible qualities assumed to be the differentiating properties of the elements on the one hand, and if these elementary characteristics themselves are determined in terms of the normal human touch sensations on the other, the fitness of the sense of touch to serve as an instrument for an objective report of all possible tangible qualities is self-evident. Since the mutual relationship assumed to exist between possible subjective and objective tactile qualities is said to prevail with regard to acts and objects of all external senses possible in the Aristotelian-scholastic world,[76] the meaning of the sensible qualities in general and of the doctrines related to them in the traditional scholastic philosophy of nature should not be mysterious either. Naturally Aquinas and his followers believe that the sense "apprehends things as they are."[77] If one projects mental phenomena into material reality and constructs this reality exclusively out of these psychic qualities, as ancient physics does, one certainly should find no difficulty in maintaining the objective reality of sensible qualities. He merely asserts of and extracts from his construction what he has put into it. The number of the senses necessarily is equal to the possibilities of specific action by the exterior real upon the physiological living being in Thomistic psychology, since the qualities of the third species, that is, the possible sensations of the normal human individual, are conceived to represent the only directly efficient dynamic physical forces of Aquinas' sublunary world.[78] The specific accidents of material things as known in the traditional scholastic physics truly constitute the structure of the intentional species, as the orthodox Thomist maintains; for these psychic structures of sensitive life are the only physical properties of the Thomistic sublunary bodies.

According to Aristotelian-Thomistic physics, material reality as sensed by a man endowed with a normal sense constitution is

---

[76] Cf. *Anima*, 3, 1, 569.
[77] Cf. *S. Th.*, 1, 17, 2: . . . (sensus) apprehendit res ut sunt.
[78] Cf. Footnote 60.

identical with the corporeal world as it is. Human sensations as the so-called proper object of the five external senses are conceived to be the physical accidents of corporeal substances.[79] They are primarily and fully actual only "outside the soul."[80] With the exception of sound which first has to be actualized in its proper subject, they have a steady and firm existence,[81] even if they are not sensed.[82] As corporeal qualities,[83] they represent the natural dynamic forces of terrestrial physical being; for only the qualities of the third species can effect qualitative physical change,[84] and thus substantial change as the end of alteration.[85] Compared with the sensory power, sensible qualities, as actual external properties, enjoy a relatively higher dignity,[86] and their natural priority demands that the structure of the senses is consequent to their natural disposition.[87] However, their psychogenic origin finds manifest expression in the definition of their nature no less than of their source. As the sense is "essentially fit to undergo change through its corresponding sensible,"[88] so a natural destination to act upon the sense represents the proper ratio of the sensible quality.[89]

Their genuine relationship is re-established in the Thomistic psychology of sensation. Projected into physical reality and identified wth physical characteristics, sensations have to be brought back into the psychosomatic subject in their original identity. The solution of this psychological problem is found in the Aristotelian notion of the passive physical potency. The conception of the sense

---

[79] Cf. *S. Th.*, 1, 18, 2: . . . intellectus noster . . . accipit a sensu, cuius propria objecta sunt accidentia exteriora.

[80] *Anima*, 2, 12, 375; Sensibilia . . . , quae sunt activa operationis sensitivae, . . . sunt extra animam.

S. Th., 1, 79, 3 ad 1: . . . sensibilia inveniuntur actu extra animam.

[81] Cf. *Anima*, 2, 16, 439: . . . habent esse permanens et fixum in suo subjecto.

[82] Cf. S. Thomae Aquinatis, *In Duodecim Libros Metaphysicorum Aristotelis Expositio* (Taurini: Marietti, 1950), *Lib.* 9, *lect.* 3, n. 1800. Hereafter referred to as *Metaph.*, followed by numbers of book, lecture, and section.

[83] Cf. *S. Th.*, 1, 78, 1.

[84] Cf. *Metaph.*, 5, 20, 1065: . . . in sola tertia specie qualitatis potest esse alteratio.

[85] *De anima*, a. 12: . . . generatio est terminus alterationis.

[86] Cf. *Anima*, 3, 3, 612.

[87] Cf. *Metaph.*, 4, 12, 681.

[88] *Anima*, 2, 13, 387.

[89] Cf. S. Thomae Aquinatis, *In Librum de Sensu et Sensato Commentarium* (Taurini: Marietti, 1949), *lect.* 15, n. 209. Hereafter referred to as *Sensus*, followed by numbers of lecture and section.

as a determined organic structure receptive of corresponding qualities guarantees that "the sense in act is the sensible in act."[90] Being in potency to the only dynamic forces of terrestrial corporeal beings, the animated sense organ together with its medium must, according to the principles of the Aristoelian morphe-dynamism,[91] either be endowed with qualities contrary to those perceptible to it,[92] or, at least, lack the qualities representing its proper object, "as the pupil which is in potency to colors and receptive of them is without any color."[93] For a natural agent which must needs produce an effect like itself,[94] can act upon a subject only inasmuch as this is not similar to it.[95] Constructed in this fashion, medium,[96] organ,[97] and/or psychic sensory power[98] are potentially what the exterior sensible quality is actually, and can be assimilated by and to the sensible,[99] without any contribution of the psychic power.[100] There is no need for a *sensus agens* which by its vital

---

[90] Cf. *S. Th.*, 1, 55, 1 *ad* 2.

[91] a) *Metaph.*, 12, 3, 2454: agens naturale agit sibi simile.
De anima, a. 13: . . . agens ad hoc agit ut similitudinem in aliis inducat.
b) *Sensus*, 10, 138: . . . corpora agunt secundum qualitates suas.
c) *Sensus*, 10, 137: . . . actio naturalis est alicuius contrarii alterantis. Cf. *Anima*, 2, 10, 351.

[92] Cf. *Sensus*, 5, 69: Organum odoratus est in potentia odor in actu, qui est per calorem vel ignem; . . . et ideo oportet quod substantia organi odoratus sit id, quod est actu frigidum, quod praecipue est in loco circa cerebrum.

[93] Cf. *Anima*, 3, 7, 680.

[94] Cf. *De subst. sep.*, cap. 15, n. 137: . . . causa naturalis per formam naturalem, per quam est actu (producit effectum): unde oportet quod agens naturale, quale ipsum est, tale producat et alterum.

[95] Cf. *Anima*, 2, 9, 338: . . . agens est contrarium patienti; non enim simile a simili patitur.

[96] Cf. *Anima*, 2, 16, 445: . . . medium in quolibet sensu, qualitatibus sensibilibus secundum illum sensum caret, ut possit omnes recipere.

[97] Cf. *Anima*, 2, 23, 547: Organum . . . sensus patitur a sensibili, quia sentire est pati quoddam: unde sensibile, quod est agens, facit ipsum esse tale in actu, quale est sensibile, cum sit in potentia ad hoc.

[98] Cf. *Anima*, 2, 21, 516: . . . sensus gustus, vel organum eius, est in potentia ad saporem . . . ; gustabile autem est, quod potest reducere ipsum de potentia in actum.
Anima, 2, 12, 382: . . . sensitivum in potentia est tale quale est in actu sensibile.

[99] Cf. *Anima*, 2, 10, 351 and 357; 2, 12, 382.

[100] Cf. *Quolib.* VIII, *q.* 2, *a.* 1: Sensus autem exteriores suscipiunt tantum a rebus per modum patiendi, sine hoc quod aliquid cooperantur ad sui formationem.—And only those qualities which "primarily and *per se*" produce this qualitative assimilatory effect in the sensory potency, that is, the exteriorized sensations or the qualities of third species, *not* physical properties like the ancient occult qualities or the modern physical correlates of sensation, are sensible qualities in ancient physics. (Cf. *Generatio*, 1, 8, 62: formae

action would transform a physical stimulus or its physiological effect in the organ and in the nervous system into a psychic representation significant for a determined animal species; for there is no physical characteristic nor a physiological effect formally different from the sensible species which as external sensible quality is the sole agent of the actualization of a sense.[101] Acting as efficient, material, and formal cause of sensation, the qualities of the third species reproduce themselves by some kind of alterating activity successively[102] and *per modum intentionis* or *spiritualiter*[103] in medium, organ, and sense, and thus cause sensation. Participating in the powers of spiritual beings,[104] material objects can by their qualitative accidents re-establish those psychic characteristics which the sensible qualities as human sensations originally had.

It is probably not necessary to give an explicit evaluation of this Thomistic conception of the physical qualities of terrestrial bodies and of the psychology of their sensation. Whoever is faintly acquainted with modern physics, physiology and comparative psy-

---

quae sunt per se perceptibiles, sunt qualitates tertiae speciei, quae ob id dicuntur passibiles, quia sensibus ingerunt passionem. *S. Th.*, 1, 78, 3 ad 2: . . . sensibilia propria primo et per se immutant sensum, cum sint qualitates alterantes.) "Directly sensible" is only what causes immutation in this Aristotelian sense of alteration, not what is recognized as stimulating a sense organ and thus leading to a sensation in an organism endowed with a corresponding sense constitution after centuries of scientific research. (Cf. *Anima*, 3, 1, 577: Quaecumque enim sentiuntur per hoc quod immutant sensum, sentiuntur per se et non secundum accidens. Nam hoc est per se sentire, pati aliquid a sensibili.—*S. Th.*, 1, 78, 3: Exterius . . . immutativum est quod per se a sensu percipitur.)

[101] Cf. *De spirit. creat.*, a. 9: Sensus . . . qui est in potentia, reducitur in actum per sensibilia actu, quae sunt extra animam; unde non est necesse ponere sensum agentem.
Anima, 2, 12, 375: Sensibilia . . . quae sunt activa operationis sensitivae, . . . sunt extra animam.

[102] Cf. *Sensus*, 16, 224: . . . sensibilia per modum cuiusdam alterationis immutant medium ita quod huiusmodi permutationes perveniunt usque ad sensum.
Anima, 3, 17, 862: . . . medium patitur et movetur a sensibili, sensus autem a medio.

[103] Cf. *Anima*, 2, 14, 148: Immutatio . . . spiritualis est secundum quod species recipitur in organo sensus aut in medio per modum intentionis.
Sensus, 19, 291: . . . sensus et intellectus recipiunt formas rerum spiritualiter.

[104] Cf. *De pot.*, q. 5, a. 9. For a more extensive presentation of the Thomistic doctrine concerning the constitution of physical reality and the psychology of its cognition cf. Marius Schneider, "The Dependence of St. Thomas' Psychology of Sensation upon His Physics," *Franciscan Studies*, Vol. 22 (1962), pp. 3 ff.

chology is aware that, with the exception of the statement: human beings are capable of sensations traditionally called sensible qualities, scarcely any of the corresponding doctrines of the scholastic physics is true. No interest in qualitative knowledge can reasonably justify the hope to defend the objectivity of the sensible qualities as conceived by St. Thomas and in the scholastic tradition. The Thomistic sensible qualities are *not* physical properties of material reality as it is known today, and those quantitative differences of, for instance, the small section of electromagnetic waves or of molecular motion, which represent physical correlates of normal external sensation, are not directly sensible. Their recognition is the result of modern scientific, i.e., intellectual effort required to disprove the common sense and traditional belief in proper or *per se* sensible qualities of the human self-world or *Umwelt*.[105] As it is rightly maintained, "rays of particular wavelength or frequency referred to as colored light . . . are not themselves colored." However, this is the case because *no* "body is actually colored, and so seen by the eye."[106] Such as a body is seen or sensed, it never is; and the actual color of the body, that is, determined frequencies of lightwaves reflected by the body—not any property of the body itself —can only stimulate a sense organ when this is attuned to it, and thus "be seen," i.e., it can elicit a vital response of vision significant for the life of a sentient being. For the sensible qualities, i.e., sensations differ in conformity with the sense constitution of animals; they are not sensory copies of the quantitative modalities of physical conditions. There is no known case of any sense organization for which the "actually colored" body, that is, all the electromagnetic waves reflected by it, still less, the microscopical elemental constitution of that body causing the reflections, would represent the specific stimulus. The traditional sensible qualities are known today as psychic phenomena which function as species specifically different *signa signata* of vital aspects of the environment in the life of sentient beings.[107] As mental, they naturally are not predicamental accidents of physical reality nor do they effect qualitative physical change. The modern physical color, sound, heat, etc., however, are not the formal object of sensation or the

---

[105] By self-world or *Umwelt* biologists and psychologists understand the phenomenal world, as it corresponds primarily to the sense constitution of a sentient being.
[106] Cf. *NSCH,* pp. 20 f.
[107] Cf. Karl F. Herzfeld, *op. cit.*, p. 42.

moving and specifying cause of allegedly purely passive sensory powers; nor is their "perception by the appropriate sense organ" the final cause of their existence.[108] The characterization given of sensible qualities in the traditional scholastic philosophy of nature does not hold true of physical characteristics of material being, as it is known today.

The morphe-dynamic conception of the sensible qualities, then, determines also the answer given in Aristotle's physics to the question concerning the existence of the elements in compounds. For, as Aquinas writes, the solution of this problem depends upon the actual mode of the realization of substantial change. "If . . . generation and corruption of bodies take place by way of congregation and segregation (of the elements), as Empedocles and Anaxagoras maintained, it follows that the elements are actually in the compound. However, if generation and corruption of bodies are effected by way of alteration, then necessarily the potential existence of the elements in the mixture has to be asserted."[109]

St. Thomas' or rather Aristotle's choice between these two alternatives was already made in the psychology of sensation. On the basis of the experience and scientific method available 2400 years ago, the view of the atomists concerning the corporeal character of light[110] and concerning atomic emissions[111] of distant objects as physical correlates of sensations had to be dismissed in favor of the traditional sensible qualities as physical properties in Aristotle's theory of sensory knowledge. Consequently, the atomistic conception of the involvement of a combination and separation of the physical elements in the formation and disintegration of composed bodies had to be replaced by the morphe-dynamic understanding of substantial change in Aristotelian physics. The way to generation is alteration,[112] which is effected solely by qualities of the third species, more precisely, by the elementary tangible qualities,

---

[108] Cf. *NSCH*, p. 18.
[109] Cf. *Caelum*, 3, 8, 600.
[110] Cf. *Anima*, 2, 14, 406.
[111] Cf. *Sensus*, 5, 60; 16, 238 f.; 8, 105 ff.; *Anima*, 2, 20, 494.
[112] Cf. S. Thomae Aquinatis, "De Mixtione Elementorum ad Magistrum Philippum," *Opuscula Philosophica* (Taurini: Marietti, 1954), n. 432: . . . alteratio est via ad generationem et corruptionem. Hereafter referred to as *Mixtio*.
Generatio, proemium, n. 1: Alteratio . . . ordinatur ad generationem sicut ad finem.

the primary dynamic forces of sublunary bodies.[113] In virtue of the vertical series of efficient causes of Aristotelian-scholastic physics,[114] the elements act by way of their specific properties, the immediate principles of physical action,[115] upon one another, and thus effect qualitative[116] and finally substantial change among themselves[117] as well as the origin of mixed bodies.[118] These latter are the result of a mixture of the elements and of their contrary qualities.[119] For all terrestrial bodies other than the elements are generated out of the four simple bodies by way of their mixture,[120] which necessarily represents a union of the altered components of the compound,[121] and thus results in a body neither identical with nor actually containing the physical elements. Since the four elements, which are conceived as the primary mutually changeable bodies and thus as the source of all qualitative and substantial change, can effect a compound only by means of their specific properties, their mixture obviously involves a simultaneous change of their sensible qualities. A combination of hot and cold, and wet and dry materials of our human self-world usually leads to an equalization of the "primary physical qualities." "Thus by a remission of the extreme degree of the elementary qualities some middle quality is

[113] Cf. Footnote 73.
[114] Cf. *De pot.*, q. 5, a. 8: Elementa . . . agunt in virtute corporum coelestium et corpora coelestia agunt in virtute substantiarum separatarum.
[115] Cf. *S. Th.*, 1, 78, 2 *ad* 1: . . . secundum qualitates activas et passivas, quae sunt naturalium actionum principia.
De pot., q. 5, a. 7 *ad* 7: . . secundum qualitates activas et passivas, quae sunt immediata principia actionis.
[116] Cf. *Sensus*, 10, 139: . . . per actionem qualitatum elementalium transmutatur materia ad formas substantiales (elementorum).
Anima, 2, 23, 539: Corruptio . . . et generatio in elementis . . . sequitur alterationem.
[117] Cf. *Metaph.*, 1, 12, 191: . . ad sensum videmus quod quatuor elementa ex invicem generantur.
Meteor., 1, 3, 16: . . . ignis et aer et aqua et terra fiunt ex invicem.
[118] Cf. *Generatio, proemium*, 2: . . . elementa, quae sunt causa generationis et corruptionis et alterationis in omnibus aliis corporibus.
[119] Cf. *Anima*, 1, 9, 140: . . . omnia corpora sunt commixta ex elementis et contrariis.
[120] Cf. *Caelum*, 3, 8, 601: . . . alia corpora generantur ex elementis, silicet per mixtionem.
[121] Cf. *Metaph.*, 1, 12, 195: . . illa sola nata sunt ad invicem misceri, quae nata sunt adinvicem transire per aliquam alterationem, eo quod mixtio est miscibilium alteratorum unio.
Caelum, 3, 8, 601: Generantur . . . ex igne caro aut lignum . . . per adjunctionem aliorum corporum simplicium simul ad mixtionem coalteratorum.

produced," as pale results from black and white, and lukewarm from hot and cold. "This *qualitas media* represents the proper quality of the mixed body, varying in each compound in accordance with the different proportion of the elements mixed . . . The qualities of the simple bodies are, therefore, contained in the proper quality of the compound according to the manner in which extreme opposites are found in the mean sharing the nature of both . . . In this way, the accidental forces of the substantial forms of the simple bodies are preserved in mixed bodies. Consequently, the forms of the elements are in the compounds not actually, but virtually."[122]

One of the essential conditions of an elementary component required by the definition of the element, i.e., that it be *in* the compound, cannot, therefore, be literally fulfilled in the case of physical elements.[123] A compound is a composition of the elements only genetically, not constitutionally. Not even the elementary qualities, still less the elements themselves can be actually present in a compound as conceived in the Thomistic philosophy of nature. "The form of the mixed body is immediately in matter in place of the forms of the elements." Accordingly, a physical substance cannot have different component parts, "as is obvious in the case of a bone, of flesh, and of a stone, each part of which receives predication according to the complete notion of the nature of the whole; *quaelibet enim pars ossis est os.*"[124]

So the "virtual presence" of Aristotelian-Thomistic physics does not mean an existence of physical elements as actual and integral parts of a compound, nor of all or of some of their properties. St. Thomas' interpretation of the doctrine of virtual presence cannot consistently "be assumed to be essentially correct"[125] by a neo-scholastic who, forced by the evidence of modern scientific knowledge, admits the falsity of Aquinas' statement that "every part of a bone is bone" or, in other words, recognizes physical elements as real parts of a compound. The doctrine of the unicity of the substantial form is a constitutive element of the Thomistic hylomorphic theory of corporeal beings. And it is necessarily so in a philosophical understanding of a physical reality which is conceived

[122] *Mixtio*, 438 f.
[123] Cf. *Mixtio*, 431.
[124] Cf. S. Thomae Aquinatis, "De Natura Generis," *Opuscula Philosophica* (Taurini: Marietti, 1954), *cap.* 7. *n.* 550.
[125] *Proceedings*, p. 162.

to be a composite of the traditional four elements and of their mixtures. These elements themselves, as the ultimate physical entities into which corporeal beings can be resolved, are not constituted atomically, but are considered as substances determined by, and supporting, the primary Aristotelian tangible qualities as their physical properties. A compound as a mixture of water, fire, air and earth, however, obviously cannot contain these elemental structures and their characteristics, as the preceding presentation of Aquinas' explanation of the process and the result of mixture has shown. If the logical analysis of the change of these corporeal entities of our human self-world nevertheless demands a composition of their substance, and if this composition, because of a systematic impossibility of an atomic structure of material reality, is determined in terms of the reified components of this analysis, the hylomorphic conception of Aristotelian physics is the necessary result. Since "in every change there must be a subject common to the terms of change,"[126] and since the subject is matter or being in potency and the terms are the succeeding substantial forms identified with the species,[127] a corporeal substance can be conceived to be composed only of primary matter and of one substantial form. As a corporeal individual of our phenomenal world pertains to one species, it can possess only one substantial form.

Thus it is understandable when, in spite of their intention to defend Aquinas' position, the neothomistic proponents of the reality of elements in compounds implicitly endorse a completely unthomistic constitutional theory of corporeal things, or when the Thomistic conception of "virtual presence," which is declared to be essentially correct, is radically different from the "virtual existence" which, in conformity with the demands of modern physical knowledge, is described as the mode of the realization of elements in a compound. The substantiality of elemental parts of the plurality of substantial forms can be consistently denied only because of an obviously unjustified identification of substance and supposite in the case of the neothomistic position which determines "virtual presence" as a preservation of "most, if not all" characteristic activities of the elements in a compound, and at the price of a confusion of "real" and of "virtual existence" with "substantial" and of "fully actual" with "subsistent," when virtual existence is

---

[126] *Metaph.*, 1688.
[127] *Metaph.*, 1278: Materia enim est ens in potentia et species est actus eius.

declared to mean to be "real, however . . . not fully actual." Since free elementary particles were established as subsistent entities and Aquinas' notion of virtual presence was implicitly dismissed as unrealistic by the recognition of physical elements as real parts of the composite, the problem of the relationship which these originally subsisting elements have to their compound when constituting its component parts, had to be solved. Instead of dealing with the problem in terms of the metaphysical notions of subsistence, complete, and incomplete substance, and determining that the subsistent element when incorporated into the complete substance of a compound loses its subsistence and becomes an incomplete substance or a substantial part, the neothomist thinks in the framework of Thomistic physics, substituting "fully actual" for subsistence and "virtual existence" and "real" for incomplete substance or substantial part, and finds that the component element "although real . . . is not fully actual" and has thus only "a virtual existence." Aquinas' respective doctrine which is essentially characterized by a denial of the actual presence of elements in the traditional mixed body is thus replaced by, and declared to be identical with a neothomistic demonstration of a virtual existence of elements which actually means a real existence of elementary particles as incomplete substances in compounds.

No less unthomistic and indefensible are neothomistic positions that insist upon the truth of the traditional hylomorphic doctrine and consequently either interpret the modern scientific evidence in terms of Aquinas' understanding of the substantial unity of bodies, or declare modern scientific conceptions as specialized instances of Aristotle's general science of nature, or simply disregard the modern world view and profess St. Thomas' physics as a consequence of his metaphysics of the act. According to Aquinas, the hylomorphic constitution holds true only of the physical reality described by Aristotle's physics, and is incompatible with an atomic structure of corporeal beings.

As has been indicated, the doctrine of the hylomorphic composition of corporeal substances is the logical result of a philosophical analysis of change observed on material entities of the Aristotelian sublunary world. The observation of the neoscholastic defender of Aristotle's general science of nature, that the recognition of its principles demands only a knowledge of logic and an experience of change in "our familiar world" is thus at least partly correct. Aristotle arrived at his notions of primary matter and substantial form through a merely logical consideration of change of corporeal objects of his experience. However, these objects which were thus found to be composed hylomorphically were entities of Aristotle's familiar world. As such, they were not simply objects of a naive "general experience" of either our age or the fourth century B.C. They were already interpreted in terms of a definite scientific theory, i.e., of the reified sensible qualities as the only immediate physical principles of change and consequently of the four elements. This identification of sensations with physical qualities was, of course, not a dictate of St. Thomas' metaphysics of the act, as the orthodox neothomist wants to believe, but the result of Aristotle's physical investigation of the related position of the atomists, on the basis of empirical facts accessible in ancient Greece.[128]

Only corporeal substances which have the normal human touch sensations as physical properties were unable actually to contain elementary physical parts and thus had to be conceived as composed of primary matter and of substantial form. It should not be too difficult to understand why Aristotle could already speak about his hylomorphic theory in the first book of his *Physics,* and why a 20th-century student of philosophy might have to overcome some resistance in accepting such ancient physical notions as philosophical truth. The world known to us differs from that of Aristotle. A neothomist who is forced to admit the fate of Hiroshima, not as a conceptual construct but as a fact of modern history, or to deny that the fire of traditional physics—that is, the illusionary corporeal substance supposedly composed of primary matter and the substantial form of fire and characterized by the sensations of hot and dry as its physical properties—is a component element of wood,[129] such a neothomist is not allowed simply to follow Aristotle and to identify the subject of his logical analysis of change with prime matter. Instead of repeating the opinions of ancient authorities that wood is a substance and its burning a substantial change, he should feel obliged to investigate whether wood truly constitutes a substance, or whether its structure and its burning really do exclude an involvement of physical elemental particles and chemical compounds, as traditional hylomorphism demands, or whether pri-

[128] Cf. Footnotes 110; 111.
[129] Cf. *Caleum,* 3, 8, 601.

mary matter as pure potency truly represents the only "reality" common to wood and ashes. Evidently a philosophical determination of substantial change in the realm of matter presupposes a knowledge of the nature of a physical substance and of the principles involved in such a change, and whatever the truth value of modern science may turn out to be, the necessary scientific presupposition of Aristotelian hylomorphism most certainly does not represent a true conception of physical being.

The traditional scholastic constitutional theory of material things can consistently be maintained only with regard to the imaginary substances of the sublunary world of Aristotle's physics. That is, it can be maintained only of a physical universe in which alteration, i.e., change effected by the elementary tangible qualities of the ancients, is the way to substantial change, as Aquinas himself asserts. It does not hold true of a physical reality that is structured atomically. For "if . . . generation and corruption of bodies take place by way of a combination and segregation (of the elements), it follows that the elements are actually in the compound."[130] The atomic and the Aristotelian-Thomistic hylomorphic composition of corporeal being are mutually exclusive. It is not only unrealistic but also unthomistic to describe modern scientific conception as detailed, specialized experiences of Aristotle's physical doctrines. The principles of Aristotelian physics cannot rightly be considered as the general science of nature in our time; they are not perennially true.

The essential association of traditional hylomorphism with the sublunary corporeal entities of Aristotle's physics finally renders futile attempts to dispose of modern scientific evidence by an appeal to the Thomistic doctrine of the unicity of the substantial form. Theory cannot prevail against obvious facts. The specious arguments for the merely virtual existence of apparently real physical elements and chemical compounds in a living body, for instance, the denial of an atomic composition of organic structures because of an alleged growth, vision, or even becoming man of tagged atoms or of nitrogen in the organism, can appear convincing only when the ultimate principles of Thomistic physics are *a priori* accepted as evident philosophical truth.

It is not surprising therefore, that such neothomistic demonstrations of the traditional notion of virtual existence can arrive at

---

[130] Cf. Footnote 109.

their conclusion only by a reversal of the realistic procedure followed by Aquinas in establishing his physical doctrine. With Aristotle, St. Thomas decides against the atomic and for the hylomorphic structure of corporeal beings on the ground of the evidence available at his age. The actual existence of the elements in the compound is denied and the composition of primary matter and substantial form asserted because the composed body, for example, flesh or a stone, did not reveal the assumed physical properties of fire, air, earth, and water. Modern defenders of Aquinas' position follow the opposite course. Instead of arriving with him at the notions of the virtual existence, and thus of the hylomorphic constitution of corporeal beings through and after an analysis of data of experience, they start by accepting Thomistic hylomorphism as their major premise and using it as a guiding principle of their interpretation of the scientific evidence opposed to related traditional physical conceptions. While Aquinas asserts the virtual existence of the four elements in the compound because there is not the least indication of their actual presence, his modern follower practically declares: The elements obviously are in compounds, since every scientific evidence speaks for their presence; yet they cannot actually be there! If asked why not? the answer actually is, because St. Thomas says so. In this fashion, obsolete physical doctrines are demonstrated as perennial, difficult, and profound philosophical truth in a philosophy of nature.

The difficulties, disagreements, and contradictions in which various neothomistic thinkers involve themselves in an attempt to reconcile modern scientific findings with Thomistic physical ideals should serve as a warning against any unreflected identification of ancient and modern physical conceptions. Aristotle's physics reflects the view of a corporeal universe radically different from material reality as it is known today. To explain facts and findings constitutive of the scientific worldview of our age by way of conceptions developed in a logical analysis of the primitive experiences and beliefs of ancient Greece, or to confirm such conceptions with insights of modern science, *a priori* seems to be questionable philosophical procedure. The notion of occult qualities,[131] for instance,

---

[131] Cf. S. Thomae Aquinatis, "De Occultis Operationibus ad Quemdam Militem," *Opuscula Philosophica* (Taurini: Marietti, 1954). Hereafter referred to as *Occult.*, followed by numbers of the sections.—The occult qualities were considered as accidents of corporeal substances in ancient physics. However, it is rather questionable generally to describe these occult virtues, for

had a meaningful place in the traditional physical theory of terrestrial bodies. Since "the world around the earth" was conceived to consist of the four elements and of bodies composed of them, characteristics of corporeal substances not reducible to the primary qualities of the elements demanded an explanation. In spite of the ingenuity Aristotle and his commentators showed in tracing the most diverse physical phenomena on earth and in the sky to the properties of the four elements, some of their experiences with the physical environment did not seem to bow to their forceful systematizing efforts. Such corporeal manifestations which did not permit a reduction to the elementary dynamic touch qualities or, as Aquinas writes, had "principles most difficult to understand"[132] were dealt with under the title of "Occult Operations of Nature." Since the required principles could not have their source in the terrestrial sphere of physical reality, it naturally had to be found in the higher level of the causal hierarchy of the Aristotelian-Thomistic physical universe: the celestial bodies and the separate substances.[133] These superior forces could produce such unexpected physical activities either directly, by exercising their own power upon a corporeal subject and thus eliciting its occult operation as, for instance, when demons perform miraculous activities by way of pictures which magicians describe as the source of the miraculous event;[134] or indirectly, by impressing upon the body a power surpassing the natural forces of the elements as a permanent intrinsic principle of such operations, for example, the ability of a magnet to attract iron,[135] or the power of gold to delight man's heart.[136] These potencies or abilities proceed from their substantial form,[137] which itself is "the product of the wisdom of the separate substance

---

instance, the power to heal by one's shadow as physical quality (cf. *Occult.* 442), or their causality, for example, that of gold which is said to delight man's heart (*Occult.*, 448) as physical change. As *occult* qualities, that is, as irreducible to the elementary and thus to the sensible qualities, they did not constitute a subdivision of sensible qualities in ancient physics any more than they do today, when "occult", i.e., irreducible physical properties are unknown. As actual physical characteristics, however, they certainly are of an essentially different nature than that ascribed to them in Aquinas' *De Occultis Operationibus*.

[132] Cf. *Occult.*, 440.
[133] Cf. *Ibid.*, 440 f.
[134] Cf. *Ibid.*, 442.
[135] Cf. *Ibid.*, 440.
[136] Cf. *Ibid.*, 448.
[137] Cf. *Ibid.*, 444.

acting by means of the power and motion of the heavenly bodies."[138] As first principles of physical reality, the spiritual substances use the celestial bodies to impress the substantial forms upon corporeal matter, according to the understanding they have of them.[139]

Aquinas' notion of occult operations is thus a logical consequence of his theory of the constitution and dynamics of terrestrial bodies. As irreducible to the elemental physical forces or to the sensible qualities, as conceived in Aristotle's physics, they have their source either directly or indirectly in the powers of pure spirits. However, it is meaningless to speak of occult qualities or powers in the context of modern physical theory. Today the ancient superiority of the heavenly bodies and the universal physical causality of separate substances are recognized as mere assumptions of an obsolete worldview and the characteristics of compounds are explained as the exclusive result of the elementary components of material reality.

For similar reasons, it is useless to refer to "a Thomistic view of the mass concept,"[140] as long as this concept is intended to be an expression of gravitational and inertial forces as known in modern physics. In the Thomistic universe, where gravity is a sensible quality formally identical with the proper object of human sensation, where heavy and light are passive principles[141] of respectively natural downward and upward movements[142] and consequently of natural places of the four elements and of bodies composed of them,[143] where the earth is the essentially immovable[144] center of the world,[145] where the heavenly bodies are neither heavy nor light[146] and moved by intellectual substances,[147] mass as a universal physical phenomenon, as understood in our age, is simply inconceivable. If this modern view of the mass concept, therefore, obviously "exists neither in the writings nor in the thought of St. Thomas, why call it Thomistic?"[148]

---

[138] Cf. *Ibid.*, 447.
[139] Cf. *Ibid.*, 446.
[140] Cf. *NSCH*, p. 13 Ftn. 23.
[141] Cf. *Caelum*, 1, 3, 22.
[142] Cf. *Caelum*, 1, 3, 29 f.; *Meteor.*, 1, 2, 11.
[143] Cf. *Caelum*, 3, 5, 575.
[144] Cf. *Caelum*, 2, 26, 527.
[145] Cf. *Ibid.*, 525.
[146] Cf. *C. Gent.*, 3, 82; *De anima*, a. 16.
[147] Cf. *De spirit. creat.*, a. 6; *Caelum*, 1, 3, 33.
[148] L. M. Régis, *op. cit.*, p. 106.

Finally, only when the meaning of the atomic structure of corporeal reality is disregarded, can one see in the fact that minimum quantitative dimensions are demanded for the existence of sensible qualities a good illustration of the "Thomist's traditional assertion of the ontological priority of quantity over quality."[149] For quantity as the immediate substratum of the Thomistic sensible qualities is necessarily conceived as continuous.[150] As already stated, hylomorphically constituted bodies are, up to their last part, of the same species as the whole; they have different parts only potentially.[151] However, these "aggregates of atomic particles" or "macroscopical domains of molecules" which are demanded as minimum dimensions for the realization of the physical sensible qualities, as they are known today, imply a discrete quantity. This latter, however, involves the existence of various "subjects" and thus a completely different conception of the sensible qualities and of their substratum than that presented in the traditional scholastic philosophy of nature. To characterize physical color or any other sensible quality as qualitative accidents of corporeal substances is therefore unjustified. What is to function as the "subject or substance" of the physical correlate of a color seen in opaque surfaces? The differences of frequency and length of electromagnetic waves reflected by a body, which represent physical color, as well as these reflected light rays themselves are certainly neither qualities nor accidents of the body seen as colored. Or what is the substance of the "quantitative modality" of the regular vibratory motion of the medium experienced as sound? Which species of quality or which kind of predicament do this quantitative modality and the vibratory movement of relatively large masses of molecules themselves represent? Can those macroscopical domains of molecules of the medium or air itself, which usually functions as the medium of human hearing, be rightly considered as one substance or that quantitative modality itself as a quality of this one substance?

The obviously negative or undecided answers to these questions reveal that a genuine, realistic philosophical evaluation of modern scientific discoveries concerning the properties and structure of

---

[149] Cf. *NSCH*, p. 24.

[150] Cf. *Sensus*, 2, 29: Qualitates . . . , quae sunt propria objecta sensuum, sunt formae in continuo.

[151] Cf. *Caelum*, 1, 3, 26: . . . continuum non habet partes in actu sed solum in potentia.

material reality is still to be desired. Certainly it will differ decisively, as St. Thomas himself indirectly admits, from that obsolete Aristotelian philosophy of nature which found its clearest expression in his writings.

When he discussed the atomistic conception of light, Aquinas had to dismiss this notion of an emanation and diffusion of physical elementary particles for the sake of that shiny property assumed to be inhering in the sun of our human self-world as a sensible quality, on the basis of the experience of his age. However, he also saw that an understanding of light as material emissions from the sun, as was asserted by the ancient atomists and is recognized as basically correct by modern science, would demand "the discovery of principles of natural philosophy different" from those of Aristotle's physics.[152] Is it too much to expect that contemporary Thomists who subscribe to the modern scientific views of the constitution of physical being and of the nature of its sensible qualities seriously reflect upon this insight of their master, finally give up the attempt to defend obsolete physical doctrines, and offer their help for the realization of a truly *neo*scholastic philosophy of nature?

[152] Cf. *In* II. *Sent.*, *d.* 13, *q.* 1, *a.* 3: Quidam enim dixerunt quod lux est corpus quod est ipsa substantia solis ex quo fluunt quaedam corpora et illa corpora dicuntur lumen, vel radius. Haec autem positio multipliciter a philosophis improbata est . . . Unde haec positio tanquam absurda et extranea relinquenda est, non enim potest sutineri, nisi aliis principiis naturalis philosophiae inventis.

THOMAS AQUINAS AND THE PROBLEM OF UNIVERSALS: A RE-EXAMINATION

by

B. Ryosuke Inagaki

1. The Problem of Universals

An attempt is made in this article to state my reasons for dissatisfaction with the existing literature on the Thomistic theory of universals. The position of Thomas Aquinas concerning the problem of universals is usually characterized as a realism, in contradistinction to nominalism and conceptualism. It is further modified as "moderate" as against "extreme" realism, which asserts the subsistence of universals.[1] Admittedly Aquinas' position may be called realistic in the sense that for him universals are neither something arbitrarily posited nor merely convenient fictions, but something real. In view of his severe criticism of Platonic realism and the explicit formulation of his own view against it, however, it is worth determining whether it is entirely justifiable to classify his position as a kind of realism, even with the qualifying note of "moderate."

A more fundamental questions arises. Have the approaches taken in the past in considering Aquinas' thought on universals been adequate? In other words, is it not the case that his thought has not been adequately understood because of improper and uncritical approaches which are really foreign to his thought? In a way, this is a commonplace question concerning the history of philosophy. It is obviously inappropriate to seek in Aquinas solutions to problems raised by Locke, Kant, or Quine. What is

[1] Although some historians of philosophy (e.g. W. Windelband) call Aquinas' doctrine conceptualism, what they mean will be better expressed by the term *realismus moderatus*. The latter expression has been widely used since M. De Wulf, J. Gredt and others.

peculiar about the present question is that an important phase in Aquinas' thought on universals, which perhaps had been presented only in an incomplete and fragmentary manner, may have been left undeveloped and forgotten because of defective approaches taken in regard to his thought. In order to sharpen the issue, I shall first briefly examine the ways in which the problem of universals has been presented in the past.

To begin with the well-known case of Porphyry, he first asks whether genera and species subsist or are they merely something posited in the mind. Then, excluding the second possibility, he asks whether they are corporeal or incorporeal, and further whether they are separated from sensible things or found in them.[2] It can be easily discerned that his question anticipates either a nominalistic or realistic answer. Moreover, although he declines to venture any solution to such a profound question, the way he states the problem suggests his preference for realism.

Porphyry's presentation of the problem seems to involve two problematics. The first is that the problem of universals is formulated with logical terms, such as genera and species. To be sure, Porphyry's concern was not confined to logical problems. His formulation shows that he has not sufficiently distinguished logic from metaphysics.[3] Rather, I am concerned with the historical fact that logicians were destined always to play the principal role in the discussions of universals.[4] I do not intend to say that the logicians' contributions to the problem of universals are not important in themselves or without significance to philosophy. On the contrary, I believe that philosophers can learn much from the theories of universals developed by modern logicians and mathematicians. At the same time we must not overlook the fact that logical discussions of the problem of universals are subjected to a definite limitation. The requirement in logic that all terms should be defined and should be used univocally makes, I submit, an adequate treatment of the problem impossible. Universal concepts, such as man and animal, are univocal. Philosophical discussion of them, however, can no longer be confined within the limit of univocity. The logicians' persistent refusal to sacrifice univocal clarity would necessarily lead to, for example, the confusion of the mode

---

[2] Migne, *P.L.*, lxiv, 82.
[3] D. Knowles, *The Evolution of Mediaeval Thought*, Longmans, 1962, p. 110.
[4] Cf. E. Gilson, *The Unity of Philosophical Experience*, Scribner's, 1950, ch. I; H. Veatch, *Realism and Nominalism Revisited*, Marquette U. Press, 1954.

of existence and that of existence and that of cognition, which will be commented on later.

Secondly, Porphyry's formula does not reveal any systematic reflection on the meaning of such terms as "subsistence," "existence," or "being." Ordinarily when we ask about being or existence, we are concerned with the existence hic et nunc. In other words, we are speaking about the existence of something perceived through our senses. Incidentally, it should be noted that we can not meaningfully say that "something is," unless the nature of that something has been grasped intellectually. Now, since it is impossible to conceive universals as something existing in time and space, their existence is bound to be denied if "existence" is taken in the sense of "existence in space and time." If we limit the meaning of "existence" to that of "existence in time and space," in other words, if we assert that there is nothing except those that can be perceived by senses, the existence of universals will be denied, and the position of so-called nominalism would follow. On the other hand, if we admit the existence of certain entities that are bound by the time-space determinations, the result will be the realistic position.

Here the problem of universals is reduced to that of a so-called Weltanschauung, or to use Quine's expression, of "ontological commitment." Insofar as Weltanschauung represents some kind of fiat, the problem cannot be solved by such reduction. Rather, it should be considered in the light of a rational reflection on the various meanings of "existence" or "being," that is, against some ontological background. Without such reflection, any discussion concerning the existence of universals will be philosophically fruitless.

Quine's discussion of "ontological commitment" promises at first sight that his theory of universals goes beyond the horizon of logic. According to him, the ontological problem of universals amounts to the question whether such (abstract) entities as attributes, relations, classes, numbers, functions exist or not. He advances as the criterion for the ontological commitment of any theory "those entities to which the bound variables of the theory must be capable of referring in order that the affirmations made in the theory be true."[5] If these entities are limited only to concrete individuals,

---

[5] Cf. "On What There Is" in: *From a Logical Point of View*, Harvard, 1961; "On Universals," *The Journal of Symbolic Logic*, XII, 3, 1947; "Steps towards a Constructive Nominalism" (with N. Goodman), *ibid.*, 4. As to certain

the theory in question is nominalistic. If, on the other hand, they include abstract entities, it will be considered realistic or Platonic.

The issue here is not, in the light of such criterion, whether Quine is a nominalist or a realist. It is the criterion itself and the validity of the approach behind it. Now, according to Quine, the question "Are there universals (abstract entities)?" is strictly a scientific question, just as is the question, "Is there life on Mars?" In other words, "existence" or "being" in these questions is taken as univocal. The "ontological commitment" as understood by Quine seems to refer to that fiat which lies behind any answers to the problem of universals. It merely reflects the lack of ontology in these theories of universals, and does not offer any positive contribution towards the solution of the problem. For its solution, we must turn to some ontology which can set the problem in a proper context, and not to some pre-philosophical ontological commitment.

R. I. Aaron's position in the problem of universals as formulated in *The Theory of Universals*[6] differs on several points from that of logicians. First, he tries to start from some basic facts of experience, avoiding the form of questioning that presupposes certain theories or interpretations. One such fact is our ability to use general terms, without which so-called conceptual thinking would be impossible. We are forced to face and answer the problem of universals in order to explain that empirical fact. Although it is debatable whether Aaron was right in his choice of the basic empirical fact as the starting point, his procedure itself seems to be valid.

Another noteworthy feature in Aaron's theory is that he distinguishes two kind of universals. The first may be called real universals. They are the recurrences of the same or similar relations, qualities, and things observed in nature which are the ultimate ground for the universal element in our conceptual thinking. The second, related but distinct from the first, is the universal as the principle of classification, and this may be called logical. This distinction is significant to the extent that it rises above the logician's tendency to treat the problem of universals exclusively from a logical point of view. As will be seen later, Aquinas clearly distinguishes these two in a different manner, limiting the philosophical

---

logicians' view on this problem, cf. *The Problem of Universals: A Symposium* (I. M. Bochenski, A. Church, N. Goodman), Notre Dame, 1956.

[6] R. I. Aaron. *The Theory of Universals*, Oxford, 1952.

consideration of universals to those we have called real universals here. Aaron is able to give to each of realism, conceptualism and nominalism a place in his theory, discerning that they represent only partial answers to the problems of universals.

Aaron's assertion that universals exist in the form of recurrences in nature calls for re-examination. He admits, it is true, that the existence of universals requires some ultimate explanation, of which the Platonic doctrine of ideas is suggested to be a significant attempt. However, the real issue is not the ultimate explanation of the existence of universals but the meaning of "existence," when universals are said to exist. We could recognize the limit of Aaron's theory in that he hastens to the ultimate explanations for the existence of universals without reflecting on the meaning of existence.

II. *Universals and the Essence*

Ordinarily, the problem of universals in Aquinas is presented not as the question of existence or nonexistence of universals, but as the question of the (objective) validity of universal concepts. Our ideas, such as "life" and movement," are abstract and universal. What we experience, on the contrary, are concrete, individual things. How then can these ideas adequately represent things? In other words, how this one-many opposition between the universal character of ideas and the individual character of sense objects be resolved? Is not the term "universal" (one-in-many) itself a mere fiction design to cover up such opposition involved in our knowledge? This is surely a serious epistemological question, and Aquinas' doctrine of universals is regarded as an answer to it.[7]

According to an interpretation accepted generally, the core of Aquinas' answer to the epistemological question is the distinction between metaphysical (or fundamental) universal and logical (or formal) universal. Aquinas observes that the nature of essence of things can be considered in three ways: (1) in itself absolutely, (2)

---

[7] Cf. M. De Wulf, *The System of Thomas Aquinas*, Dover, 1959, p. 40; R. P. Phillips, *The Modern Thomistic Philosophy*, Newman, 1950, II, p. 84. As to Aquinas' own discussion of the meaning of the term *universale*, see: *De Ente et Essentia*, c. 3; *Summa Theologica*, I, 16, 7, ad 2; 79, 5, ob. 2; 85, 3, ad 1; *In Libros Metaphysicorum Expositio*, VII, 13, 1570, 1572; *Quaestio Disputata de Anima*, 3, ad 8; *In Peri Hermeneias Expositio*, I, 10, 122; *In Libros Posteriorum Analyticorum Expositio*, I, 42, 6.

as it is found in individual things, and (3) insofar as it is known by the intellect, that is, as it is in the intellect.[8] To explain this in more detail, our intellect grasps concerning the nature of things what belongs to this nature in itself before adverting to the mode of its existence. The nature thus grasped cannot be said to be either one or many, but at the same time it does not exclude the possibility of being one or many. This way of grasping the nature is called by scholastics as simple apprehension, in which the subject and object are not yet, as it were, divided. Next, the intellect proceeds to its second act, judgment, as it is there that the subject and object are first divided. It implies that the nature of things is grasped as being in individual things as well as in the intellect, the knowing subject. At this stage, however, the nature of things does not assume the character of universality. The nature as it is found in the intellect is often said to be universal, but this is misleading as an interpretation of Aquinas' position.[9] The conceptualist view that universal concepts—concepts as universals—are found in the intellect does not represent, as will be shown later, the intention of Aquinas.

When, in the next stage, we reflect explicitly upon the nature of things as known, we recognize that the universal has a uniform relation to individual things, that is, it is common to "many" while being "one." We say "explicitly," in order to distinguish the reflection by which the notion of universal is reached from the reflection or *reditio*, involved in every judgment, upon the nature known by the first act of intellect.[10]

Here we have the universal in the strict sense, referred to as the logical universal by scholastics. It is the so-called metaphysical universal that provides the ground for this logical universal. That the metaphysical universal possesses actually neither the oneness as the mark of intellectual knowledge nor the manyness as the mark of sense knowledge, being neutral to both of them yet excluding neither of these possibilities, as the interpretation goes, is the ground for the formation of logical universal as "one-in-many."

---

[8] Cf. *De Ente et Essentia*, c. 3; *Quaestiones Quodlibetales*, VIII, 1, 1.

[9] Aquinas says that the nature of things in our intellect does not derive its universality from the fact that it is in the intellect. Cf. *De Ente et Essentia*, c. 3.

[10] As to the notion of reditio or reflectio, see: P. Hoenen, *La théorie du jugement d'après St. Thomas d'Aquin*, Gregorian, 1946; K. Rahner, *Geist in Welt*, Kösel, 1958.

According to this interpretation, by recognizing the metaphysical universal, abstracted from actual existence, the truth in each doctrine of nominalism , conceptualism, and realism can be saved without falling into their onesided assertion, thus making a synthetic solution to the problem of universals possible. The interpretation, which can be supported by some texts in Aquinas' writings, is valuable insofar as it shows that his approach to this problem transcends those of logicians.[11] However, is it not more appropriate to say that Aquinas has made it clear, by exposing confusions involved, that the problems of universals as discussed by logicians are pseudo problems, rather than that he has synthesized their views on a higher plane?

First, he distinguishes three so-called universals: (1) the nature of things considered in itself absolutely, (2) the nature of things insofar as it is known, (3) the universal in the strict sense. Of these three, since the first is abstracted from actual existence, the questions, "Is there a universal, and if so, how?" do not apply to it. So also to the third, any discussion concerning its actual existence is meaningless. By definition it is not a real being—that which is divided into ten categories—but a being of reason.[12] In this latter sense, even privation and negation are said to be being. Thus, for Aquinas, there can be no question of actual existence as to the universal as the objects of logic, such as genera and species. Here too the so-called problems of universals is a pseudo problem.

What about the question of the existence of the second kind of universal? It is here that I find conventional Thomistic interpretations unsatisfactory. Sometimes the proposition that there are universal concepts in our mind is presented in the name of Thomas Aquinas. The thought behind this proposition is that when something is intellectually known a universal concept signifying its nature is formed in the intellect as a certain entity. This concept is called "universal" in the sense that it is common (identical or similar) in many knowers.[13] Such a conceptualist interpretation, I submit, is extremely misleading as to the intention of Aquinas. For him, since there is no intellectual knowledge apart from a

---

[11] *Summa Theologica*, I, 55, 3, ad 1; *Summa Contra Gentiles*, III, 24; II *Scriptum Super Sententiis*, d. 3, q. 3, a. 2, ad 1.

[12] Cf. *De Ente et Essentia*, c. 1; as to the object of logic, see R. M. McInerny, *The Logic of Analogy*, Martinus Nijhoff, 1961, pp. 37-48.

[13] Cf. J. Gredt, *Elementa Philosophiae Aristotelico-Thomisticae*, Herder, 1953, I, p. 93, Thesis VI.

connection with senses, there can be no intellectual concept separated from manifold phantasms. In other words, the intellectual concept always involves a relation with the phantasm, and is formed as the abstraction from the phantasm is being made. The so-called universality of intellectual concept is found in its relation to manifold phantasms from which it has been abstracted, not among many knowers. This "radical empiricism" of Aquinas is often overlooked, thus opening the way to the conceptualist interpretation described above.[14]

The conventional interpretation is problematic also in its identification of Aquinas' position as a kind of realism, insofar as realism involves the confusion of the mode of being with that of cognition. His position is generally summarized as follows: the universal is formally in the intellect only, with its foundation in things. The question with regard to this formulation is: In what precise sense does the (formal) universal have its foundation in things? Obviously, the universal does not exist in things as universal.[15] However, realism seems to imply that the object of our intellect is intelligible in itself. Thus, if this logic of realism is applied to the above formula, it would lead to the conclusion that the intelligible nature as known is somehow found in things in the same way as it is in the intellect. This is precisely the fundamental epistemological error rejected by Aquinas.

These two problematics are related to Aquinas' view of the nature of intellectual knowledge. Now it has been generally overlooked, and it is a serious omission, that intellectual knowledge in its proper sense—the grasp of the nature or essence of things—presupposes a grasp of being (*ens universale*), which is to be distinguished from the intellectual knowledge in the strict sense.[16] In order to understand the nature of intellectual knowledge in Aquinas, then, it is necessary to consider this knowledge of being. As the problem of universals is that of intellectual knowledge, it is necessary to turn to *ens universale* which lies behind or beneath universals, if we are to interpret Aquinas' thought on this problem correctly. The observation made before that it is neces-

[14] As to the "empiricism" of Thomas Aquinas, see B. R. Inagaki, "Intellectus Agens and the 'Empiricism' of Thomas Aquinas," *Studies in Mediaeval Philosophy*, VII, 1965; *ibid.*, "The Object of Knowledge," *Academia* 53, 1966.

[15] As observed before, in calling the recurrences in nature universals, Aaron asserts the existence of universals as universals in reality.

[16] See my articles mentioned in n. 8.

sary to reflect on the meaning of being before asking whether universals exist or not, receives here a fresh confirmation. The neglect of this consideration has been the basic defect in the past interpretations on Aquinas' theory on universals.

III. The Universal and Abstraction

The core of past interpretations of Aquinas' thought on universals has been the notion of essence or nature abstracted from actual existence, which is neither one nor many in itself. This notion has been made the basis for the solution of the problem of universals, and the theory of abstraction has been designed to answer the problem of the formation of universals.

Such an interpretation is unsatisfactory insofar as it is not set within an ontological background or context. Because of this, universal concepts and universal natures, alleged to correspond to the former in things, tend to be reified, or regarded as a certain kind of entity, thus giving rise to conceptualist and realist interpretations. As already noted, the so-called problem of universals, namely, the problem of knowledge of universals and that of their reality or "ontological status," should be considered in the light of ontology in the sense of consideration of various meanings of being. In the following pages I shall examine in regard to the problem of the knowledge of universals the conceptualist and realist interpretations. The problem of the reality of universals for Thomas Aquinas, I suggest, is in the final analysis the problem of divine causality.[17] Though it is indispensable to consider this problem for a full understanding of Aquinas' thought on universals, I shall not attempt it here.

Aquinas points out repeatedly that the term universal may be taken in two ways. First, universal refers to the nature of the thing known by us. This is what scholastics inadequately term the metaphysical universal, and is not a universal in the strict sense.

[17] There are many references to the universals as causes in Aquinas' writings. *S.T.* I, 78, 4, ad 1; I-II, 90, 2; II-II, 58, 6; *De Veritate* 7, 6, ad 7. The ultimate explanation for the reality of universals, however, may be found in his teaching that the diversity of things is contained in the higher being in a more simple and perfect manner, and finally contained in God as the First Cause in an absolutely simple manner. The following article discusses this question on the basis of Aquinas' *Exposition super Librum de Causis:* L. Elders, " 'Contineri' in Aquinas' Ontology," *Studies in Mediaeval Philosophy*, VIII, 1966.

Secondly, universal refers to a universal as a universal, that is, the very concept *(intentio, ratio)* of universal.[18] As to the relationship between these two, Aquinas observes that when the intellect reflects upon the nature of things as known, it recognizes its uniform relation to individuals and accordingly attributes the accident of universality to it.[19] Therefore, for Aquinas, as has been said before, the nature of things as known—intelligible species as the means of knowledge—is not universal in itself, but is a singular species.[20] Thus, Aquinas has nothing to do with apriorism which seeks the basis of the universal validity of our knowledge in the very structure of knowledge. He is rather radically empiricistic. For him, cognitive activity is above all the self-perfecting of the knowing subject through acquiring species or forms which it was not endowed with innately.

Aquinas usually names genus, species, and difference as the universal in the strict sense. This is an indication that Aquinas' principal concern is the knowledge of the nature of things. The name "universal" is given only to those essences which signify—implicitly and indistinctly—some individual as a whole, in other words, those essences which can be predicated of some individual.[21] The universal in this sense is formed through comparison, namely the knowledge of similarities and differences, and not through abstraction. It presupposes the knowledge of nature or essence gained through abstraction. This distinction between comparison and abstraction is generally overlooked in modern theories of abstraction, what is called there abstraction being really comparison. This omission deserves deeper reflection than is usually given to it.

The core of the problem of the knowledge of universals, therefore, is not the formation of universals in the strict sense, but the grasp of that to which the accident of universality is attributed, namely, the so-called universal nature. The great question is, how is abstraction possible?

Abstraction, according to Aquinas, is an act which makes what is potentially intelligible actual as such, by abstracting the nature or form of things from their matter and material conditions.[22]

---

[18] *S.T.* I, 85, 2 ad 2; 85, 3 ad 1; I-II, 29, 6; *In Met.* VII, 13, 1570.
[19] *De Ente et Essentia*, c. 3.
[20] *Ibid.*, *S.T.* I, 76, 2, ad 3; 79, 5, ad 2.
[21] Cf. *De Ente et Essentia*, c. 3.
[22] Cf. Inagaki, "Intellectus Agens."

This statement implies that it is impossible to seek the cause of abstraction in things. It is impossible to suppose that the nature of things is found—in things or apart from things—in the same way as it is known. To suppose so would amount to the identification of the mode of the existence of things in themselves with the mode in which they are known. This identification would involve us in that aporia which troubled all forms of Platonism from the one criticized by Aristotle in his *Metaphysics* down to modern logicism. We must, therefore, seek the cause which makes abstraction possible in the intellect itself.

Since Aquinas explains abstraction as immaterialization, we shall begin with a consideration of the character of immaterialization. The proposition that the abstraction is immaterialization presupposes the knowing subject's awareness of itself as an immaterial being, and the idea of knowing as the act whereby things to be known are received into the knowing subject according to the (immaterial) mode of the latter, thus enriching and perfecting it.[23] In other words, knowing is the actualization of the knowing subject, which, as an immaterial being, can reflect upon or return to itself completely. The receiving of things known and their presence in the knowing subject are to be understood within the framework of such complete self-return of the knowing subjects.[24] I cannot here elaborate on it at any greater length.

The immaterialization meant here is that of the phantasm, which is the immediate object for the intellect to act on. Plantasms represent things insofar as they are individuals and are their similitudes. They do not signify actually what things are. In other words, they represent individuals which can be perceived by senses, signifying whatness—this can be grasped by the intellect—only potentially. That phantasms represent the whatness of things only potentially—its limitation or lack of transparency, as it were —is what is meant by its materiality. It will be immaterialized by the act of abstraction. How will this be done?[25]

Epistemologically speaking, it is done by coming to recognize the materiality of phantasms as materiality, that is, as limitation. Through this, what is materialized and limited by phantasma, namely, the form or nature as the limited, is brought to aware-

---

[23] *S.T.* I, 75, 5; 76, 2, ad 3; *Q.D. De Anima*, 14 c.
[24] *De Veritate*, 1, 9.
[25] *S.T.* I, 84, 3.

ness. In other words, the form or nature, which was signified in manifold and potential ways by phantasms, is then first actually grasped, when the limitation is recognized as limitation, thereby bringing the limited into consciousness. The question, then, is: how is phantasm recognized as limitation?

It must be the work of certain principles pre-existing in our intellect. It is empirically unverifiable to suppose that the intellect possesses naturally forms or natures as the means of knowing. Again, to assert that the intellect is immaterial by definition, or that it possesses the so called "light" of agent intellect is insufficient as epistemological explanation. The immaterialization in question must be explained in terms of our cognitive experience.

Now, Aquinas says that that which is first known by the intellect and which is the principle of the knowledge of all other things is being. This knowledge of being is sometimes called natural or innate in the sense that it is gained not through something else but through itself (per se), and that it is not acquired through a repeated use of intellect, but arises at the very beginning of the intellectual activity. Aquinas emphasizes repeatedly that the whole of our intellectual knowledge presupposes such grasp of being, which finds its explicit expression in the form of so-called first principles.[26]

I take this knowledge of being—it is not knowledge in the strict sense in as much as the latter is the knowledge of the nature or essence of things—to be the principle which makes abstraction possible. The being spoken here is related to the nature or essence signifying "whatness" of things as the limited to the limitation. Our intellect is able to recognize nature as potentialities limiting the actuality of being, in virtue of the notion of being which preexists in it. In other words, being is that which actualizes nature, and thus the cause of the intelligibility of the latter. The nature of things signified potentially by phantasms is actualized by such a cause of intelligibility. It is this cause of intelligibility that makes the recognition of the materiality or limitation of phantasm possible. Actually, this process takes place in the form of a reduction to the so-called first principles or other principles established through them, the details of which cannot be discussed here. The preceding short analysis is an attempt to show that abstraction presupposes the notion of being as the actuality of nature or intelligibility (to which the concept of universality is attributed), and that consequently

[26] Cf. Section V (also my articles in II, 8).

the problem of abstraction cannot be adequately discussed without a reflection on being.

It is clear, in the light of these considerations, that Aquinas does not hold that abstraction is the formation or making of universal ideas as certain entities. Rather, the species abstracted from phantasms are forms perfecting the knowing subject in the order of essence. Thus, his position is not conceptualistic, which asserts the existence of universal concepts in the intellect. To make this point clearer, let us examine his view on the knowledge of universals. When he states that while senses are of individuals, intellect is of universals,[27] and that the object of our intellect is the nature of material things,[28] he states the same thing. "Universals" and "nature" here refer to the result of abstraction, that is, the thing insofar as it is immaterialized, and not the thing in itself from which abstraction is made.[29] What is to be known, however, is the latter. How can it be known? The answer becomes obvious when we realize that abstraction belongs to the first act of our intellect. In its second act, judgment, our intellect returns to the phantasm as that from which abstraction is made, and thereby knows the thing itself. Or, when it reflects upon being, limited by the nature grasped through abstraction—the complete self-return of the intellect—the thing or being itself is known.

Thus Aquinas views the act of knowing as a circle involving two movements in opposite directions, namely, abstraction and return. However, in the final analysis, it is the knowing subject's self-return as its mode of existence. To know does not mean to make something universal concepts, for instance, or to act upon something other than the knowing subject itself, but to perfect the knowing subject itself in its act of self-return by way of abstraction.

IV. The Subsistence of Universals

Aquinas' repeated statement that universals do not subsist[30] is usually taken as rejecting extreme realism, which asserts the subsistence of universals apart from individuals. Let us re-examine this interpretation through a reflection on his basic thought on universals.

---

[27] *S.T.* I, 85, 3.
[28] Inagaki, "The Object of Knowledge."
[29] *S.T.* I, 86, 1; *Q. D. De Anima*, 20, c.
[30] *In Met.* III, 9, 455; VII, 13, 1571; *Q. D. De Anima*, I, ad 2; 4, c.

First, the term "universals" in the proposition "Universals do not subsist" refers to the nature of things as known and consequently as found in the intellect. Such natures cannot exist in the same mode (that is, an intelligible), the proposition states, not only apart from individuals, but also in individuals. As to universals in the strict sense formed through a reflection on such known natures, their subsistence is out of question. The problem of the subsistence of universals, therefore, is really the problem of whether intelligible objects as such exist or not.[31]

There are two grounds on which Aquinas rejects the existence of intelligible objects as such, both of which are based on direct experiences. The first is that the whole of human knowledge—including its first principles—has its origin in sense, that its range is co-extensive with that of senses, and that no knowledge is possible unless connected with sense.[32] If intelligible objects as such are presented to us and grasped by our intellect directly, the essential role of senses, and consequently that of bodily elements, will be denied. Aquinas can never accept such view in the light of his basic notion of man as well as of the evident empirical facts he refers to. In one passage he observes that if we admit the existence of intelligible objects, there will be no necessity of positing an agent intellect. What he really emphasizes is the essential role of senses in human knowledge.[33]

Another ground for denying the existence of universal or intelligible objects is the distinction of the mode of a thing's existence in itself and that of its being known by us. This distinction is repeatedly emphasized and used as a principle of explanation by Aquinas and may be described as follows. First, from the fact that we receive the object of knowledge according to the mode of our own existence, it does not follow that the object thus received exists in itself in the same mode.[34] Secondly, this distinction is supported by empirical evidence.[35] Especially, the necessity of making this distinction becomes clear in the light of the undeniable fact that human knowl-

---

[31] According to Aquinas, though in themselves intelligible, God and separate substances are not the immediate object of human knowledge. That a being is more intelligible in itself, does not mean that it is more intelligible to us.
[32] I plan to discuss the meaning of these "empiricistic" propositions in my next paper.
[33] *Q. D. De Anima,* 4, c.
[34] *In Met.* III, 9, 445; *S.T.* I, 84, 1, *et passim.*
[35] *S.T.* I, 81, 1.

edge does not reach its completion at once but only progresses gradually. In other words, it is *in via* and *in motu*. If intelligible objects existed and were presented to us directly, such facts would be inexplicable. It is true that knowledge requires a fundamental similitude between that which is known and the knower. In the case of human knowledge, however, this similitude is not a datum but an objective to be achieved.

The final ground for the assertion that universals do not subsist is that nature or essence does not have its reality in itself but receives it in being actualized by that ultimate reality, *esse*. The nature considered absolutely in itself is separated from *esse*. Nature in itself, in other words, is nonbeing, in need of receiving *esse* in order to exist. To complete this summary consideration of Aquinas' thought on universals, then, we must turn to the *esse* which, being limited by natures or essences as universals, gives reality to them.

V. Universals and Ens Universale

First, we must avoid the pitfall of taking the being in question as a supreme genus. Logical arguments showing that being cannot be one of the genera had already been formulated by Aristotle.[36] The deeper ground for this impossibility is that being is not a nature or essence to which the accident of universality may be attributed. According to Aquinas, our intellect grasps the nature of things by its first act, and by its second act (judgment) the *esse* itself of things.[37] He calls the second act a separation, in order to distinguish it from the first which is properly called abstraction. It is called separation on the ground that, although the *esse* grasped is always found in the nature of sensible-material things, and is limited by it, this does not belong to the very nature of *esse*, but *esse* is separable from material nature. On the other hand, it is impossible to grasp *esse* by itself, "abstracting" it from a certain nature. In other words, it is impossible to form a concept of being, an impossibility implied by the assertion that being cannot be a genus. When our intellect reflects upon itself as it knows a certain nature, it grasps being as that actuality limited by that nature. Thus being is grasped as that which actualizes nature, or as the cause of nature's intelligibility. It is impossible, therefore, to grasp being

---

[36] *Metaphysica* III, 998 b 20-; *In Met.* III, 8, 433.
[37] *In Boethii De Trinitate*, 5, 3.

apart from its connection with the nature or intelligibility of some concrete thing. If we attempt this impossibility, that is, if we try to grasp being, not in the act of judgment but in the same way as nature or essence is grasped, being becomes an empty notion. In fact, the attempt to conceptualize being, or to determine it univocally by Duns Scotus, is a step towards such direction.[38] When being is called *ens universale,* the word *universale* does not signify that it is universal in the strict sense, but that being in itself involves no particular determination.

The being in question is not that mere being which holds for such acts or perfections as living and knowing, but being as the highest perfection or actuality, which embraces living and knowing as its particular determinations or modes.[39] It is the highest perfection and transcends all perfections capable of being univocally determined, and at the same time embraces them all in a higher dimension of *esse.*[40] Aquinas' reflection on the richness of the perfection, *esse,* can be found in his discussion on the so-called transcendental properties of being, namely, true, good, one, and so on.

According to Aquinas, however, the human intellect regards *ens universale* precisely insofar as it is an intellect.[41] This does not mean that human intellect knows being as its proper object. In the strict sense, the intellect knows only the nature of material things, and this knowledge takes the form of a circular movement, consisting abstraction from phantasm and return to the individual represented by the phantasm. That our intellect is able to know its proper object, namely, the nature of things. In other words, the very possibility of abstraction depends, as seen before, on our intellect's grasp of being.

This grasp of being, which is the so-called light of the agent intellect, is brought to consciousness (the operation of agent intellect is experienced by us, Aquinas says) in the consideration of being ranging from the first of intellectual knowledge ("that which first falls into intellect is being"[42]) to the ontological study of being as such. It is that radical experience in our cognitive life, expressed

---

[38] Cf. C. L. Shircel, *The Univocity of the Concept of Being in the Philosophy of John Duns Scotus,* Washington, 1942.
[39] *S.T.* I-II, 2, 5, ad 2; I *Sent.* d. 17, q. 1, a. 2, ad 3.
[40] *S.T.* I, 4, ad 3; *Q. Q. D. D. de Potentia,* 7, 2, ad 9.
[41] *S.T.* I, 76, 1, ad 1; 76, 2, ad 3; 76, 5, ad 4; 78, 1; 79, 2 c.; 79, 2, ad 3; 79, 7; 87, 3, ad 1; *S.C.G.* II, 83.
[42] *S.T.* I, 5, 2; 78, 1; I-II, 94, 2; *De Verit.* 1, 1; 24, 4, ad 9.

by the Aristotelian dictum, often quoted by Aquinas, that *anima est quodammodo omnia* or Aquinas' own proposition that "intellect has a capacity to infinity."[43]

Being cannot be known, therefore, in the same way as the nature of things is known. Consequently, knowledge of being is excluded from so-called scientific knowledge. However, through reflection on the ground of the knowledge of nature it can be established that it is being that makes that knowledge possible and that our intellect is in essential relation with being. In the final analysis, natures and essences are nothing else than so many modes whereby being is revealed to us. In other words, human knowledge does not stop at the knowledge of natures (or laws in empirical sciences). While directly concerned with the knowledge of nature, the human intellect is directed to something beyond. Such is the meaning of Aquinas' proposition that "intellect is concerned with *ens universale*."

In past theories of universals, the universal has been considered in relation with individuals subsumed by it, and the "existence" asked of the universal is that of individuals. Such defects in the presentation of the problem of universals have not been sufficiently taken into consideration in past interpretations of Aquinas' thought on universals. The universal (nature or essence) can be adequately understood only when it is considered in relation to being, which gives reality to it. The universal is a particular determination or limitation of being. What has obstructed the way to such understanding of universal is an interesting question in itself. Perhaps one hindrance is the so-called scientific attitude which tends to limit the knowledge to that of nature (or laws), and another is the logical demand that the equivocity (or analogy) of being must be reduced to univocity. However, the univocal clarity of so-called universal concepts may demand the equivocity of being as its context. Such is a prospect suggested by the argument presented in this paper.[44]

---

[43] *S.T.* I, 76, 5, ad 4; 76, 7, 2, ad 2; 86, 2, ad 4; I-II, 2, 6. Also see: J. Pieper, *Was Heisst Philosophieren*, 1959, II.

[44] As to the equivocity of being, see the following study in addition to numerous studies on analogy: J. Owens, "The Accidental and Essential Character of Being in the Doctrine of St. Thomas Aquinas," *Medieval Studies*, XXXVI, 4, 1959.

11

RADICAL REALITY ACCORDING TO JOSÉ ORTEGA Y GASSET

by

Felix Alluntis, O.F.M.

The purpose of this study is to expound and evaluate Ortega's ideas on the "object of first philosophy," or on what he calls radical reality, namely, that reality which is the root, the foundation, and the justification of all other realities.[1]

[1] The principal works in which Ortega deals with radical reality are the following:
Historia como sistema, Obras completas (Madrid: Rivista de Occidente, 1954-1963), VI, pp. 11-50 *(History as a System,* in *Towards a Philosophy of History,* trans. Helene Weyl, New York: Norton, 1941).
Meditación de la técnica, l.c., V, pp. 317-375 *(Man the Technician,* in *Towards a Philosophy of History,* trans. Helene Weyl, New York: Norton, 1941).
"Prólogo a veinte anos de caza mayor," l.c., VI, pp. 419-492.
Misión del bibliotecario, l.c., V, pp. 207-234.
Guillermo Dilthey y la idea de la vida, l.c., VI, pp. 165-214 *(A Chapter from the History of Ideas—Wilhelm Dilthey and the Idea of Life,* in *Concord and Liberty,* trans. Helene Weyl, New York: Norton, 1946).
En torno a Galileo, l.c., V, pp. 9-164 *(Man and Crisis,* trans. Mildred Adams, New York: Norton, 1962).
"Prólogo a la historia de la filosofía por Emile Bréhier," l.c., VI, pp. 377-416 ("Prologue to a History of Philosophy," in *Concord and Liberty,* trans. Helene Weyl, New York: Norton, 1946).
"Un rasgo de la vida alemana," l.c., V, pp. 184-210.
Ideas y creencias, l.c., V, pp. 377-409.
"Filosofía pura," l.c., IV, pp. 48-59.
Apuntes sobre el pensamiento, l.c., V, pp. 517-547 *(Notes on Thinking—Its Creation of the World and Its Creation of God,* in *Concord and Liberty,* trans. Helene Weyle, New York: Norton, 1946).
El tema de nuestro tiempo, l.c., III, pp. 141-203 *(The Modern Theme,* trans. James Cleugh, London: C. W. Daniel, 1931; New York: Norton, 1933).
Goethe desde dentro, l.c., IV, pp. 395-420 *(In Search of Goethe from Within,* trans. Willard R. Trask, in *The Dehumanization of Art and Other Writings on Art and Culture,* Garden City: Doubleday Anchor Book, 1956).
On Ortega's philosophy of life see Julián Marías Aguilera, *La Escuela de Madrid* (Buenos Aires: Emece, 1959); José Ferrater Mora, *Ortega y Gasset* (New Haven: Yale University Press, 1957); Santiago Ramirez, *La filosofía de Ortega*

I

EXPOSITION

Life

Radical reality, according to Ortega, is life, each man's life, since all other realities are rooted in it in the sense that in one way or another they must all appear in it.[2] Life is a task, a constant *fieri* in an unceasing struggle with the difficulties that man's environment presents.[3] The reason why human life is a constant *fieri* is that man's being and nature's being do not fully coincide. Man's being is partly akin to nature and partly unlike it; man is at once natural and extranatural, "a kind of ontological centaur, half immersed in nature, half transcending it." What is natural in man is realized by itself and presents no problem. For this reason he does not consider it as his true being. On the other hand, his extranatural part is but an aspiration, a project of life. Yet he feels that this is his true being, his personality, his self.[4]

Life consists in an attempt to carry out, in the light of circumstance, that project or program which each man or ego actually is. For Ortega, human life is what he calls "production." He denies that it is what it has long been thought to be, contemplation, thought, or theory, and holds that it is action. It is "fabrication," an act of making, and it is thought, theory, or science only in so far as they are necessary for "autofabrication," or self production. They are necessary not primarily but only secondarily; for one of us to live, means to find ways to realize the program that each of us is in.[5] In other words, human life is not an entity that changes accidentally but rather an activity whose "substance" is change. It is a drama and the subject to whom this drama happens is not something apart from and prior to it, but its very function; the " 'substance' of this drama is its argument, and since this changes, the variation is 'substantial.' "[6]

---

y Gasset (Barcelona, 1958); Jean-Paul Borel, *Raison et vie chez Ortega y Gasset* (Neuchatel, A la Baconnière, 1959).

[2] *Historia como sistema*, p. 13.
[3] *Meditación de la técnica*, p. 341; *Historia como sistema*, p. 13.
[4] *Meditación de la técnica*, pp. 388 and 341; *Historia como sistema*, pp. 32 ff.
[5] *Meditación de la técnica*, p. 341; *Historia como sistema*, p. 26.
[6] *Historia como sistema*, pp. 31 and 35; "Prólogo a veinte anos de caza mayor," pp. 468 ff.; *Misión del bibliotecario*, p. 212. At times Ortega writes of

Ego

As pointed out above, life is an interaction between ego and circumstance. Each man's ego or self is a program or project. Thus man begins by being something that has no reality, either corporeal or spiritual, something that as yet is not but aspires to be. To the possible objection that there can be no program "without somebody having it, without an idea, a mind, a soul, or whatever it is called," Ortega replies that he cannot discuss this point thoroughly because it would require a course in philosophy. He then adds: "But I shall say this: although the project of being a great financier must be conceived in an idea, nevertheless being the project is different from holding the idea. In fact, I find no difficulty in thinking this idea, but I am very far from being this project."[7]

Man is an entity whose being consists not in what it already is, but in what it not yet is, whereas everything else in the world is what it is. An entity whose mode of being consists in what it already is, whose potentiality coincides with its actuality, is called a *thing*.[8] Man is not a thing in this sense but an aspiration: he is an aspiration to be this or that. He is an entity found by traditional ontology at the conclusion of its work but left unexplained, viz., a *causa sui*. However, there is this difference: the *causa sui* of traditional ontology needed only to strive to be the cause of itself and had no need to determine what self it was going to be, whereas man must decide what to be, and must choose among the different possibilities of being that at every moment are open to him.[9]

---

man and life without making any distinction. However, when he writes precisely, he clearly distinguishes between the ego or man, who is a project, and life, which is a task, action, or drama, and includes both ego and circumstance. Ortega points out the difference between his theory and Bergson's in the following passage: "Bergson . . . emplea constantemente la expresión 'l'être en se faisant.' Mas si se compara su sentido con el que mi texto da a esas mismas palabras se advierte la diferencia radical. En Bergson, el término *se faisant* no es sino un sinónimo de *devenir*. En mi texto, el *hacerse* no es sólo *devenir* sino además el modo como deviene la realidad humana, que es efectivo y literal hacerse, digamos *fabricarse*."

[7] *Meditación de la técnica*, p. 338.
[8] *Ibid*.
[9] *Historia como sistema*, p. 33. In earlier texts Ortega states that although we are physically free to choose this or that project, we are morally bound to follow our vocation or destiny which has been imposed on us by we do not know whom. *Goethe desde dentro*, p. 400; *En torno a Galileo*, pp. 137-138. Yet in later texts he drops all reference to the apriorism of the self or project every man is, and writes that man is the novelist of his own being insofar as he must create the figure of being he wants to be. Ortega speaks, it is true, of

These possibilities are not presented to a man. He must find them either by his own personal efforts or by the help of his fellow men. Once found, he must then choose among them, which means that he is free, necessarily free *(libre por fuerza)*, whether he wishes to be or not. Or better, it means that man is freedom. Freedom should not be conceived as a property or activity of an entity that already possesses a fixed being. To be free means to lack constitutive identity, to be able to be other than what one is, to be unable to install oneself once and for all in any given being. The only fixed, stable element in a free being is his constitutive instability.[10] Therefore, "in order to speak ... of man's being we must elaborate a non-Eleatic concept of being, as others have elaborated a non-Euclidian geometry. The time has come for the seed sown by Heraclitus to bring forth its mighty harvest."[11]

Since man must decide what he is going to do and to be at each instant, he has to justify to himself why he chooses one possibility rather than another. If in his choice he is faithful to his "self," to the project he is, his life will be authentic. On the contrary, if he abandons himself to the customary and topical and is unfaithful to his project, his life will be false and be inauthentic. Hence morality consists in authenticity in the full realization by each man of the figure of being he has decided to be.

Man's constitutive freedom implies that he is in an infinitely plastic entity of which he may make what he will. In fact man has been many things. We can set limits to "human plasticity." Ortega holds that Madame Pompadour and Lucile de Chateaubriand have come from the most primitive ancestors and so also Sir Isaac Newton and Henri Poincaré. He notes that within a few decades John Stuart Mill and Herbert Spencer have been followed by Stalin and Mussolini.[12]

---

limitations imposed upon man's freedom by circumstance, viz., the past and existing technology. Yet they only reduce the possible number of figures that he can choose in a given situation; within that number he remains free to create his ego. In reading Ortega's work, *The Modern Theme*, we may get the impression that when he opposes vital values to cultural values, by the former he primarily means biological and animal values. Such an interpretation cannot be reconciled with his subsequent description of life as the effort to realize the project that each man is.

10 *Ibid.*, p. 34; "Vives," *Obras completas*, V, pp. 495-6; *Misión del bibliotecario*, p. 211.
11 *Historia como sistema*, p. 34.
12 *Ibid.*, pp. 34-35.

It is laughable in the extreme that historicism should be condemned because it implies that human life is changeable in every way, that in it there is nothing concrete that is stable. For substantial change is the condition of progress, which is possible to man only because he is not linked today to what he was yesterday and trapped forever in a being that is already but can move from it into another. "The mutable condition has thus its ontological virtue and grace, and invites one to recall Galileo's words: *I detrattori della corruttibilità meriterebber d'esser cangiati in statue.*"[13]

Two of Ortega's preceding statements have probably perplexed the reader. On the one hand, Ortega repeats that each ego consists in a project or program and this is also the meaning of his assertion that the subject of the drama in which man's life consists is not prior to the drama itself. On the other hand, he constantly affirms that each man, each ego, must create the figure of his own life. Does he admit two egos? His early formula, "I am I and the circumstance," seems to favor such an interpretation. If he admits two egos, what would the first ego be, the one that plans the project, i.e., the second ego? Ortega alludes to the problem in the objection already mentioned before, "there can be no program without somebody having it," which he leaves unanswered. In another place he defines man as a desire, as an absolute desire, to be. He holds that to subsist means that each man desires to realize his own particular ego. Obviously, such a being already exists, since otherwise, it could not desire to be. Yet such a being is in jeopardy, as it were, since only a being that is uncertain of being in the next instant can experience to be.[14] Ortega again leaves the difficulty unsolved.

His commentary on a text of Aristotle concerning the structure of thought may perhaps throw some light on the question, for he holds that both thought and life possess the same type of reality. Thought consists in a progress towards itself; it is a movement *sui generis*. Movements in the strict sense—alteration, quantitative change, local movement—have a terminus and cease when they reach it. Thought, on the contrary, consists in a constantly restarted motion. It also reaches its goal, but its goal is the potency itself once liberated or actualized, which always emerges as potency

---

[13] *Ibid.*, p. 43.
[14] *En torno a Galileo*, p. 32.

demanding new actualizations. Hence thought is a type of motion that does not end when it reaches its goal because its terminus *ad quem* is identical with its terminus *a quo,* and when the former reaches its perfection in the latter, it emerges as a potency that demands new actualizations. Since life is a movement of the same kind as thought, Ortega perhaps conceives the entity that strives to be as life itself in a moment of its actualization, emerging anew as potency that demands further actualizations *in infinitum.*[15]

One thing is certain, Ortega does not and cannot admit any substantial and permanent entity behind the project that is the ego. He cannot think of the body, or the soul, or the substantial unity of both as the entity that plans to be this or that, for body and soul pertain to or are parts of circumstance. Nor does he refer to spirit, understood as substance, as a permanent and essentially identical nature. "I am not interested in the so-called spirit, a confused idea laden with magical reflexes."[16] In another passage, where he speaks against those whom he calls knights-errant of the spirit, such as Descartes, Hegel, and others, he writes: "But it happened that in the effort to comprehend the human element as a spiritual reality, things did not go any better: human phenomena showed the same resistance, the same stubborn reluctance to let themselves be hemmed in by concepts."[17] The reason for this failure is that Descartes and the others conceived spirit as *res.* In traditional ontology the term *res* is always connected with the term nature, either as synonymous with it or in the sense that nature is the true *res,* and, of course, nature is conceived as something stable, fixed, and identical—properties that pertain only to a concept. If anything, in the world, spirit is identity and, therefore, a *res,* no matter how subtle or ethereal. Spirit has a static consistency; it is already what it is and can be.[18]

Man's authentic being is not a nature. "Man has no nature."[19] What could be called man's nature is, first, his body and soul, which are not man, but a part of circumstance, and, secondly, the past which lives in the present in the form of having been, and includes the belief on which man is grounded, subjectively considered—objectively they pertain to circumstance. Man's body and

---

[15] "Prólogo" a la *Historia de la filosofía* de Emile Brehier, pp. 409 ff.
[16] *Meditación de la técnica,* p. 338.
[17] *Historia como sistema,* pp. 25 ff.
[18] *Ibid.*
[19] "Vives," pp. 495-496.

soul can be called this nature, for they experience scarcely any mutation, whereas life changes substantially. But man is not his body; he finds himself with a body and he must live with it, whether it is weak or strong, healthy or sick. Nor is a man his soul; he finds that he has a soul, and that he must use it in order to live. Body and soul are things, whereas the ego is not a thing but a project, an unending struggle to be what he has to be.[20]

The past is a part of life. Before us lie the different possibilities of being, but behind us lies what we have been, preserved by memory and accumulated in our actual reality. This knowledge negatively acts on what we are or can be. A man's experience in life is made up not only of his past personal experiences but also of the past of his ancestors, transmitted to him by society. The past forms a part of present life in the form of having been. Life as reality is absolute presence, and nothing can be said to be unless it is present and actual. Therefore, if there is a past, it has to be as present and presently acting in us. In fact, if we analyze what we are now, we discover that our present life is composed of what we have been personally and collectively. If being is understood in its traditional sense as something that already is, as something fixed, static, and invariable, man's only being is his past, what he has been.[21]

Man's beliefs are not actually distinct from his past. They are the convictions he possesses concerning the nature of things, of other men, and of himself. Only in the light of such convictions can he choose among the different possibilities open to him and live. Beliefs constitute the basic stratum of our lives; they are the ground beneath our feet, and for this reason we say that man is grounded on them.[22] Beliefs are not merely ideas, but rather ideas in which a man firmly believes. As ideas, or from the intellectual point of view, they may be incoherent, but as beliefs they always

[20] *Historia como sistema*, p. 35; *Meditación de la técnica*, p. 339.
[21] *Historia como sistema*, p. 39; "Un rasgo de la vida alemana," pp. 199 ff.
[22] *Ideas y creencias*, p. 392: "El hombre, en el fondo, es crédulo o, lo que es igual, el estrato más profundo de nuestra vida, el que sostiene y porta todos los demás, está formado por creencias." *Ibid.*, pp. 387-388: "Las creencias constituyen la base de nuestra vida, el terreno sobre que acontece. Porque ellas nos ponen delante lo que para nosostros es la realidad misma. Toda nuestra conducta, incluso la intelectual, depende de cuál sea el sistema de nuestras creencias auténticas. En ellas 'vivimos, nos movemos y somos.' Por lo mismo, no solemos tener conciencia expresa de ellas, no las pensamos, simo que actuan latentes, como implicaciones de cuanto expresamente hacemos o pensamos." Cf. also *Historia como sistema*, p. 18.

constitute a system. In other words, even if from the logical point of view they lack articulation, they nonetheless possess a vital structure. Hence they always possess an architecture and function as a hierarchy. In every human life there are beliefs that are basic, fundamental, and radical, and there are others that are secondary, derived from the former and upheld by them. Their structure and hierarchy make it possible for us to discover their hidden order and to understand our own life and the life of others, both present and past. Hence the diagnosis of any human existence, whether of an individual, a people, or a culture, must begin by analyzing its system of convictions, and above all by establishing the fundamental and decisive belief, sustaining and vivifying the others.[23] To the affirmation that beliefs constitute the deepest stratum of our lives Ortega adds a note: "Let us leave the question of whether beneath this deepest stratum there is still something else, a metaphysical ground that not even our beliefs reach untouched."[24] It is evident that once again Ortega refuses to discuss a problem of capital importance.

Circumstance

Circumstance, as a dimension of life, means everything except the ego. We are not allowed to preselect the circumstance in which we must live, for we find ourselves submerged in it. Circumstance is constituted by the contents of our beliefs, namely, by "what is true reality for us." Not only our environment, or the world in which we happen to live, but also our body and soul belong to circumstance. Body and soul are not the ego, which is a project or program that must be realized or actualized, but things with which the ego finds itself and which it must use in order to live.[25]

Although beliefs are the authentic reality for us, they are not primary and pure reality.[26] The terms nature, world, and circumstance are man's interpretations of what he primarily encounters

[23] *Historia como sistema,* pp. 14-15.
[24] *Ideas y creencias,* p. 392, n. 1: "Dejemos intacta la cuestión de si bajo ese estrato más profundo no hay aún algo más, un fondo metafísico al que ni siquiera llegan nuestras creencias."
[25] *Historia como sistema,* pp. 32 ff.; *Meditación de la técnica,* p. 339.
[26] *Ideas y creencias,* p. 405: "Lo que solemos llamar realidad o 'mundo exterior' no es ya la realidad primaria y desnuda de toda interpretación humana, sino que es lo que creemos, con firme y consolidada creencia, ser la realidad."

in life—a sum of helps and obstacles *(facilidades y dificultades)*. Nature and world are two concepts that qualify their content as something that is there and that exists by itself, independent of man. The same is true of the term thing, which means something endowed with a fixed, determinate, and independent being. All this is an intellectual interpretation of what we originally meet around us. What first confronts us has no being apart from and independently of us; it consists in helps and obstacles regarding the project each of us is. Only in relation to our program or project is a thing an advantage or a difficulty, and according to our project the advantages or difficulties which make up the pure and primary circumstances will be such and such, greater or smaller. Why the world is different for each epoch and each man is explained by this fact.[27] For example, the authentic reality of the earth is without figure or mode of being. It is an enigma. If it is considered in its pure and primary consistence or "essence," it is the ground that momentarily sustains us. It is something that has helped us to escape from danger, but at the same time it separates us from our wife and children. At times it is laboriously uphill and at other times invitingly downhill. Hence in itself, and stripped bare of our ideas, earth is not a thing but an uncertain complex of advantages and difficulties in relation to our lives.[28] In this sense the authentic and primary reality has no figure; it is an enigma. Man reacts to it by releasing his intellectual mechanism which primarily is imagination.[29]

Solution of the Realism-Idealism Antinomy

A philosophy that starts from human life as from radical reality, Ortega contends, *a radice* surpasses the realism-idealism antinomy. For realism things are the primary reality while for idealism the primary reality is the ego, which projects the world. Life is neither the ego nor things, but an interaction between both. The ego has no reality independent of life nor do things, which are man's interpretations of what he finds in life. He denies that a "I myself" exists except vis à vis other things. At the same time such other things exist only insofar as they exist for me. While I am not such things and they are not me, nevertheless I do not exist

[27] *Meditación de la técnica*, pp. 339-340.
[28] *Ideas y creencias*, p. 400.
[29] *Ibid.*

without them nor do they exist without me. Hence Ortega opposes both idealism and realism.[30]

Thus in a philosophy that finds its starting point in life the antinomy between idealism and realism disappears. Ortega, it seems, does not have exact ideas of these epistemological positions and their different historical nuances. If his attempted solution of the antinomy realism-idealism is to have any meaning, he must write "enigma" instead of "things," for, according to him, the terms thing and circumstance are subjective, idealistic interpretations of pure reality.

Identical Essential Structure of Man

Although Ortega describes life as substantial change, he writes that "there is an identical essential structure of life," for otherwise the history of human lives would be impossible.[31] In the first place, man's life starts from certain radical convictions concerning world and his own position in it. Moreover, every life finds itself in a given circumstance that includes a given technology. Thus ideology and technology are two essential factors of human life; a comprehensive study would discover other dimensions in our life, but "for the moment these two will suffice."[32]

History does not consist in investigating the characters of men, but in finding out how men have lived their lives, since life is not man or the subject who lives, but the interaction between the ego and the world. History is not primarily psychology, but a reconstruction of the drama that has taken place between men and the world. In a given world or circumstance men of the most different psychologies face a common and unavoidable repertory of problems that give their existence an identical fundamental structure, while their subjective differences are merely subordinate and accidental.[33]

At first sight the reader may get the impression that there is a contradiction between this and Ortega's repeated assertion that the substance of life is change and instability and that there is no "permanency of forms in human life."[34] However, it is possible to

---

[30] "Filosofía pura," *Obras*, p. 58.
[31] *En torno a Galileo*, pp. 26 and 19; "Vives," pp. 29 ff.
[32] *En torno a Galileo*, pp. 29 ff.
[33] *Ibid.*
[34] *Apuntes sobre el pensamiento*, p. 538.

reconcile these affirmations. First, in the context of Ortega's philosophy it is possible to admit an abstract and "unreal" structure of life which is identical in all men. Thus in every human life there are at least an ideology and a technology, even if their concrete contents are different. Ortega's statement on the generic and specific identity of human life should also be interpreted in a formal or unreal sense, since genus and species are abstract concepts and for him such concepts are not real. Secondly, life's real content itself can be fundamentally the same in a given period and place because of the fact that the beliefs and ideas by which men live, the figures of being they have decided to be, and consequently the helps and obstacles they meet, are fundamentally identical. It is obvious that in this case the identity would be relative to a given period or place, and that it would not imply a substantial stability in the vital reality, which would continue being a task and a "substantial" change.

Generations

Some modifications occur in the world that do not affect its general figure. In such cases man does not get the impression that the world has changed but that something has changed in the world.[35] However, there are other modifications that affect the existing world itself and the structure of the vital drama. Such changes are properly historical. How can they be explained or what is their cause? Normally up to the age of twenty-five a man is dedicated to learning, to assimilating the already made world which consists of the systems of convictions prevalent at the time. At about twenty-five he begins to live an independent life, and since he is not satisfied with the existing world for the simple reason that his problems and needs are distinct from the problems and needs of those who made it, he also starts to remake or reshape the world. This is true not only of the few but of all young men living at a given time. Each one of them intervenes in one field or another; some act upon art, others upon religion, the different sciences, industry, or politics; yet all together act upon the whole world. Even if the modifications caused in each field are small, the world will present a different profile to the following generation.

[35] *En torno a Galileo*, pp. 29 ff.

Therefore, the reason of historical changes is the fact that some men die and other are born, and that life is time and limited time, as Dilthey says and Heidegger repeats. In other words, in a given period of time there exist the young, the mature, and the old.[36] This implies that every historical actuality, every present, involves three distinct times or three great vital dimensions. For some today is a period of twenty years, for others forty years, for still others sixty years. All those who live at the same time are contemporary but not all are coetaneous, for the coetaneous are only those who coincide in their problems and ideas and consequently contribute to the formation of the world in an equal or similar fashion. The same chronological time includes three different vital times. History changes because of this internal lack of equilibrium. If all those who are contemporary were coetaneous, no basic or radical change would be possible, and history would come to an end.

All those who are coetaneous constitute a generation,[37] which, according to Ortega, lasts fifteen years. When historical changes are greater than usual, the existing generations are decisive and mark historical epochs.[38] Ortega very effectively uses the idea and the method of generations in his interpretation of historical events.[39]

Life and Philosophy

What compels man to philosophize is his concrete life as radical reality existing previous to all theories. Philosophy has a real meaning when it is a task imposed upon man by the circumstance he encounters in his life. A man usually knows what to do because he has a system of beliefs on which he is grounded. However, sometimes such beliefs fail either totally or partially, and he is at a loss about what to do. Yet he cannot cease to act, for life consists in doing something concrete here and now, in having to choose here and now among different possibilities. What can a man do in such a situation, where he does not know what to do and yet must do something? He releases the mechanism of his thought so as to find out what to do. Historically, thought has adopted different forms: the sapiential, the magical, and so on. Knowledge

---

[36] *Ibid.*
[37] *Ibid.*, pp. 38 ff.; *El tema de nuestro tiempo*, pp. 145 ff.
[38] *En torno a Galileo*, pp. 69 ff.
[39] *Ibid.*, pp. 43 ff.

or philosophical thought is one of these forms, and it emerged in Greece in the seventh or sixth century before Christ. In other words, Western man was compelled to philosophize at that particular period because he had to continue living, and other types of thought failed to help him in his vital struggle.[40]

The method of philosophy, or the instrument by which man captures radical reality, is vital reason. In the last analysis, vital reason is identical with life itself, in the sense that since life is a continuous making, it must constantly consider and weigh the advantages and difficulties of the situation, and must choose among the possible alternatives. In other words, it must reason. Because life is essentially time, history, vital reason is also historical reason. Its method is narration, and it uses concrete and "occasional" concepts of variable content rather than Eleatic—that is, universal and identical—notions.[41]

II

EVALUATION

Life, each man's life, is the radical reality, Ortega holds, because every other reality is rooted in it in the sense that every other reality must in one way or another appear within it. This argument is surprising. It implies, first, that nothing is or can be a reality unless in one way or another it appears within life, and, secondly, that life itself is not rooted in any more basic reality. As regards the first implication, it is true that in a man's vital dealings with the world things must actually appear in his life or must be referred to it. But to conclude from this fact that nothing is or can be a reality unless it appears within life, is arbitrarily to change and restrict the meaning of the term reality. Of course, in the epistemological order a thing can only be a reality for an individual if it is present to his mind. But epistemology should not be confused with ontology. The second implication, namely, that life is a radical and not a derivative reality, is likewise

---

[40] *Apuntes sobre el pensamiento*, pp. 529 ff.
[41] Cf. Felix Alluntis, "The 'Vital and Historical Reason' of José Ortega y Gasset," *Franciscan Studies*, XV (March, 1955), 60-78

arbitrary. Every man's life appears in the world and consequently is rooted in it.

Ortega describes life as autofabrication and the ego or man as a project, as something that as yet is not but aspires to be. An obvious objection to this is that there can be no project without someone who fashions it. Ortega is aware of this difficulty and refers to it, but he leaves it unanswered. However, even if he should admit a previous subject, such a subject would not be for him the real man, whom he defines as something that as yet is not. Here is seen Ortega's radical error. Obviously, we can speak of an ego, a personality, or a character that is the result of man's actions. But such a personality is accidental and presupposes a permanent subject or ego. This permanent ego constitutes man and does not "find itself with a body and a soul," as Ortega says, for without body and soul there is no ego or man, who is the substantial and intelligent unity of both.

Doubtless, man is a historical being; in large measure he decides the course of his life and his actions and he can project a given personality. However, he is not a mere capacity to be or a mere potency; he has an actuality, an essential entity, that is the subject of his accidental realizations. From its very beginning, human life or existence possesses an essence, or nature, and meaning that is universally valid for all men, that does not come from us, and that cannot be altered in any way by human choice or decision. Far from excluding each other, essential identity and historicity imply each other. To have stressed freedom of the human person against all types of determinism, as many representatives of recent philosophies do, is one of Ortega's merits. But like many of his contemporaries he exaggerates when, in accordance with his fundamental tenet that man has no stable being, he affirms that the ego does not "enjoy or suffer" freedom, but is essentially freedom. Man is not freedom, which presupposes a subject, but a free being.

Because man is constitutively free, Ortega adds, he is a moral being. He can make his life either in an authentic or in an inauthentic way; in the first case his life will be morally good, in the second case it will be morally evil. Taken in itself, the statement that moral goodness is authenticity can be interpreted in an acceptable sense. If life is authentic, that is, if it is in agreement with human nature adequately considered, it will be good. However, Ortega, who denies that man has a nature, does not understand authenticity in this sense. For him authentic or morally good life means a life that is faithful to the project or program every man is or rather has decided to be. It is not easy to understand the meaning of this statement. If man freely creates the figure of being he is going to be, why may he not act against it and even change it? The statement would make sense if each man's authentic being, the project he is, did not depend on him but had been imposed upon him, as Ortega held in earlier texts. In any case, for Ortega morality is relative, there are as many moralities as there are men. He explicitly affirms the relativistic character of his vital morality even in his earlier works.[42] Those who have attempted to prove that Ortega is not a moral relativist have failed to prove their point.[43]

The writer has no quarrel with Ortega's affirmation that circumstance in a sense is a dimension of human life or existence—*dasein*—but he cannot accept the denial of objective value in our concepts implied in his thesis that primary and pure reality is an enigma and that the terms world, circumstance, and thing are subjective interpretations of ultimate reality. In view of such Kantian subjectivism it is hard to accept or even to understand Ortega's contention that his philosophy *a radice* overcomes the antinomy between realism and idealism. With regard to this asserted solution of the realism-idealism antinomy several further observations are in order. First, Ortega inaccurately asserts that realism professes the primacy of things over the ego. Most certainly moderate realism has never held such a thesis, since by being or *res* it has always understood everything that is or can be, including the ego. By conceiving being as something fixed and stable Ortega has retained only the Parmenidean concept of being. Secondly, it has been previously noted that the foundation of his attempted solution of the antinomy, namely, that everything deserving the name or reality must appear in one way or another in life, cannot be accepted. Thirdly, Ortega's reason for his rejection of idealism, namely, that our life includes both the ego and things,

---

[42] Cf. *Meditaciones del Quijote, Obras completas*, I, pp. 305 and 316; *España invertebrada*, l.c., p. 102; *El espectador*, IV, l.c. II, pp. 359 and 407.
[43] Cf. Pedro Laín Entralgo, "Los Católicos y Ortega," *Cuadernos hispanoamericanos* 101 (1958), p. 289; José Luis L. Aranguren, *La ética de Ortega* (Madrid: Taurus, 1958), pp. 45-49; Felix Alluntis, "Social and Political Ideas of José Ortega y Gasset," *The New Scholasticism* XXXIX (October, 1965), pp. 467-491.

that the ego never finds itself without things, is not conclusive. Idealism holds that things derive from the ego or are its projections, and this contention is not refuted by the fact that the ego always finds itself together with things. There is no contradiction in saying that the ego finds itself with things elaborated by itself—which, in the final analysis, is what Ortega himself holds since for him things are subjective interpretations of pure reality, which is an enigma.

Ortega speaks of the essential structure of life. However, with regard to concrete forms of life, which are for him its only real forms, he can only admit an identity of vital structure that is relative to a given period of history. This is a consequence of his initial theses that radical reality is life and life is substantial change. In such a case what explanation can be given for the constant emergence of identical conceptions of life and circumstantial reality in different periods of history, or the subsistence of identical values in the estimation of most diverse individuals and peoples throughout the centuries? It cannot be replied that such a uniformity can be explained by men's generic and specific identity, for according to Ortega the generic and specific are abstract and unreal.

Ortega's explanation of the origin of knowledge contains a great deal of truth. Many readers will possibly accept it with regard to empirical sciences and practical philosophy, but not with regard to speculative philosophy, which, it is said, seeks knowledge for the sake of knowledge. The writer is of the opinion that all knowledge, including so-called theoretical philosophy, is practical. Rational exigencies are also vital, and man needs to solve speculative problems in order to satisfy his inner needs and live an integral human life. Ortega's analyses concerning historical changes and crises, as well as his idea of generations and the use of it in historical exegesis, offer positive and lasting contributions.

12

SCHOLASTICISM, NOMINALISM, AND MARTIN LUTHER

by

RICHARD P. DESHARNAIS, C.S.C.

The Second Vatican Council's call for a re-evaluation of many historical and philosophical positions was anticipated in part by several works that investigated late scholasticism, and in particular the nature of nominalism. Traditionally, this latter mode of thought has been considered highly influential in the formation of Lutheranism. However, despite the many monographs written on individual late scholastics, few of them did anything but hint at the precise influence that nominalism exerted on the actual formation of Luther's thought. The purpose of this article is to review certain of these works on late scholasticism and to indicate a way in which Luther was related to both.

Over the past thirty years, the work of Etienne Gilson and others has stressed the fact that scholasticism, far from being a single monolithic system, involves a great deal of uniqueness in its various currents and individual contributors.[1] This conclusion, grounded on painstaking research into medieval manuscripts, has paved the way for considering anew several late scholastic currents, and nominalism as well, in terms other than they have hitherto been investigated.

Most recently, it has been discovered that former opinions of nominalism would vary, depending upon whether one belonged to the Thomistic, Scotistic, or Ockhamistic school. It was found likewise that opinions of its influence on Luther would differ according

---

[1] A representative statement to this effect is that of A. Maurer, *Medieval Philosophy* (N. Y.: Random House, 1962), p. 374: "The term 'Medieval Philosophy' does not designate one particular type of philosophy. It is simply a name for the philosophizing that took place within the historical period called the Middle Ages, and this philosophizing exhibits great variety and diversity. There is no one philosophical system called medieval philosophy."

to this "school approach," if one would choose to characterize his thought from the viewpoint of reformation history.[2]

Adherents to the Thomistic school, for instance, would hold that medieval philosophy reached its apex in the works of Aquinas. Due to the accidents of history, since men of sufficiently high intellectual calibre to perpetuate his doctrine were lacking, a great decline set in after the construction of his masterly synthesis. Consistent with this view, Thomists have held it as a ruling principle that this decline of Thomistic learning contributed to the development of the specifically reformation doctrines of Martin Luther.

Contrary to the Thomistic position, those belonging to Franciscan schools, whether of Scotus or Ockham, would tend to defend the philosophico-theological orthodoxy of their masters. They sought for the beginnings of Lutheran doctrine in the later developments made in their doctrines by such men as Peter of Ailly and the so-called "Last of the Scholastics," Gabriel Biel. Such Franciscan scholars, like the members of the Thomistic School, insisted generally that nominalism was a corruptive influence on Martin Luther and eventually prepared for logically necessary doctrines found within the German reformation.

A totally different course of study was pursued by the historians of the reformation. They looked upon the movement, not at all from the viewpoint of scholasticism and nominalism, but rather as a conscious departure from both and a return to the thought of St. Paul and St. Augustine.

As can be seen, none of these approaches exemplifies a wholly unprejudiced perspective for scientifically coming to grips with the questions of either the precise nature of nominalism or its reputed influence on Luther. Steps towards a more impartial approach on these questions were taken by men such as Cardinal Franziskus Ehrle and Paul Vignaux. Their pioneer work finally made way for a totally new assessment of late scholasticism by today's authors. Ehrle, for instance, was the first to call attention to the fact that nominalism ought not to be approached from an overly onesided treatment of Ockham alone, nor solely from the viewpoint of his

---

[2] For this school interpretation of late scholasticism, cf. H. Oberman, *The Harvest of Medieval Theology: Gabriel Biel and Late Medieval Nominalism* (Cambridge: Harvard University Press, 1963), pp. 1-4. Hereafter cited as *The Harvest* . . .

logic.³ With like perspicacity, Vignaux voiced the opinion that it must not be seen simply as a way of reasoning based upon a specifically epistemological theory.⁴ Similar findings indicated that nominalism need not necessarily be considered as being opposed to a valid metaphysics⁵ or to the principle of causality.⁶ With these cautions well spelled out, authors were led to question the positive nature of nominalism and how practically it influenced Luther.

A partial response to these inquiries came as a result of the work done on the manuscripts of the reputed founder of nominalism, William of Ockham, and his followers. Done largely by Franciscan scholars under the leadership of Philotheus Boehner, this work yielded that nominalism was far more sophisticated and broader in influence on late scholasticism than had been thought and that, so far as Ockham was concerned, it was far from being a destructive force in philosophy. Indeed, Ockham was demonstrated to be traditional on several scores. The difference between his system and those preceding it lay more in the new emphases called for by the ecclesiastical condemnations of Paris and Oxford in 1270 and especially in 1277. As a result, the philosophies of Ockham and his followers were not, and, indeed, could not be, the presentation of neat, precise, and calm categories. Rather, they exemplified the dynamism and broadness called for by the Church, and stressed more than ever before the full liberty of God over all the beings of creation. In Ockham's case, at least, there is evidence of a very positive and rich metaphysics that has been aptly described as a "realistic conceptualism."⁷

It should be immediately noted that "conceptualism" in this context does not in the least imply that Ockham's metaphysics was divorced from contact with real things. It neither destroys men's capacity to arrive at the natural knowledge of God's existence nor

---

[3] F. Ehrle, "Der Sentenzenkommentar Peters von Candia," *Franziskanische Studien* IX (1925), p. 106.

[4] This view, for instance, was held, though not exclusively, by P. Vignaux, *Nominalisme au XIVe siècle* (Montréal: Lycée S.-Albert le Grand, 1948), p. 11.

[5] L. Meier, "Research done on the Ockhamism of Luther at Erfurt," *Archivum franciscanum historicum* XLIII (1950), pp. 56-67.

[6] G. Manser, "Drei Zweifler am Kausalprinzip im XIV. Jahrhundert," *Jahrbuch für Philosophie und spekulative Theologie* XVII (1912), pp. 291-305 and 405-437.

[7] Ph. Boehner, "The Metaphysics of Ockham," *Review of Metaphysics* I (1947-1948), pp. 57-86.

prevents them from achieving some worthwhile cognizance of the divine nature and God's dealings with the world.

After vindicating Ockham of unorthodoxy and anti-traditionalism, there still remained the question as to whether the subsequent development of his thought might account for some of the origins of the Protestant reformation within the years 1347-1517. Work has been done in this area, but the precise nature of nominalism has not at this date been made fully clear.

Two efforts towards assessing the nature of post-Ockhamist thought have been executed, one by Heiko Oberman of Harvard University[8] and the other by Damascus Trapp, editor of the official Augustinian review for the German provinces of his order.[9] While Oberman advocates four distinct currents within nominalism and Trapp insists that only two such divisions are discernible, their studies point out that, on extrinsic evidence at least, two different spirits animated scholastic and nominalist writing at the end of the medieval period. One of these was traditional in tone and was respectful of the work done in previous ages. The second, far from presenting a unified and absolutely consistent or logical doctrine, evidently favored daring in criticism and questioned even the most sacrosanct of traditional scholastic doctrines.

From these researches and in an effort to characterize the precise nature of nominalism, there appear three alternatives. First, there is the opinion of those who hold that it is a form of thought which would declare natural reason completely insufficient to attain any knowledge of God and suprasensibles. In this view, nominalism would be an escapist system in which its adherents turn to faith as the only means of security in an utterly uncertain and unknowable world. A second view considers nominalism as that system which, while preserving the supremacy of faith, makes philosophy its true handmaiden. Still a third alternative holds nominalism to be that mode of thinking which is, at one and the same time, preoccupied with the critical issues of certitude and truth, while attempting to build a better and more solid philosophical underpinning for orthodox theological views. In this last position, the critical spirit of nominalists is not such that they consider themselves as abandoning

---

[8] H. Oberman, "Some Notes on the Theology of Nominalism," *Harvard Theological Review* LIII (1960), pp. 47-76.

[9] D. Trapp, "Augustinian Theology in the Fourteenth Century" *Augustiniana* VI (1956), pp. 146-274.

traditional thought but rather as improving upon it. Its criticism, then, would not necessarily be negative but constructive.

The first of these assessments is insufficient to explain the complexity of what has come to be understood as the major task of the nominalist enterprise. It is not based on a study of the sources and has largely been disregarded by the research already done on late scholasticism. Nominalism cannot be considered as a system which negates the whole of philosophy.

The second view is good, but it implies that late scholastics were seeking for an entirely new philosophy. Recent scholarship has indicated that the majority of nominalists, while at times severely critical of much of earlier scholasticism, were conscious of their fundamental agreement with the substance of traditional thinking and gave evidence of such agreement. For this reason the second position must be disregarded together with the first.

Only the third opinion seems to fit the case for an adequate description of nominalism. It accounts well for the critical dimension in late scholastic thought as well as for the possibility of some of its weaknesses so as to form two divergent streams within the nominalist movement. This opinion likewise could account for the broad scope of argumentation that is so frequently based on the classic distinction between God's absolute and ordained power. It was under the dialectics of this philosophical distinction that late scholastics, with growing frequency, brought forth their views upon man's knowing and willing powers as well as demonstrating to what extent he could naturally know God's existence, nature and his legislative powers over the world and man.

It has been said that this distinction is produced by the human mind for the purpose of understanding more about God's nature as well as the extent to which God can influence the present world order.[10] While it was utilized from the dawn of scholasticism[11] and its terms were deemed especially helpful to indicate something of the limits discernible among the actually un-

[10] H. Oberman, *The Harvest* ..., p. 466.
[11] While it is preferred here to treat of the general nature and influence of this distinction in late scholasticism, a fairly complete handling of it from Hugh of St. Victor to and including St. Thomas Aquinas may be found in the unpublished thesis of R. Desharnais, *History of the Distinction between God's Absolute and Ordained Power and Its Influence on Martin Luther* (Washington, D. C.: Catholic University of America, 1966), pp. 38-110.

limited and varied capacities God has in dealing with a contingent order of things, it was used widely by late scholastics as a guide in much of their philosophical and theological inquiries.

The divine ordained power *(potentia ordinata)* is posited by men to indicate both God's dealing with the order which he has definitely established as well as the ways in which he may choose to act towards his *opera ad extra*. As generally understood, this is a power which is regulated by both the natural and revealed laws established by him and discoverable by men. It has been determined that this power is understood to be executed together with God's wisdom, goodness, and justice. Wherever scholastics use the terms: *in statu isto, stante lege, secundum leges ordinatas et institutas a Deo*, they refer in context to this ordained power of God.[12]

The divine absolute power *(potentia absoluta)* signifies the illimitable ways in which God can act towards creatures. It implies that the actual, contingent order of things is not under discussion. It is a way of acting, rooted in the freedom of the divine nature itself, which theoretically can *in se* either suspend or transcend the *modus essendi et operandi* of all finite things. It is conditioned only by the principle of noncontradiction.[13]

Research done into the use of this distinction in late scholasticism indicates that it was not because of any variant interpretation of it that two separate nominalist schools might be distinguished. Rather, it seems more probable that it was because of a peculiar type of speculation deriving from it which made way for them. This speculation concerns itself with many philosophical and theological issues. For instance, despite their sometimes unscientific attitude towards William of Ockham, Bengt Hüggland has indicated the utility this distinction had for his delineating of the precise limits of faith and reason or of philosophy and theology,[14] while Carl Feckes, in his pioneer work on the subject, speaks of the utility of it for late scholastic theories of justification,[15] and Erwin Iserloh finds a similar function for it as regards late scholasticism's theories of grace and the sacraments.[16]

---

[12] H. Oberman, *The Harvest* . . . , p. 473.
[13] *Ibidem.*
[14] B. Hägglund, *Theologie und Philosophie bei Luther und in der occamistischen Tradition* (Lund: C. Gleerup, 1955), pp. 34f and 40.
[15] C. Feckes, *Die Rechtfertigungslehre des Gabriel Biel und ihre Stellung innerhalb der nominalistischen Schule* (Münster: Aschendorff, 1925).
[16] E. Iserloh, *Gnade und Eucharistie in der philosophischen Theologie des*

However, it was not until Oberman had determined the areas in which this distinction was used by nominalists that a properly philosophical assessment of its fuller influence could be written.[17] With its help, Oberman has said, nominalists were able to speculate not only upon the precise relationship between reason and faith, but also to verify the contingency of the world, and to indicate clearly how God's liberty exceeds the present world order as well as the order of his revelation. Because of this distinction scholastics could move out, over, and beyond the circle of revealed facts to deal precisely with the various possibilities and changes God could effect in the observable world order as well as in the order of grace. Finally, it was largely due to the use of this distinction that reason, or philosophy, in the late Middle Ages enjoyed an independence it never experienced before.

These general areas have been appreciated by other scholars who would specify the influence this distinction had as to how it affects the outlook of late scholastics on man's knowing capacities and his power to know about God, how man's will acts might be affected, and finally how they viewed the contingency of the present world order. Several monographs on those scholastics who may be termed major, because of their prominence in the later Middle Ages, namely, Ockham (1280-1350), Peter of Ailly (1350-1420), Gabriel Biel (1410-1495), Jodocus Trutvetter (1460-1519) and Batholomaeus Arnold of Usingen (1465-1532), have indicated that despite their repeated and insistent use of the distinction they maintained a link with and even furthered a deepening of the metaphysics of God which was characteristic of earlier medieval thought. Webbering,[18] Boehner,[19] and Oakley[20] are among the many who now defend the cogency and validity of Ockham's epistemology and metaphysics and his position on the natural moral law. Similarly, after a long period of doctrinal misinterpretation and misrepresentation, Peter of Ailly has emerged in recent study as having a rich

---

Wilhelm von Ockham: Ihre Bedeutung für die Ursachen der Reformation (Wiesbaden: F. Steiner, 1956).

[17] Cf. note 8 above.

[18] D. Webbering, *The Theory of Demonstration According to William of Ockham* (St. Bonaventure, New York: Franciscan Institute, 1953).

[19] Ph. Boehner (E. Buyaert ed.), *Collected Articles on Ockham* (St. Bonaventure, New York: Franciscan Institute, 1958).

[20] F. Oakley, "Medieval Theories of Natural Law: William of Ockham and the Significance of the Voluntarist Tradition," *Natural Law Forum* VI (1961), pp. 65-83.

theory of knowledge and metaphysics through the efforts of such writers as Meller,[21] Oakley,[22] and others. Oberman's work on Gabriel Biel settles for once and all the orthodoxy and richness of Biel's contributions to the topics under discussion.[23] Although monographs on Bartholomaeus of Usingen and Jodocus Trutvetter are rather old, they indicate, after a thorough study of the manuscripts, that a similar exoneration from any taints of unorthodoxy holds for their doctrine. Again, far from being unusual or out of keeping with the high attainment of their predecessors in epistemology, metaphysics, and ethics, their doctrine stands in sharp contrast to other nominalists of their time.[24]

In brief, then, all the writings of these men who are termed major scholastics are traditional in character because of the balanced effect their use of the distinction produced in their work. This distinction guided their epistemological theory and their defense that man could have a natural awareness of God's existence and a certain knowledge of his nature. The distinction was a formidable aid to them as well in their metaphysics where there were questions pertaining to the contingency of the present world order and the stability of the moral law in face of the divine liberty.

Less thoroughly investigated, but sufficient for drawing some conclusions as to its effect on Reformation thought, is the work that has been done on that stream of minor scholastics who utilized the distinction between God's absolute and ordained power to reach totally different conclusions from those of the men just mentioned. This trend of thought has been found to begin from a time immediately subsequent to Ockham in the anonymous work entitled the *Centiloquium*, or in its longer title, the *Summa seu tractatus de principiis et philosophicis*.[25] This work of one hundred propositions or "sayings" evidently was meant to be the introduction to a larger

---

[21] B. Meller, *Studien zur Erkenntnislehre des Peter von Ailly* (Freiburg im Breisgau: Herder, 1954).

[22] F. Oakley, *The Political Thought of Pierre d'Ailly* (New Haven: Yale University Press, 1964).

[23] Cf. note 2 above.

[24] N. Paulus, "Der Augustiner Bartholomäus Arnoldi von Usingen, Luthers Lehrer und Gegner," *Strassburgher theologischer Studien* I (1893), pp. 207-342; and G. Plitt, *Jodokus Trutfetter von Eisenach der Lehrer Luthers in seinem Wirken geschildert* (Erlangen: A. Deichert, 1876).

[25] A critical edition of the *Centiloquium* is contained in *Franciscan Studies* I (March, 1941), pp. 58-72; (June), pp. 35-54; (September), pp. 62-70; II (March, 1942), pp. 42-60; (June), pp. 146-157; (September), pp. 251-301.

treatise and includes many statements on epistemology, man's knowledge of God, man's moral duties, and the distinction between the absolute and ordained power of God.

After an impassioned debate between Philotheus Boehner and Erwin Iserloh on the authorship of the *Centiloquium*, it was determined that, because of its imprecise and impersonally worded text and its careless use of the distinction between God's absolute and ordained power, the *Centiloquium* ought no longer be attributed to Ockham.[26] On the basis of both internal and external evidence, when its thought and his were compared they were found to be unalterably opposed.

Studies on the *Centiloquium* are reticent to name a candidate for its authorship. However, in his manuscript study and notes for a more critical edition, Boehner found that it must be the work of an Englishman. His suspicions became crystallized when he was able to discover many parallels in both literary style and doctrine with the work of Robert Holcot, an English Dominican. He unearthed passages which tend to promote a fideism and a scepticism in almost the exact wording of the text of the *Centiloquium* and identifies them with Holcot's works. More recently, it was discovered that, while Holcot protests his fidelity to the epistemological principles, he has a radically different point of departure for the object of human knowledge from Ockham. While Ockham holds that scientific knowledge consists in the direct proportion between real things and our concepts formed from them, Holcot reverses this position. Human knowledge, he contends, is and can only be of mental propositions without any necessary reference to things. Surprisingly, Holcot attributes this position to Ockham.[27] Other studies of Holcot's doctrine of the divine attributes and the distinction between God's absolute and ordained power in particular indicate that he has adopted a very inconsistent and fideistic doctrine.[28] In addition, he proposed a positivistic moral theory which states that

---

[26] The records of this debate are contained in Ph. Boehner, "The Medieval Crisis of Logic and the Author of the *Centiloquium* attributed to Ockham," *Collected Articles on Ockham*, pp. 351-372, and E. Iserloh, "Um die Echtheit des Centiloquium," *Gregorianum* XXX (1949), pp. 78-103; 309-346.

[27] E. Moody, "A Quodlibetal Question of Robert of Holcot on the Problem of the Objects of Knowledge and Belief," *Speculum* XXXIX (1964), pp. 53-74.

[28] This opinion has been voiced by A. Meissner, *Gotteserkenntnis und Gotteslehre nach dem englischen Dominikanertheologen R. Holkot* (Limberg: Lahn Verlag, 1953), and B. Smalley, *English Friars and Antiquity* (Oxford: At the Clarendon Press, 1960).

man, on his own efforts, can merit eternal beatitude if he does the best that is in him as a human being.[29] In other words, he holds that if one lives according to this standard and fulfills the law, man's final end is achieved.

The conceptualism and Pelagianism evident in both the *Centiloquium* and Robert Holcot's works were furthered by Nicholas of Autrecourt and John of Mirecourt at the University of Paris. While Autrecourt's main preoccupation was with the more speculative questions of man's knowledge of God, Mirecourt's lay with the more practical or ethical questions of man's capacity to achieve his final destiny. The records of the University of Paris indicate that both were condemned for their views which were arrived at largely through their particular use of the distinction between God's absolute and ordained power.[30]

The continuing development of a divergent form of nominalism is easily ascertainable from the same records of the University of Paris which present the thought of Autrecourt and Mirecourt. Under the rectorships of Albert of Saxony, Peter of Bercorio and Simon of Brossa were condemned for "making use of proscribed dialectics on man's knowledge of God,"[31] as were Aegidius of Medun,[32] a Franciscan, Louis of Padua, John of Calore, and Dennis Foullechat.[33] One of the last representatives to bring this deviationist nominalist current up to the time of Luther was John Montesson, over whose doctrines a celebrated inquest was adjudicated under the rectorships of Peter of Ailly and John Gerson, the last leaders of the University of Paris before it lost its pontifical status in the fifteenth century.[34]

Two inevitable conclusions derive from the presentation of this multiplicity of facts. First, there is doctrinal evidence throughout the fourteenth and fifteenth centuries of two different types of nominalism. Secondly, their divergence of viewpoints on the central

---

[29] H. Oberman, "*Faciente quod in se est, Deus non denegat gratiam:* Robert Holcot and the beginnings of Luther's Theology," *Harvard Theological Review* LV (1962), pp. 317-342.

[30] For Nicholas of Autrecourt this record is dated May 20, 1346, and is contained in the *Chartularium Universitatis Parisiensis*, (J. Denifle and A. Chatelain, eds.), (Paris: Delalain, 1889-1897), Volume II, pp. 576-584. For John Mirecourt, it is dated in 1347, and is found in the same volume, pp. 587-590.

[31] *Ibid.*, Volume III, pp. 5ff and 11ff.

[32] *Ibid.*, pp. 21-22.

[33] *Ibid.*, pp. 95f, 108f, and 114-124.

[34] *Ibid.*, pp. 486-496.

issues of late scholasticism rests on their different applications of nominalist demonstrative techniques and on their speculations deriving from the distinction between God's absolute and ordained power. Thus, by the sixteenth century, scholastics were faced with an alternative. Either they could pursue the more orthodox and traditional implications of nominalism or they could use nominalism and in particular the distinction between God's absolute and ordained power to reach conclusions totally out of harmony with these implications for man's knowing and willing capacities, for his knowledge of God's nature, and the stability of the moral law.[35] This is the situation which obtained when Luther came to compose the works for which he remains famous.

Martin Luther and Nominalism

Recent research has uncovered the fact that under the influence of repeatedly using the distinction between God's absolute and ordained power nominalism's characteristic preoccupation with God took two significantly different turns in doctrine. The first, found in the works of all the major scholastics, constitutes a body of doctrine in the high Middle Ages which both harmonizes with and advances the metaphysical aspects of the distinction. The second, found in the works of the minor scholastics, relied excessively on probable reasoning, provoked much agitation under the pretext of being scientifically critical, derogated from man's intellectual power to know God, and, while undermining the very stability of the moral law, paradoxically exalted man's natural, moral sufficiency to attain his own final end. With this background established by the most recent scholarship, it is surprising that so few of the works in question did not even attempt to indicate what relation there is between the two nominalist currents and Luther's thought. This can be done here, it seems, if one is willing chronologically to subject Luther's main works from 1509-1525 to even a simple examination.

Despite a brief interruption in 1505, Luther was under the constant tutelage of Trutvetter and Usingen from 1501-1508. If the information presented on the thought of his teachers is correct,

[35] G. Leff has drawn a clear picture of this secondary, deviationist and nominalist trend in the doctrine he presents in *Gregory of Rimini: Tradition and Innovation in Fourteenth Century Thought* (Manchester, England: University Press, 1961), pp. 20-26.

then Luther certainly had the best that traditional nominalist thought could provide. When he came to study theology in 1507 he was still under the tutelage of these same men. It can therefore be seen that he had a full opportunity to be thoroughly schooled in the traditional type of nominalism. In addition, although his teachers' tradition apparently did not antedate the works of John Buridan, they were fond of citing Ockham, Scotus, and Aquinas. There are no grounds for supposing that they did not faithfully represent the thought of these earlier scholastics. Luther himself was proud to claim Ockham as his beloved master,[36] but it is more probable that he was neither in possession of Ockham's works nor enjoyed a first-hand acquaintance with the other scholastics of the preceding era. It has been claimed that he knew the doctrine of Aquinas, Scotus, and Ockham only from the quotations and notes which he received from his teachers.[37] This still does not imply that Luther received an inferior education, nor does it militate against the fact that he won distinction in all his academic grades.[38]

More important than details of his education are the works which Luther produced from the year 1509, since it is largely by these works that his understanding of scholasticism and its influence upon him can be assessed. Moreover, it appears that from an analysis of his writings, from the marginal notations on St. Augustine's opuscula to his more mature work *On the Enslavement of the Human Will (De servo arbitrio)* in 1525, a fairly complete picture can be drawn of Luther's relationship to scholasticism, nominalism and the distinction between God's absolute and ordained power.

The marginals on Augustine indicate his attachment to Ockham, but they insist that both authors are in agreement.[39] Both are admired for their preoccupation with viewing how God must ultimately fit into the answer to any question. This must be done, it is stated, apart from useless and time-consuming struggles over the meaning of words, figures of speech, or over-reliance on the rules

---

[36] Cf. Luther's *Tischreden* (Weimar: H. Boehlau, 1912-1921), Volume II, p. 516: "Occam, magister meus"; *Werke* (Weimar: H. Boehlau, 1883-1948), Volume VI, p. 195: "Sum occamicae factionis"; *ibid.*, p. 600: "Occamistae meae sectae." Other references are easy to find in the *index nominum* of the *Weimarer Aufgabe*, volume LXXXIII.[1] Hereafter this edition is cited as *WA*.

[37] K. Meissinger, *Der katholische Luther* (München: Leo Lehnen, 1952), p. 109.

[38] Cf. E. Schwiebert, *Luther and His Times* (St. Louis: Concordia Publishing House, 1950), pp. 128ff for documentation on this matter.

[39] Luther, "Randbemerkungen zu Augustini opuscula" (1509), in *WA* IX, pp. 3-27.

of logic. In this, his earliest work, Luther shows forth a view which was to become characteristic of all his thinking, namely, a detestation for Aristotle and the whole position of moderate realism. He calls Aristotle a mere storyteller and his defenders nothing but a group of frivolous men. Reason, he insists, is a very poor help for men to know anything of genuine value about God. While philosophy can to some small extent nourish man's intellect with truth about created things, it can give the will some direction in its quest for goodness in this world.[40]

These statements offer no convincing proof that Luther thought differently from his teachers. But it is significant that he holds to a preference for nominalism at the beginning of his writing career. This is shown by his reverence for Ockham, who had become famous for beginning this mode of thought, and by his opposition to a reliance on logic where there is question of human knowledge about God and his dealings with men.

Beginning in 1510 and continuing into 1511, the years of Luther's most intense studies, there appeared what is unquestionably the chief accomplishment of his early writings, namely, his marginal notations on the *Sentences* of Peter Lombard.[41] As with his previous work, Luther protests on five different occasions in such writing that he intends to respect the epistemological and psychological principles of Ockham.[42] Any other course of argumentation, he states, would serve only to hinder and obscure man's vision of God as well as the proper view of human nature and how man can achieve his final destiny. He protests against those whose philosophy is so tinged with logicism that they can convince men that what is false is true and what is true, false. He likewise scores a point against any philosophy based on a realistic, Aristotelian foundation, and here he mentions Scotism by name as well as men "of our own company," namely certain Ockhamists, who subtly act and write as though nothing were unknown when a question of man's knowledge of God is at issue. Such men, he claims, are truly more subtle than genuinely wise.[43]

---

[40] *Ibid.*, p. 14: "Sic ergo voluntatis in hac vita non potest haberi perfectio, ita nec intellectus. Unde omnis philosophia de rebus tali ac tanta pascit intellectum veritate, quali ac quanta bonitate pascit voluntatem eadem creatura."

[41] Luther, "Randbemerkungen zu Sentenzen des Petrus Lombardus," in *WA* IX, pp. 29-94.

[42] *Ibid.*, pp. 33, 40, 54, 83, and 91.

[43] *Ibid.*, p. 47, *In I Sent.*, d. 23: ". . . nihil est nostris (i.e. occamistae) incomprehensibile et ineffabile. . . . nostri subtiles quam illustres."

While Luther criticizes certain members of his own Ockhamist school for their excessive curiosity in matters pertaining to God, there does not appear to be any reason for saying that he has separated himself from their company. Neither does he appear to have lost all confidence in reason's power to achieve some knowledge of God or the ability of the human will to conform itself to a moral law which is capable of leading men to their final end. Throughout these notations, then, he steers clear of any frivolous wordplay where a knowledge of God is concerned, and he rejects the utility of entering into speculation based on the possibilities open to God. This Sentence-Commentary, then, makes him appear to present as positive and definite a natural theology as did his professors.

It is not certain whether Luther had any direct knowledge of Gabriel Biel's *Commentary on the Sentences* at the time he wrote his own marginals on Peter Lombard. He makes no reference to Biel in his own work, and it is known that he did not have access to its first edition of 1501. Deggering is apparently correct when he suggests that Luther knew this only second-handedly through the notes of his teachers, Trutvetter and Usingen, and in its original form only after its edition of 1514.[44]

Prior to his preoccupation with Biel's *Collectorium,* Luther composed two of his celebrated Scriptural commentaries. In that on the *Psalms,* which was begun in the summer of 1515,[45] he held it for certain that man was able to attain beatitude by observing all of the moral laws established by God. To be sure, man cannot in strict justice coerce God into granting him a supernatural reward for the exercise of his will-activity. However, simply because of the promise and ordinance of God's mercy, men can fittingly expect to be rewarded for a virtuous life and for doing the best that is in them. By implication, at least, Luther felt quite confident that the moral law could both be recognized by men as a stable code, and that it could, under the express will of God, infallibly lead men to achieve their final end.[46]

---

[44] H. Deggering, *Luthers Randbemerkungen zu Gabriel Biels Collectorium in quottuor libros Sententiarum* (Weimar: H. Boehlau, 1933), pp. viii-ix.

[45] Luther, "Erste Psalmenvorlesung," in *WA* IV, pp. 1-462.

[46] *Ibid.,* p. 262: "Hinc recte dicunt doctores, quod homini facienti quod in se est, Deus infallibiliter dat gratiam, et licet non de condigno sese possit ad gratiam praeparare, quia est incomparabilis, tamen bene de congruo propter promissionem istam Dei et pactum misericordiae. . . . Ideo omnia tribuit gratis et ex promissione tantum misericordiae suae, licet ad hoc nos velit esse paratos quantum in nobis est."

No sooner had Luther completed this commentary on the *Psalms* than he completely reversed his opinion on the nature of the law and the human will. Commenting on St. Paul's Epistle to the Romans, he declares that it is a most absurd thing to rely on the oft-repeated sayings of philosophers and theologians to the effect that men can achieve their end by living according to the prescriptions of the law. Man, he says, can do nothing on his own to achieve final beatitude.[47] He repeated this same teaching in a series of propositions written for one of the usual scholastic disputations at the University of Wittenberg, held on September 25, 1516. Luther states that without a very special concursus of God—even granting that a man do the best that is in him—all avails absolutely nothing. Man's nature is wholly corrupt and capable only of evil and sin.[48] This doctrine also found its way into his marginals on Biel's *Collectorium*.

Such doctrine has been well reviewed in even the most ancient of Lutheran studies, but unfortunately the motive which provoked this turn of mind has not been sufficiently explored. A continuing résumé of Luther's work seems to supply the reasons.

Of one piece with Luther's *Commentary on Biel's Sentences* is his work entitled *Disputation against Scholastic Theology*, which was completed on September 4, 1517.[49] Its 97 cryptic statements indicate his attitude towards several scholastics, reason, and philosophy. It presents his particular evaluation of realism, symbolized by Aristotle, and a conception of man's cognitive and volitional powers in relation to God. While there is a precise doctrinal parallel between this work and the *Commentary* on Biel,[50] even a cursory reading of its text will provoke wonder as to whether Luther had remained at all faithful to the nominalist masters to whom he owed all his training. The majority of the theses are directed against

---

[47] Luther, "Vorlesung ueber den Romerbrief, November, 1515 bis September, 1516," in *WA* LVI, p. 503: "Absurdissima est . . . sententia usitata per doctores qua dicitur 'Faciente quod in se est, infallibiliter Deus infundat gratiam,' intelligendo per 'facere in se est', aliquid facere vel posse."

[48] Luther, "Disputations Thesen fuer Bartholomaeus Bernhardi," in *WA* I, pp. 145-151. Cf. p. 147: "Homo, Dei gratia exclusa, praecepta ejus sevare nequaquam potest, neque se vel de congruo vel de condigno ad gratiam praeparare, verum necessario sub peccato manet," and p. 148: "Homo quando facit quod in se est, peccat, cum nec velle aut cogitare ex seipso possit."

[49] Luther, "Disputatio contra Scholasticam Theologiam," in *WA* I, pp. 224-228.

[50] P. Vignaux has indicated these parallels in his, "Luther lecteur de Gabriel Biel," *Eglise et théologie* XII (1959), pp. 22-59.

the very men who have already been singled out as laying the groundwork for a nominalist philosophy. Nineteen propositions, for instance, are directed against Gabriel Biel, and six objections are against Peter of Ailly, who is listed together with Robert of Holcot as a "recent dialectician." Ockham's name is listed twice, while Scotus appears twelve times either explicitly or in context. Besides these scholastics, Luther raises general objections to certain "common opinions of philosophers," "against scholastics in general," and "against moralists."

Luther's opinion of realistic philosophy is summed up in his judgments on Aristotle, whom before this work he had frequently termed "the light of nature" and the "guide of all scholastics." He is now unequivocal in declaring that a theologian who wishes to know God's attitude towards men should have nothing whatsoever to do with Aristotle and asserts that even the most useful of his definitions "beg the question." His evaluation of human nature is no less caustic than that of realism. He equates reason with human nature eleven times and shows nothing but scorn for the intellect's capabilities. The intellect teaches men nothing but error, and the scholastics are wrong when they say man is capable of choosing between good and evil. The reason for this latter remark is that the will can neither naturally conform itself to right reason nor assist men in performing good deeds without the special help of God.[51] It seems that the ultimate basis for these statements on man's nature lies in Luther's remarks that all the scholastic efforts tend both to exalt man's will-power and thus derogate from the supremacy of God and his absolute liberty in dealing with creatures. Their opinions, he states, only serve to feed human pride.

This stand on the total corruption of human nature in face of God—first adopted in his *Commentary on Romans*—appears firmly embedded in the text of this disputation. Subsequent developments indicate, however, that the distinction between God's absolute and ordained power has guided his thought on this matter. Just short of two months after this disputation, Luther exploited his thought on human will-acts in a series of ninety-five theses which he proposed to debate publicly. This text, properly called the *Theses for the*

---

[51] Luther, "Disputatio contra Scholasticam Theologiam," theses 5-7: "Falsitas est quod appetitus liber potest in utrumque oppositum, imo non liber; Voluntas non potest se conformare dictamini recto naturaliter; Elicit actum difformem necessario et malum sine gratia Dei."

Disputation on the Power and Efficacy of Indulgences, and publicized beyond all due proportion, was never used. Reports of its contents reached Rome and then Luther's superiors. The result of this confused reporting was that Luther was ordered to write up some resolutions of the theses and to acquaint his Augustinian confrères with his new thinking at the next general chapter of the order. This latter took place in Heidelberg by way of a disputation on April 25, 1518.[52] The text for this program consists of 28 theological and 12 philosophical propositions and elaborates upon his motives for holding the doctrine in *Disputation against Scholastic Theology* as well as the *Disputation on Indulgences.*

At Heidelberg, Luther insisted that realistic, Aristotelian philosophy speculates on and intrudes upon God's liberty and thus is too inquisitive. All realistic categories, he stated, bear the same stamp of constricting God's freedom and serve only to puff up men's pride.[53] For these reasons, Luther urged his confrères to distrust their reason and will, to abandon realistic philosophy, to reject vain speculation on the possibilities open to God's liberty, and then, positively, to rely in faith in what God in fact has ordained and revealed in the Scriptures. By speaking thus, he clearly divorced himself from traditional scholasticism, and thereby urged them to stop following those who insisted on guiding their thought according to the classic distinction between the divine absolute and ordained power.

He himself refused to follow out the implications of the distinction, attributed nothing to human effort, and fashioned what to his mind is the only sure way for men, namely, a sort of positivism and theocentricism. This, he felt, leaves God's absolute liberty intact and yet relies on an individual interpretation of what God has freely ordained for them. Luther repeatedly had said that man can know nothing genuinely worthwhile of the inner secrets of God's freedom, but in faith has surety that God, in Christ, has once and for all mapped out clearly the way man is to make his way back to himself. This involves that men, who are truly and totally corrupt in nature, must have a trust and confidence that God is simply on their side.

---

[52] Luther, "Disputatio Heidelbergae habita," in *WA* I, pp. 350-374.

[53] *Ibid.*, theses 34 and 22: "Si Aristoteles absolutam cognovisset potentiam Dei, adhuc impossibile asseruisset materiam stare nudam; Sapientia illa, quae invisibilia Dei ex operibus intellecta conspicit, omnino inflat, excaecat et indurat."

It is possible to trace Luther's absolute divorce from an orthodox nominalism and his espousal of a certainly determinist and fideist thought from his correspondence as well as by unravelling the complicated religious and political intrigues which occurred over him between the years 1518 and 1524.[54] During this time Luther incurred the enmity of his teachers, Trutvetter and Usingen, and succumbed to the provocation of others to engage in bitter polemics over his views on human nature and, in particular, his position on the will. Much of this struggle centered around the undebated, but widely published theses on indulgences of 1517. Through the insistence of his opponents, he debated at Leipzig in 1519, and gradually clarified his ideas on these subjects. His condemnation in 1520 only served to strengthen his resolution to get a hearing for his views and in the next three years propelled him to compose several polemical bookets. Finally, after a year's debate with Erasmus he wrote the work which he considered until the time of his death[55] to be his best, that *On the Bondage of the Human Will.*[56] This work gives clear reasons both for why he held to the determinism of the will, and why his attitude towards scholasticism was what it was. Both these positions are based on the distinction between the divine absolute and ordained power.

Early in the work, Luther states that one must distinguish sharply between the doctrine of God as presented in the Bible and that of God as he is in himself.[57] There is a great deal of mystery in the second part of this distinction, he says, and all those who attempt to pry with their speculations into the "unrevealed God of Majesty" are to be repudiated. Continuing, it is said that God's attributes are as incomprehensible to men as is his innermost essence. These absolutely surpass all and any created concepts. While Luther insists repeatedly that it is faith that sufficiently makes known the meaning of God's omnipotence, he is clear to say that God is powerful in a way that is beyond all rightful human conceptualization. It is sufficient for men to realize that in the Scriptures God has

---

[54] This complicated area has been clarified in R. Fife, *The Revolt of Martin Luther* (New York: Columbia University Press, 1957), pp. 266ff.

[55] Luther stated that his *De servo arbitrio* was his best work in the last and most complete of his scriptural commentaries on the Pentateuch of 1545. Cf. *WA* XLIII, p. 458.

[56] Luther, "De servo arbitrio," in *WA* XVIII, pp. 551-787.

[57] *Ibid.*, p. 685: "Distinguendum est inter praedicatum, hoc est, inter verbum Dei in Scriptura sacra et Deum ipsum."

in fact made known the dictates of his omnipotence.[58] Further, Luther states that it is on the basis of his divine concursus that God effects everything in the world. This concursus is uninterrupted, continuous, and unable to be thwarted. It and it alone moves agents to act and human wills to will properly. Since it is ridiculous to say that anything can be done without God's concursus, the safest and surest way men have is to rely on what he has done, to believe that he cannot lie or deceive, and to realize that whatever God has freely foreknown and forewilled will necessarily and infallibly be brought about.

In this work, Luther refuses to enter upon the elaboration of any distinctions within the divine attributes and states that he will not engage in "plays upon the various possibilities" open to the divine liberty, as the nominalists have done. These possibilities, for him, are all hidden within the secrets of the divinity. It is not at all the business of men to investigate them. Such speculations would not be conducive in any way to the welfare of a truly religious man.

While Luther refuses to enter into such speculation, he is not at all reticent to say that his conception of God has very definite consequences for man's relationship toward him. Any thought of the quality of human deeds as being strictly or fittingly meritorious of eternal beatitude is for him a matter of sophistical word play. It suffices to say that human works are weighed in the mysterious unknown divine balance and not to be rated by any human standards. Everything a man does on earth, even though it appear to be done freely, is not done so in reality. Everything done or accomplished by man must be looked at from the viewpoint of the fulfilment of the divine will, which alone is free. God is God for whose will no cause or human reason may be assigned as its rule and measure. Nothing is on a level with it, and nothing is superior to it. In itself, it is the measure of all things. If any rule or measure or cause or human reason existed for it, it could no longer be the will of God. On the basis of his understanding of the divine will and man's present state, Luther concludes that it has been ordained by God, and indeed it is even evident in the Scriptures, that man is totally corrupt in nature. Free will is not in any way attributable

---

[58] *Ibid.*, p. 718: "Omnipotentiam vero Dei voco illam potentiam qua multa facit (i.e. absolutam) sed actualem illam (ordinatam) qua potenter omnia facit in omnibus, quomodo Scriptura vocat eum omnipotentem."

to man, but to God alone. Were such done, it would constitute a sacrilege, the magnitude of which there could be no greater.[59]

The *De servo arbitrio* sheds much light on Luther's earlier thought, as well as on his motivation for teaching the fundamental corruption of human nature. Formerly, it was concluded too hastily that this doctrine on the will, the nature of law, and the contingency of things, and even his usage of the distinction between God's absolute and ordained power, were Scriptural or theological in origin. That such is not the case seems evident from the above cursory survey of his works.

In his early marginals on St. Augustine, Luther shows himself fully consonant with the teachings of nominalism and appears preoccupied to develop a theocentricism by rejecting what he felt was an over-emphasis on logic and realism on the part of scholastics. Similarly, in his marginals on the *Sentences,* he indicates his dislike for realism and places severe restrictions on the capacity of human reason. By the time he came to comment on Biel's *Collectorium,* he had already taken a definite stand on the total incapacity of the human intellect to acquire any genuinely worthwhile knowledge of the divine nature and became concerned with disproving the ability of the human will to achieve deeds worthy of divine reward.

His *Disputation against Scholastic Theology* serves as a recapitulation of his thinking on man's intellectual and volitional powers, but it is especially in the *Heidelberg Disputation* that this doctrine is not only repeated but strongly insinuated as being founded on his understanding of the distinction between God's absolute and ordained power. Luther explicitly situates this distinction among those theses labeled as philosophical. It was not until he was forced into it by Erasmus' *Diatribe* that Luther explicitly brought forth the distinction and explains it as the basis for his views.

While Luther's thought is very often couched in theological phraseology, he is well aware that this distinction had involved a philosophical conception of created human nature which has kept its essential integrity for the majority of scholastics before him,[60] and he finally rejects any freedom of the human will on the same

---

[59] *Ibid.,* p. 636: "Sequitur liberum arbitrium esse plane divinum nomen, nec illi posse competere quam soli divinae majestati . . . quod si hominibus tribuitur, nihilo rectius tribuitur, quam si divinitas quoque ipsa eis tribueretur, quo sacrilegio nullum esse majus possit."

[60] P. Vignaux, "Sur Luther et Occam," *Franziskanische Studien* XXXI (1950), p. 27.

basis as his predecessors had defended it. He states that he will have nothing to do with scholastic speculation, and yet he actually does interpret the distinction in a way no other scholastic in either of the two nominalist traditions had given before him. The absolute divine power, he states, is beyond all human knowledge. It is in very truth the hidden majesty of God. However, the ordained power of God is for him a combination of what he finds revealed in Scripture and in his own reasoning. What he finds in both of these sources is the total corruption of human nature.

Vignaux, who was among the first to consider the importance of this distinction for Luther, states that it had relevance only for his theological questions on grace and justification.[61] A similar preoccupation with the theological implications of the distinction is evident in the works of Link,[62] Auer,[63] Meller,[64] Dettloff,[65] and Grane.[66] Other writers, concentrating on Luther's theological doctrines, have stated that it exerted no influence on them whatsoever. Among these may be numbered Weijenborg[67] and Rupp.[68] Still others who have written most recently on this distinction, namely, Leff[69] and Oberman,[70] have either stated that it had definite philosophical "implications" in late scholasticism or have been somewhat vacillating on this point. Neither of these authors, it may be remarked here, has formally or explicitly studied the distinction in any specific part of Luther's works. While it cannot be denied that the distinction allows Luther to make certain theological points, there does not seem to be any justification for saying that it is a purely theological distinc-

[61] P. Vignaux, "Occam," *DTC*, Tome XI,1 columns 888ff; "Nominalisme," *ibid.*, columns 764ff; and his *Justification et prédestination au XIVe siècle* (Paris: E. Leroux, 1934).

[62] W. Link, *Das Ringen Luthers um die Freiheit der Theologie von der Philosophie* (München: C. Kaiser, 1940), pp. 270-308.

[63] J. Auer, *Die Entwicklung der Gnadenlehre in der Hochscholastik* (Freiburg in Breisgau: Herder, 1942).

[64] B. Meller, *Studien zur Erkenntnislehre des Peter von Ailly* (Freiburg in Breisgau: Herder, 1942).

[65] W. Dettloff, *Die Lehre von der Acceptatio Divina* (Werl: D. Coelde, 1954).

[66] L. Grane, "Gabriel Biels Lehre von der Allmacht Gottes," *Zeitschrift fuer Theologie und Kirche* LIII (1956), pp. 53-76.

[67] R. Weijenborg, "La Charité dans la première théologie de Luther," *Revue d'histoire ecclésiastique* XLV (1950), pp. 617-669.

[68] G. Rupp, *The Righteousness of God: Studies on Luther* (London: Hodder and Stoughton, 1953), pp. 91f.

[69] G. Leff, *Gregory of Rimini: Tradition and Innovation in Fourteenth Century Thought* (Manchester, England: University Press, 1961), pp. 18-28.

[70] H. Oberman, *The Harvest* . . . , pp. 30-56.

tion for him. Like its function in previous times, it is seen to be Luther's guide for the many observations he makes on man's knowledge of God, of human nature and of the moral law.

There remains one last point for the completion of this article and this concerns Luther's relationship to nominalism. From the very beginning of his writing career, his low estimate of the human intellect clearly dissociates his thought from the mainstream of tradition-conscious nominalists. While Ailly, Biel, Trutvetter and Usingen place definite limitations on the capacity of reason, they never rejected its ability to achieve some genuinely worthwhile knowledge of God, nor did they fail to use reason to demonstrate the stability and effectiveness of the moral law to assist men reach final beatitude. In his estimate of the human will, Luther is seen to have dissociated himself from the lesser current of nominalism. Holcot, Mirecourt and their followers used the distinction between God's absolute and ordained power precisely to assert the self-sufficiency and strength of the will to achieve man's final beatitude. Luther rejects this position as well.

It seems, then, that no other conclusion can be reached but that Luther's position on this distinction must be rated as original with himself. While thoroughly trained in nominalism, while showing its characteristic preoccupation with the divine liberty, and while intent on fashioning what to his mind was a positive and theocentric doctrine, he finally arrived at a position never before held by any scholastic, Everyone knows that his philosophical position led him to the formation of an ecclesiology, a sacramental theology, and a view of justification which last to this day. These latter remain as the most potent factors in the perduring and tragic division within Christendom.

NOTES ON CONTRIBUTORS

Felix Alluntis, O.F.M., has been a member of the philosophy faculties of The Catholic University of America and Santo Tomas de Villanueva University, Havana, Cuba. He has translated and edited the *De primo principio* of John Duns Scotus for the BAC series (Madrid, 1960), has completed a Spanish translation of Scotus's *Quaestiones quodlibetales,* and has published extensively in Spanish and English philosophical journals.

Gilbert B. Arbuckle, Ph.D., is a graduate of the College of the Holy Cross and The Catholic University of America (M.A., 1954; Ph.D., 1962). The author of *A Critique of the Thomistic Doctrine of Definition* and other works, he is engaged in full-time philosophical research and writing.

Bernardino M. Bonansea, O.F.M., professor of philosophy in The Catholic University of America's School of Philosophy, is the author of many articles on medieval and renaissance thought. He is translator and editor of *Duns Scotus: the Basic Principles of His Philosophy* by Efrem Bettoni (Washington, 1961) and his *Thomas Campanella: Renaissance Pioneer of Modern Thought* is in press. He is a *Lector Generalis* in the Franciscan order, has taught in China, and has been Visiting Professor at St. John's University.

Antonio S. Cua is professor and chairman of the Department of Philosophy, State University College, Oswego, New York. He received his doctorate from the University of California and is the author of *Reason and Nature: The Ethics of Richard Price* (Ohio University Press, 1966) and other works on philosophy.

Richard P. Desharnais, C.S.C., is a member of the philosophy faculty of King's College. Both his M.A. and the Ph.D. degree were earned at The Catholic University of America. He is the author of *The History of the Distinction Between God's Absolute and Ordained Power and Its Influence on Martin Luther.*

Jude P. Dougherty is Dean of the CUA School of Philosophy and has taught at Marquette University and Bellarmine College. He is the author of *Recent American Naturalism: An Exposition and Critique* (Washington, 1960), *American Naturalistic Thought: James, Dewey, Edel, Hook, Romanell, Dennes* (New York, 1966), and has contributed numerous articles to the *New Catholic Encyclopedia* and other publications.

B. Ryosuke Inagaki is associate professor of philosophy at Nanzan University,

Showa-Nagoya, Japan. After undergraduate studies in Japan, he came to the United States and received the M.A. and Ph.D. degrees at The Catholic University of America. He has contributed to philosophical journals in Japan, has translated works by Josef Pieper into Japanese, is the author of *The Constitution of Japan and the Natural Law* (Washington, 1955) and *Scholastic Bibliography in Japan* (Nanzan, 1957), and contributes to Japanese philosophical journals. He has twice held Fulbright grants and during the academic year 1967-1968 has taught at King's College, Wilkes-Barre, Pennsylvania.

Thomas Prufer is associate professor in the CUA School of Philosophy. He did his undergraduate work at the University of Virginia, received the Ph.D. from the University of Munich in 1959, and spent the following year in postdoctoral work on a grant from the German Academic Exchange Program. He has contributed to *Philosophische Rundschau*, SPHP, and IPQ.

Mother Caroline Canfield Putnam, R.S.C.J. teaches at Newtonville College of the Sacred Heart. An artist as well as a philosopher, she holds M.F.A., M.A., and Ph.D. degrees from The Catholic University of America, and is the author of *Beauty in the Pseudo-Dionysius* (Washington, 1960).

John M. Quinn, O.S.A., is a member of the philosophy faculty at Biscayne College and has taught at Villanova University. He received his Ph.L. degree from Laval University and the Ph.D. from The Catholic University of America. His doctoral dissertation is *The Doctrine of Time in St. Thomas Aquinas: Some Aspects and Application*.

John K. Ryan is Elizabeth Breckinridge Caldwell Professor of Philosophy at The Catholic University of America and served as Dean of the School of Philosophy from 1956 to 1967. He is the author of numerous books and articles on philosophy and is Advisory Editor of the Encyclopedia Americana.

Marius G. Schneider, O.F.M., is professor in the School of Philosophy, The Catholic University of America, and has also taught in China and Germany. Besides the M.A. and Ph.D. degrees he holds the Diplompsychologe of the University of Munich and is a *Lector Generalis* of the Franciscan order.

INDEX

Aaron, R. I., 177, 178
Adams, H., 40
Ailly, Peter of, 213, 216, 222
Albert of Saxony, 216
Albertus Magnus, 39, 46
Anselm, St., 128-141 passim
Aristotle, 37, 42, 46, 47, 61, 71, 72, 105, 117, 122-127, 143-173 passim
Augustine, St., 46, 47, 75-127 passim, 226
Auer, J., 227
Autrecourt, Nicholas of, 216

Bacon, R., 39, 43, 44
Bark, W. C., 36, 40, 41
Benedict, St., 37, 38
Bercorio, Peter of, 216
Bergson, H., 78, 117-127
Berkeley, G., 97
Biel, G., 208, 213, 220, 221, 226
Boehner, G., 209, 215
Bolzano, B., 45
Bonaventure, St., 135
Boyer, C., 45
Bradwardine, T., 46
Brussels, Gerard of, 46
Buridan, J., 47
Butterfield, H., 48

Caius, 9-15
Calore, John of, 216
Cantor, G., 45
Cavalieri, B., 45
Cellini, B., 58
Chan, Wing-tsit, 27
Christ, Jesus, 1, 4, 10, 14, 15
Clagett, M., 36, 46
Coerver, R. F., 58
Collingwood, R. G., 26
Confucius, 18-21, 26-28, 30
Coyré, A., 36

Creel, H. E., 30
Crombie, A. C., 36, 41-44, 46, 48
Cusa, Nicholas of, 46

Dawson, C., 43, 44, 47
Demophilus, 9
Denis the Pseudo-Areopagite, 3-17
Descartes, R., 102, 117
Dettloff, W., 227
Duhem, P., 36, 47
Duns Scotus, John, 46, 128-141 passim, 189, 208

Eadmer, 129
Erasmus, 226

Farrington, B., 40
Feckes, C., 213
Foullechat, D., 216
Freiburg, Theodoric of, 46
Fung Yu-lan, 18

Galileo, 42, 44, 195
Gaunilo, 130
Gerson, J., 216
Gilson, E., 99, 102
Grane, L., 227
Grosseteste, R., 40, 45, 46

Hägglund, B., 212
Harvey, W., 42
Heidegger, M., 78, 115, 116
Hobbes, T., 73
Holcot, R., 215, 216
Holzman, D., 19, 22
Hume, D., 71-74, 97
Hu Shih, 28

Isenloh, E., 212, 215

James, W., 53

231

Kant, I., 78, 96-97, 102, 174
Kennedy, J. F., 93, 116
Klemm, F., 39

Ladner, G., 113
Lady, Our, 40
Lefebvre des Noëttes, Comm., 37, 41
Leff, G., 227
Legge, J., 19
Leibniz, G. W. F., 139, 141
Lin Yutang, 33
Link, W., 227
Locke, J., 174
Lombard, P., 218
Lun Yü., 18
Luther, M., 207-228

Maier, A., 36, 46
Maxwell, C., 74
Medun, Aegidius of, 216
Meller, B., 227
Meng Wu-po, 25
Merlie, W., 46
Michel, V., 142
Mill, J. S., 194
Mirecourt, John of, 216
Montesson, J., 216

Nakamura, Hajime, 18
Neckham, A., 39
Nemorarius, J., 45, 46
Newman, J. H., 49
Newton, I., 42, 194

Oakley, F., 213, 214
Oakesmith, J., 2
Oberman, H., 210, 214
Ockham, W., 46, 47, 208, 209, 213-18, 222
Oresme, N., 46
Ortega y Gasset, J., 191-206 passim

Padua, Louis of, 216
Paul, St., 4, 221

Pecham, J., 46
Peregrinus, P., 46
Pinckaers, S., 53, 54
Pisa, Leonard of, 45
Plato, I., 19, 29, 38
Plotinus, 104-106
Plutarch, I., 38
Poincaré, H., 194
Polycarp, 8
Popper, K., 49
Porphyry, 175, 176

Quine, W. V., 174, 176, 177

Rupp, G., 227

Shun, 21
St. Armand, John of, 46
Struid, D. J., 45

Tacquet, A., 45
Thomas Aquinas, St., 46, 48, 133, 142, 173, 174-190
Thorndike, L., 36, 43
Trapp, D., 210
Trutvetter, J., 213, 217, 224
Tseng-Tzu, 21
Tzu-Chang, 21
Tzu-Kung, 21
Tzu-Yu, 25

Usingen, Bartholomaeus Arnold of, 213, 217, 224

Vanneste, J., 3, 4, 10
Vignaux, P., 209, 227

Wang Yang-ming, 20
Whitehead, A. N., 38, 42, 43, 48
Whyte, L., 36, 37, 41
Witelo, 46
Wolf, A., 35, 36, 40, 44

Yao, 21, 26

www.ingramcontent.com/pod-product-compliance
Lightning Source LLC
Chambersburg PA
CBHW031413290426
44110CB00011B/366